John Lydgate

Fabula Duorum Mercatorum and Guy of Warwyk

MIDDLE ENGLISH TEXTS SERIES

The Middle English Texts Series is designed for classroom use. Its goal is to make available to teachers, scholars, and students texts that occupy an important place in the literary and cultural canon but have not been readily available in student editions. The series does not include those authors, such as Chaucer, Langland, or Malory, whose English works are normally in print in good student editions. The focus is, instead, upon Middle English literature adjacent to those authors that teachers need in compiling the syllabuses they wish to teach. The editions maintain the linguistic integrity of the original work but within the parameters of modern reading conventions. The texts are printed in the modern alphabet and follow the practices of modern capitalization, word formation, and punctuation. Manuscript abbreviations are silently expanded, and *u/v* and *j/i* spellings are regularized according to modern orthography. Yogh (ȝ) is transcribed as *g*, *gh*, *y*, or *s*, according to the sound in Modern English spelling to which it corresponds; thorn (þ) and eth (ð) are transcribed as *th*. Distinction between the second person pronoun and the definite article is made by spelling the one *thee* and the other *the*, and final *-e* that receives full syllabic value is accented (e.g., *charité*). Hard words, difficult phrases, and unusual idioms are glossed either in the right margin or at the foot of the page. Explanatory and textual notes appear at the end of the text, often along with a glossary. The editions include short introductions on the history of the work, its merits and points of topical interest, and brief working bibliographies.

This series is published in association with the University of Rochester.

Medieval Institute Publications is a program of
The Medieval Institute, College of Arts and Sciences

John Lydgate

Fabula Duorum Mercatorum and Guy of Warwyk

Edited by
Pamela Farvolden

TEAMS • Middle English Texts Series • University of Rochester

MEDIEVAL INSTITUTE PUBLICATIONS
Western Michigan University
Kalamazoo

Printed and bound in the United States of America

**Library of Congress Cataloging-in-Publication Data
are available at the Library of Congress**

ISBN 978-1-58044-246-6
eISBN 978-1-58044-247-3

To Doris M. Farvolden

and

M. A. Whitaker

Gladly wolde she lerne and gladly teche

CONTENTS

Acknowledgments

My deepest thanks go to Russell Peck, the General Editor, for his patience and invaluable comments, and to Pamela Yee, Assistant Editor, for her astute, perceptive, and friendly advice. I would also like to thank Jenny Boyar, Alison Harper, and Sharon Rhodes, staff editors; Pat Hollahan and her staff at Medieval Institute Publications, and the NEH for funding the project. I also thank Martha Johnson-Olin whose careful manuscript reading and early advice were very much appreciated. Thanks are due also to Benjamin Garstad for his translation of Gerard Cornubiensis and to the librarians and staff at MacEwan University Library, and especially to Nick Ursulak and Sean McCready. I wish particularly to thank Stephen R. Reimer and M. A. Whitaker, who read parts of the manuscript in draft form, and to whom I am deeply grateful for comments and suggestions, and my colleague Carolyn Ives. I am grateful to the Bodleian Libraries at the University of Oxford for permission to quote from Oxford, Bodleian Library, MS Laud Misc. 683 and to the British Library Board for permission to quote from British Library, MS Harley 2255 (© The British Library Board, Harley 2255, fols. 72r–88r). I thank all the libraries that provided me access to the manuscripts whether in person or by means of microfilm or CD: the British Library, London; the Bodleian Libraries, Oxford; Cambridge University Library, Cambridge; Leiden University, Leiden; and Peterborough Central Library, Peterborough, England. I would like to extend a special thanks to Richard Hunt and Richard Hillier of the Peterborough Central Library, where I spent several pleasant days examining the Peterborough manuscript. Finally, I am also grateful for the online access to digitized manuscripts provided by Houghton Library, Harvard, MA; and Trinity College Library, Cambridge.

I am deeply thankful to my husband and children for their unflagging support through what has been a long process, and to my mother for her steady faith in me. To her, and to M. A. Whitaker, who first introduced me to medieval literature, this volume is dedicated.

General Introduction

The two narrative poems in this volume by John Lydgate (ca. 1371–1449) might at first seem an unusual pairing. The *Fabula Duorum Mercatorum*, an English poem despite its Latin title, has at its narrative core the conflict between *amor* and *amicitia*, love and friendship. Drawing on medical lore, courtly love convention, and Boethian philosophy,[1] it is a polished and accomplished romance. *Guy of Warwick*, on the other hand, relates in chronicle fashion the final episode in the life of the titular pilgrim knight, one of England's greatest and most familiar heroes. The *Fabula* is set in the exotic east, its central characters presented as courtly lovers; *Guy* is firmly anchored in England, its central character presented as a real-life Warwick ancestor and his story as part of "real" history. Although they differ in subject matter, style, and genre, the two poems have several features in common. Both are relatively short, accessible narrative works that deserve to be better known but have received little scholarly scrutiny.[2] Both are very likely from the same period in Lydgate's career, the 1420s; both exhibit typical features of Lydgate's style, though to different effect; and both exhibit a mixture of genres. Both have at their heart an exemplary thrust and both are based on an earlier source, the *Fabula* on a very brief twelfth-century exemplum and the *Guy* on a Latin prose chronicle.[3] In each case, Lydgate's treatment of his source governs his purposes, style, and approach.

---

[1] My discussion of the *Fabula* centers on Lydgate's specific use of Boethius' *Consolation of Philosophy* rather than on the more general fifteenth-century Boethianism so cogently described by David Lawton in "Dullness in the Fifteenth Century," whereby, in a world governed by Fortune, the poet-speaker humbly protests his rhetorical inadequacy while also offering advice and warnings to princes. Both the *Fabula* and the *Guy* may be seen as participating generally in this "pervasive Boethianism" (Lerer, *Chaucer and his Readers*, p.13; see also Sponsler, "Lydgate and London's Public Culture," p. 21). In *Guy*, for example, Lydgate briefly protests his "dullness" in the humility topos which ends the poem (lines 583–92), and the *Fabula*, in its depiction of the Syrian merchant's fall, offers itself as a "mirror," though not particularly for princes (lines 664–65). Neither poem is of the same scale, scope, or purpose as the major Lydgatean works, particularly the *Fall of Princes* or the *Troy Book*, as discussed by Lawton.

[2] Each is given some attention in the book-length treatments of Lydgate by Pearsall, *John Lydgate*, Schirmer, *John Lydgate: A Study in the Culture of the XVth Century*, and Ebin, *John Lydgate*. Articles including discussion of the *Fabula* are Cooper, "'His guttys wer out shake,'" Farvolden, "'Love Can No Frenship,'" and Stretter, "Rewriting Perfect Friendship." Treatments of Lydgate's *Guy* are included in V. Richmond, *Legend of Guy of Warwick*, A. S. G. Edwards, "*Speculum Guy de Warwick*," and Hardman, "Lydgate's Uneasy Syntax."

[3] The *Fabula* is based on a tale from Petrus Alfonsi's *Disciplina Clericalis*, the *Guy* on the chronicle of Gerard Cornubiensis. See the individual introductions in this volume, pp. 8–9 and p. 88.

In the *Fabula*, Lydgate completely transforms his source, expanding a short didactic tale exemplifying the perfect friend into an elevated narrative. In its literary allusiveness and its treatment of love, friendship, and fortune, the *Fabula* takes up a number of significant medieval themes and bears comparison with the best works of its type. In its resolution of the love triangle, it can be seen as an answer to Chaucer's Knight's Tale, for example,[4] and in its explicit evocation of the *Consolation of Philosophy* it invites comparison to Chaucer's *Troilus and Criseyde*. In genre it most closely resembles a romance, as I have termed it above, but it retains something of the exemplum it is based on, and it is often described under the label of a fable or didactic poem,[5] though it is certainly more complex than these labels imply. The poem's exemplarity and moral thrust arises from the conduct of the two merchants who rise above their own self-interest in the service of a larger ideal, which at poem's end elicits a murderer's confession and prompts a "wise, worthy king" (line 857) to see into the truth of things and render true justice. In *Guy of Warwick*, by contrast, the tone and approach are meant to evoke history and chronicle. Here, Lydgate does not so much transform as shape his source to articulate the political desires of a patron. The poem is, at least in part, designed to assert the Warwick ancestral claims of Margaret de Talbot, daughter of Richard Beauchamp, thirteenth Earl of Warwick. A number of its significant features are attributable to this patronage, including the choice of a chronicle rather than a romance source, an insistence on the authority of the chronicler,[6] and the presentation of Guy himself as noble hero, brave knight, devout pilgrim, and Warwick ancestor in equal measure. He is an exemplar of all that is best in a particularly English hero. The exemplary and moral thrust of the poem arises from this balanced presentation as well as from its warnings about pride and tyranny, against which only the virtuous, with God's help, may stand. Like the *Fabula*, *Guy of Warwick* is also difficult to pin down generically. Many medieval versions of the Guy legend were romances that often had strong hagiographical elements, but Lydgate's *Guy*, based on the chronicle tradition that had inserted Guy into actual history, downplays hagiography.[7] The poem resists categorization into one particular

---

[4] See Farvolden, "Love Can No Frenship," and Stretter, "Rewriting Perfect Friendship."

[5] See, for example, Pearsall, *John Lydgate*, pp. 202–04, Ebin, *John Lydgate*, pp. 111–12, and Schirmer, *John Lydgate: A Study* (who classifies it as a "pious tale," p. 268).

[6] Medieval historical writing emphasized accuracy and "truth." See Given-Wilson, *Chronicles*, especially the first chapter, "Telling the Truth," pp. 1–20. See also Galloway, "Writing History," for a useful introduction to English medieval historical writing.

[7] Susan Crane Dannenbaum usefully analyzes the co-mingling of hagiography and romance in Anglo-Norman and Middle English romance versions of the Guy legend and other exemplary or pious romances, including a detailed comparison between the AN and ME versions of *Guy* and the *Life of St. Alexis*, which share several striking parallels. See Dannenbaum, "Exemplary Romance," especially pp. 357–63. See also her *Insular Romance*, pp. 92–133, which expands her discussion. On the co-mingling of romance and hagiography see also Childress, "Between Romance and Legend"; Hopkins, *The Sinful Knights*, pp. 20–31 and pp. 70–118 (on the romance *Guy*); Wogan-Browne, "'Bet . . . to . . . rede'"; and Woodcock, "Crossovers," pp. 146–50. Dalrymple's discussion of pious formulae in Middle English romance is also relevant; see *Language and Piety*, especially pp. 120–38. Dalrymple twice very briefly mentions Lydgate's *Guy*. Both times, he interestingly asserts that the poem is a hagiographic treatment of the Guy tale. See pp. 121, 139–40.

genre; it is neither romance nor saint's life, though in the view of A. S. G. Edwards, it contains "elements of both."[8]

The rhetorical style of each poem suits its subject matter and purpose. The *Fabula* is a good example of Lydgate's elaborate, rhetorical style, consisting of — though not necessarily limited to — elevated, aureate diction, amplification, didactic digression, wide-ranging, often encyclopedic references and allusions, and loose, paratactic syntax.[9] In the *Fabula*, Lydgate successfully harnesses these devices to transform the original exemplum into something new. The poem is, as Pearsall says, a superb exercise of style.[10] In the *Guy*, on the other hand, the digressions and amplifications are often more overtly didactic, and the syntax is particularly problematic. Sentences are loose and paratactic in the extreme and often substitute infinitives or participial phrases for finite verbs. Josef Schick's oft-quoted criticism of Lydgate's excessive anacoluthon uses an example from *Guy*: "There is . . . no instance of the anacoluthon in [the *Temple of Glas*] quite so bad as the beginning of *Guy of Warwick* where . . . not only the predicate of the sentence is wanting, but the subject as well."[11] This difficult syntax may be due in part to Lydgate's source, which Lydgate was translating from convoluted medieval Latin prose into English poetry. The style and approach suit a poem that seeks to embed its hero firmly in history and underline Margaret's ancestral claims.

Guy of Warwick also illustrates Lydgate's position as a sought-after poet who wrote many poems on commission for some of the most important and powerful people in England. Lydgate wrote several of his lengthiest and most important works for members of the royal family, for example: the *Troy Book* for the future Henry V, the *Fall of Princes* for Henry's brother, Humphrey of Gloucester, *The Lives of SS Edmund and Fremund* for the young Henry VI.[12] He also wrote in a variety of genres for other nobility, gentry, civic officials, and merchants; as Robert Meyer-Lee puts it "[n]o other English poet was patronized so consistently by the dominant political figures of his day nor by so broad a spectrum of society."[13] Margaret's father, Richard, Earl of Warwick, was himself a patron of Lydgate's.

---

[8] Edwards, "*Speculum Guy de Warwick*," p. 89.

[9] Lydgate's style has occasioned much discussion, from early editors of his work (see, for example, Schick's introduction to the *Temple of Glas*, or Schleich and Zupitza's introduction to the *Fabula*), to the present. An essential work is still Pearsall, *John Lydgate*. See also Pearsall's "Lydgate as Innovator." Among the many discussions of this multi-faceted topic, see Lois Ebin, *Illuminator*, on the components of Lydgate's high style, pp. 19–48; Hardman, "Uneasy Syntax"; Lerer, *Chaucer and his Readers*, on Lydgate's aureation and laureate poetics, pp. 35–46; Mitchell, "Gower and Lydgate," on rhetorical context, pp. 576–83; Meyer-Lee, *Poets and Power*, on Lydgate's laureate style, pp. 54–61; Norton-Smith, *John Lydgate: Poems*, pp. 192–95; Scanlon, "Lydgate's Poetics"; and D. Vance Smith, "Lydgate's Refrain."

[10] Pearsall, *John Lydgate*, p. 204.

[11] Schick, Introduction to *Lydgate's Temple of Glas*, p. cxxxvi.

[12] Lydgate's first major work, the *Troy Book*, was commissioned in 1412 by the future King Henry V, the *Fall of Princes* in 1431 by Humphrey, Duke of Gloucester, *Edmund and Fremund* for Abbot Curteys, who commissioned it as a gift for Henry VI, in 1433. Many scholars discuss Lydgate's patrons. A useful recent summary is provided by Meyer-Lee, pp. 50–51. See also the chapter in Pearsall's *John Lydgate*, entitled "Laureate Lydgate," pp. 160–91.

[13] Meyer-Lee, *Poets and Power*, p. 51.

A powerful political figure and guardian of the infant Henry VI, Richard commissioned *The Title and Pedigree of Henry VI*, designed to demonstrate Henry's rightful kingship over England and France. Lydgate's *Guy* implicitly alludes to Richard in its praise of the "Olde erle of Warwik" (line 316).[14] The *Fabula*, by contrast, offers no evidence with respect to a possible patron, circumstances of composition, or occasion, aside from a possible suggestion of a contemporary situation in its final lines.[15] Both poems were probably written during the decade of the 1420s, and though more is known about the context and occasion of *Guy* than of the *Fabula*, there is no real certainty about the specific date of either one.

If both poems do belong to the 1420s, they were written during a particularly busy and productive period of Lydgate's life, after he had written the massive *Troy Book*, *Life of our Lady*, and the *Siege of Thebes*, all complete by 1422, and before he began the *Fall of Princes* in 1431.[16] During the 1420s, Lydgate produced many shorter works on commission, shorter political and occasional poems as well as the dramatic entertainments known as mummings or disguisings. During this period, as Pearsall says, Lydgate "had the *de facto* status of an 'official' poet . . . who could be relied upon to produce something appropriately dignified for any occasion."[17] Lydgate seems to have led "an active and public life."[18] Born in about 1371 in the small village of Lydgate, Suffolk, and becoming a Benedictine monk when he was about fifteen at the great monastery of Bury St. Edmunds in Suffolk, he attended Gloucester college in Oxford where he met the future King Henry V, traveled to Paris, spent time in London, and was for several years prior at Hatfield Broad Oak.[19] His poetic output is extraordinary for its quantity (over 145,000 lines)[20] and its variety. Lydgate wrote in every genre: historical epic, *de casibus* tragedy, saints' lives, dramatic entertainments, courtly works, political poetry, religious verse, and numerous short didactic poems. His long career — he seems to have died in 1449 — is punctuated by many major works, among them the *Troy Book* (1412–20), the *Siege of Thebes* (1421–22), the *Fall of Princes* (1431–38), and the

---

[14] See further the Introduction to *Guy* in this volume, p. 92n43.

[15] See the Introduction to *Fabula*, pp. 23–25.

[16] See Pearsall, *Bio-Bibliography*, pp. 50–51.

[17] Pearsall, *John Lydgate*, p. 160. On Lydgate's unofficial laureate status and connections with the Lancastrian court, see Pearsall's chapter "Laureate Lydgate," pp. 160–91, and his *Bio-Bibliography*, pp. 28–32. See also Meyer Lee, *Poets and Power*, pp. 49–87; Mortimer, *Narrative Tragedy*, especially pp. 51–94; Nolan, *Public Culture*, especially pp. 10–20, 71–75; Patterson, "Making Identities"; Straker, "Propaganda"; and Strohm, "Lancastrian Court." Most introductions to Lydgate and his poetry also include discussion of the social and political culture. See, for example, Ebin, *John Lydgate*, especially pp. 1–16; Gray, "Hoccleve and Lydgate"; Mitchell, "Gower and Lydgate"; Simpson, "Energies"; and Simpson, "John Lydgate."

[18] Sponsler, ed., *Mummings and Entertainments*, p. 4. Pearsall, however, suggests caution in "assuming too readily that [Lydgate] was a frequent visitor in society" (*Bio-Bibliography*, p. 22), noting that his absences from the monastery, other than those periods when he was at Oxford or Hatfield Broad Oak, would have been the exception rather than the rule. See pp. 21–22.

[19] See Pearsall, *Bio-Bibliography*, pp. 15–28 for an overview of these parts of Lydgate's life.

[20] This oft-quoted number can be found in any number of sources. See, for example, Pearsall, *John Lydgate*, p. 4; Renoir and Benson, p. 1809; Simpson, "Energies," p. 44; Mitchell, "Gower and Lydgate," p. 583n2; and Strohm, "Lancastrian Court," p. 652.

Lives of SS Edmund and Fremund (1434–36) and of *SS Albon and Amphibalus* (1439).[21] These achievements cannot be underestimated, but as John Norton-Smith has remarked, "it is the shorter, occasional poems treating public and private matters that show Lydgate at his best."[22] It is not the purpose of this edition to maintain that these two shorter poems do indeed show Lydgate at his best — though I would argue that the *Fabula* comes close to fitting the bill — but rather to present two works that are each in some way representative of Lydgate and that together illustrate some of his most characteristic moves.

EDITORIAL PROCEDURE

The *Fabula* and the *Guy of Warwick* survive in seven manuscripts each,[23] suggesting that both enjoyed some contemporary popularity.[24] In preparing this edition, I have examined all of the manuscripts, either in person or by means of digital, online, or microfilm copies. Both poems were first edited in the late nineteenth century, *Guy* in 1873 by Julius Zupitza (though this is not a critical edition) and the *Fabula* in 1897 by Zupitza and Schleich.[25] The standard critical edition of both poems is that of H. N. MacCracken, who included both works in his 1934 edition of Lydgate's shorter poems.[26] None of the previous editions collate

[21] These dates are taken from Pearsall's *Bio-Bibliography*, pp. 50–51.

[22] Norton-Smith, *John Lydgate: Poems*, p. x.

[23] For these manuscripts, along with brief descriptions, see the introductions in this volume. For the *Fabula*, see pp. 25–28, and for *Guy*, see pp. 100–104.

[24] The *Fabula* and a work that may be Lydgate's *Guy* both appear in the inventory of books owned by Sir John Paston. See Lester, "Books of a Fifteenth-Century English Gentleman," p. 202. Among these books are two that contain works entitled "Warwyk," "Balade [. . .] off Guy & Colbronde," and "[. . .] Marchauntes" (Items 1 and 5). It is impossible to say whether these first two refer specifically to Lydgate's poem of *Guy*, but the reference to "Marchauntes" is almost certainly to the English version of the *Fabula*'s title, "A/The Tale of Two Marchauntes." See Lester, p. 204, and Breeze, "Libelle," pp. 230–31, who does not mention Lester. Other books in Sir John's inventory include works on heraldry and chivalry as well as didactic and other courtly works, including romances, suggesting that the *Fabula* and *Guy* appealed to contemporary taste, particularly, perhaps, to a family like the Pastons, social-climbing gentry who enjoyed rubbing shoulders with nobility and seemed particularly to enjoy works on chivalry and romance. See the lists in Lester, pp. 202–06, 211–12; see also Johnston, *Romance and the Gentry*, pp. 30–32, who provides a brief overview of the Pastons' books. The Pastons and their circle seem to have been particularly interested in Lydgate; the *Temple of Glas* was at one time thought to have Paston connections, and Lydgate's "Epistle to Sibille" was probably written for Sibille Boys, a member of the Paston circle. See Bale, "A Norfolk Gentlewoman." On the Pastons, see Davis, ed., *Paston Letters and Papers*; Barber, ed., *The Pastons: A Family in the Wars of the Roses*; Castor, *Blood and Roses*; and C. Richmond, *The Paston Family in the Fifteenth Century* (3 vols).

[25] See J. Zupitza, ed. "Lydgate's *Leben des Guy von Warwick*" and G. Schleich and J. Zupitza, Lydgate's *Fabula Duorum Mercatorum*. Zupitza's edition of *Guy* (based on British Library, Laud Misc. 683) is not collated with that of other *Guy* manuscripts, though he provides a brief introduction and notes. F. N. Robinson's 1899 printing of *Guy* from Cambridge, MA, Harvard University, Houghton Library MS Eng 530 should also be noted here. Robinson collated the text with Zupitza as well as with that of Leiden, University Library MS Vossius Germ. Gall. Q.9 and provided a useful, though now dated, introduction. See Robinson, "On Two Manuscripts."

[26] MacCracken, ed., *The Minor Poems of John Lydgate*. Part II. Secular Poems. Items 21 and 22.

all seven of the extant manuscripts for each poem.[27] Though I have followed H. N. MacCracken in my choice of base texts, I have newly edited each poem from the manuscript, collating the text with the other six manuscripts in each case. I have checked the texts and collations against MacCracken, from whose readings I sometimes differ.

I have tried to present each poem in an accessible, readable form, following modern English capitalization and punctuation conventions, and providing what I hope are helpful glosses and commentary. Each text follows the reading of the base manuscript, in each case the best of the seven manuscripts within which each poem is extant; these choices are explained in the "Notes on the Text" in each individual introduction. I have emended each text very little and only when not to do so would compromise meaning or cause confusion. These few emendations are recorded in the textual notes to each work, which also record substantive variants from all other manuscripts. In accordance with METS editorial guidelines, I have used modern English spelling conventions for words with *v/u* and *i/j*, and have provided modern equivalents for thorns, yoghs, and eths. I have also brought into conformity with modern English spelling *y/g*, *f/ff*, *w* when it is a vowel, *the/thee* and *of/off*. Where they occur at the beginning of a word and signal a capital letter, double *ff*s become *F*, and when *e* at the end of a word receives syllabic value it is marked with an accent (e.g., *cité*). Where the scribe has used Roman numerals, I have spelled them out. Word division is also regularized; examples specific to each text are detailed in the individual "Notes on the Text."

---

[27] Schleich and Zupitza omit the Leiden manuscript (V) from their edition of the *Fabula*, and MacCracken omits Cambridge MS Hh.4.12 (C) from his. MacCracken omits the Peterborough manuscript (P) from his edition of the *Guy*. See further the "Manuscripts" section of each individual introduction in this volume (pp. 25–28 and 100–104).

INTRODUCTION TO *FABULA DUORUM MERCATORUM*

Lydgate's *Fabula duorum mercatorum [The Tale of Two Merchants]*[1] is a 910-line poem that exemplifies the extraordinary friendship between two merchants. Lydgate's source is a short, straightforward twelfth-century exemplum which becomes in Lydgate's hands a courtly and philosophical romance shot through with allusions — both implicit and explicit — to Boethius's *Consolation of Philosophy,* Chaucer's *Troilus and Criseyde,* and Chaucer's Knight's Tale.[2] Although the poem stands apart from Lydgate's other short narrative poems[3] in its narrative sophistication, and its survival in seven medieval manuscripts suggests some contemporary popularity, it has received little critical attention.[4] Yet it is one of the best medieval treatments of the popular theme of male friendship, and in its rhetorical complexity and overall quality, it deserves to be better known.

The tale centers on two merchants, one from Egypt and the other from Baldac (in Syria),[5] who become acquainted through trade. Knowing each other only by hearsay, they are delighted to meet when the Syrian travels to Egypt on business. After eight days of entertainment and socializing, the visitor falls ill. All the doctors of the land are summoned, who, after much deliberation, diagnose love sickness. After bringing forth all the women in his household, the Egyptian finally summons a woman he has brought up in his house with

---

[1] The title is scribal, appearing in London, British Library, MSS Harley 2251 and Additional 34360. Since the edition of Schleich and Zupitza, the poem has been known as the *Fabula duorum mercatorum*.

[2] On the relationship of the *Fabula* to Chaucer's Knight's Tale, see Farvolden, "'Love Can No Frenship,'" and Stretter's response, "Rewriting Perfect Friendship."

[3] Under MacCracken's still useful classification of Lydgate's works, the other short narratives are "The Churl and the Bird," "Guy of Warwick," "The Debate of the Horse, Goose, and Sheep," and "Isopes Fabules" as well as the *Fabula*. See MacCracken, ed., *Minor Poems*, 2:v.

[4] Only one other recent article focuses specifically on the *Fabula,* L. Cooper's "His guttys wer out shake." L. Cooper examines the merchants' relationship as mercantile and commercial, and compares the *Fabula* to Lydgate's "Letter to Gloucester." Earlier criticism of the poem is scarce and brief: Schirmer treats the poem briefly and somewhat inaccurately in his 1952 study *John Lydgate: A Study*. Ebin is also brief, and focuses on the poem's digressions, which "emotionalize the action and give the simple plot a new intensity [and] . . . magnify the characters' sense of loss and their dilemmas in an uncertain and transitory world" (*John Lydgate,* p. 112). Pearsall is even-handed; though he feels the story "sinks" beneath the weight of its digressions and is "lost from sight," he goes on to note that "as an exercise of style it is superb . . . [and] must stand . . . as a warning against any underestimation of the range of Lydgate's skills" (*John Lydgate,* p. 204). For an earlier view of Pearsall's, see his "English Chaucerians."

[5] According to Ormrod, *Baldac* is Old French for Baghdad. See "John Mandeville," p. 337.

the intention of marrying her, and his guest confesses that she is the woman he loves. The Egyptian unhesitatingly gives her to the Syrian, along with her dowry and the gifts he had intended for her when she became his wife.

Some years later, the Egyptian, having lost all of his wealth, travels to Baldac, seeking his friend's help. Arriving in the middle of the night, ashamed of his penury and afraid of being turned away, he spends the night in a mosque where, during the night, a man is murdered. In despair, the Egyptian confesses to the murder. As he is led to the gallows, his friend recognizes him and seizes the opportunity to repay the Egyptian's previous kindness by crying out that he himself is the murderer. As the Egyptian is taken to the scaffold, the real murderer feels such contrition and guilt that he confesses, and all three are brought before the king, who marvels at this extraordinary display of loyalty, love, and friendship. The Egyptian, after receiving half his friend's goods, then chooses to return home, although his friend has offered him a home in Baldac.

SOURCE AND NARRATIVE CONTEXTS

Lydgate's narrative source is the second tale from the *Disciplina Clericalis,* a collection of exempla compiled and translated from Arabic to Latin in twelfth-century Spain by Petrus Alfonsi, a Jewish doctor and scholar.[6] This collection of thirty-four didactic tales is, according to Eberhard Hermes, the "oldest collection of novelle in the Middle Ages,"[7] and it became well known throughout Western Europe, serving, as "a sort of bridge or literary medium through which Eastern, predominantly Arabic popular stories, proverbs and sayings, [were] transmitted or transplanted to Europe."[8] The *Fabula* is based on the second tale of the collection, "The Perfect Friend."[9]

This tale became the source for a number of continental and English tales of friendship, which developed along two different but analogous lines. One of these is represented by Boccaccio's prose tale of Titus and Gisippus in the *Decameron* (eighth day, tenth story). While Alfonsi's tale remains at the core, Boccaccio made some significant changes and

---

[6] Moses Sefardi, who took the name Petrus Alfonsi when he converted to Christianity in 1106. See Hermes, ed., *Disciplina,* especially pp. 36–43, and Schwarzbaum, "Folklore Motifs," p. 268. For an overview of Petrus Alfonsi and his works, see also Tolan, *Petrus Alfonsi*. Tolan does not mention, however, Lydgate's or other adaptations of this particular tale. See also Jones and Keller's useful introduction to *Scholar's Guide.*

[7] See Hermes, ed., *Disciplina,* p. 5.

[8] Schwarzbaum, "Folklore Motifs," p. 269.

[9] Also known as "The Whole Friend," in contrast to the first tale, "The Half Friend." This tale with its motif of perfect male friendship has ancient origins; it combines two folktale motifs which can be found separately or together in numerous analogues in Classical Greek, Roman, and Arabian literature. See Thompson, *Motif-Index,* P315 ("Friends offer to die for each other") and P325 ("Host surrenders his wife to his guest"). H1558.2 ("Test of friendship: Substitute as murderer") is also relevant. See also Lee, *Decameron,* pp. 334–38, for a particularly full list of ancient analogues to Alfonsi's tale as well as Hermes, ed., *Disciplina,* p. 180n25, and Schwarzbaum, "Folklore Motifs," pp. 288–90.

additions to plot details and setting,[10] and his version of the story became itself a source for many subsequent retellings. In fact, English writers treated it in verse, prose, and drama up until the nineteenth century,[11] and it seems still to be the best known version of Alfonsi's story. The other line of development, to which Lydgate's poem belongs, contains tales that more closely follow the narrative details of Alfonsi's tale, and examples can be found in many early European and Middle English exempla collections, for example, in the *Alphabet of Tales* and Caxton's *Aesop* (the first of the "Fables of Alfonce").[12] The version of the tale closest to Lydgate's is contained in the *Gesta Romanorum*, a collection of exempla probably compiled in the late thirteenth century that circulated throughout Western Europe.[13]

GENRE AND THEME

The difference between these very short, didactic, exemplary works and Lydgate's poem is profound. Lydgate's thematic concerns go beyond simply illustrating a perfect friendship and extend to an examination of the linked themes of fortune, love, and friendship. The first part of the *Fabula* — for it falls neatly into two parts, each anchored by a test of friendship — shares with The Knight's Tale an examination of the claims of friendship and

---

[10] For example, the principals are named, the setting is Athens, and the two parts of the tale are more closely connected, the poverty of the original lover being caused by his yielding the woman to his friend.

[11] The first English appearance of the tale of Titus and Gisippus was either William Walter's poem *Tytus and Gisyppus,* which may have been published in the 1530s, or Sir Thomas Elyot's prose version, inserted in his *Boke Named the Governour,* published in 1531 (Chapter 12, Book 2). Other versions of this popular tale include, for example, Edward Lewicke's "The most wonderful and pleasaunt History of Titus and Gisippus . . ." (1562), Edward Jenynges' "Notable Hystory of two faithfull Louers named Alfagus and Archelaus . . ." (1574), Thomas Deloney's "of the faithfull friendship that lasted betweene two faithfull friends" in *Garland of Good Will* (1631), Thomas Durfey's "Titus and Gissippus" in *Stories, Moral and Comical* (1706), Oliver Goldsmith's story of Alcander and Septimus (*The Bee* 6 October 1759), Charles Lloyd's "Titus and Gisippus" in *Desultory Thoughts on London, Titus and Gisippus,* with other poems (verse, 1821), and Gerald Griffin's *Gisippus* (drama, produced at Drury Lane 23 February 1842). See Wright, *Boccaccio in England.*

[12] It is #57 in *Alphabet of Tales*. See Banks, ed., *Alphabetum Narrationum,* pp. 126–27. For Caxton's version, see Lenaghan, ed., *Caxton's Aesop*. pp. 194–95.

[13] See Herrtage, ed., *Early English Versions of the Gesta Romanorum,* pp. vii–xxviii, for an explanation of the complex textual history of the several versions of the *Gesta*. For analogues to this tale, see #47, #28, #11, and #55. Although Herrtage thought that Lydgate was "probably indebted" (p. 482) to the Anglo-Latin *Gesta*, the differences in narrative detail and overall approach clearly indicate that this is an analogue and not a source. Schleich and Zupitza show that Lydgate knew Petrus Alfonsi's version directly (see *Fabula Duorum Mercatorum*, pp. lxxx–vi). And we know that there was a Latin text of the *Disciplina* in the Bury library, now London, BL, MS Royal 10 B XXII (for a list of contents, see the British Library's online *Catalogue of Illuminated Manuscripts*: http://www.bl.uk/catalogues/illuminatedmanuscripts/record.asp?MSID=5373&CollID=16&NStart=10021). See also Warner and Gilson, *Catalogue of Western Manuscripts,* 1:322. Two other of Lydgate's short poems, "Stans puer ad mensam" and "A Ballade of Jak Hare" (MacCracken, ed., *Minor Poems* 2:739, 445) are also adapted from the *Disciplina,* as is "The Churl and the Bird," although in this case Lydgate tells us that he got it from a "Frenssh . . . paunflet" (MacCracken, ed., *Minor Poems* 2:468, lines 34–5). Wolfgang's "Out of the Frenssh," posits a different source for "Churl."

those of love but offers an alternative to the potential clash engendered when two men fall in love with the same woman. In the case of Palamon and Arcite, the clash is deadly, but in the *Fabula* it is averted when the Egyptian relinquishes to his friend the woman they both love.[14] In the second part of the poem, an even more severe test of the friendship mirrors the first. The Egyptian merchant, finding himself friendless and impoverished, seeks death in his misery and despair. Confessing to a murder he has not committed, he is saved by the Syrian, who offers his own life for that of his friend. There are many Boethian echoes in this part of the *Fabula,* as the Egyptian merchant moves from despair to consolation and understanding that only true friendship can provide stability in an unstable world. Both parts of the poem are also steeped in allusion to Chaucer's great romance *Troilus and Criseyde,* which elevates the doomed love of Troilus to tragedy and provides, like The Knight's Tale, a Boethian framework within which to understand human experience.

While Lydgate sticks to the basic narrative details of his original, he elevates it significantly with the addition of a variety of material. He infuses the first part of the poem with romance convention, casting the merchants as noble lovers and the object of their affection as a courtly lady, and creating, then solving, a conflict between the duties of love and friendship that was not present in Alfonsi's version. He also adds a good deal of contemporary medical lore, mainly on the symptoms and diagnosis of the Syrian merchant's illness, that may seem out of place. Yet the merchant's malady, lovesickness, is at the heart of this part of the poem, and the very experience of falling in love and nearly dying from the condition, as well as the noble friendship that allows the Egyptian to relinquish the object of his affection, contribute to the elevation of the poem to romance. In the second part of the poem, Lydgate's expanded descriptions and additions of detail impart a clear Boethian sensibility to the whole, contrasting worldly instability with the enduring quality of the merchants' friendship: in the face of sublunary change and the fickleness of fortune, true friendship is the only thing that can be counted upon. Lydgate's skilful synthesis of a variety of materials — romance and courtly love convention, classical and medieval friendship ideals, medieval medical lore, and Boethian ideals — effectively transforms the original short, simple exemplum on perfect male friendship into an elaborate and complex narrative linking the themes of friendship, fortune, and love.

ROMANCE AND FRIENDSHIP

The *Fabula*'s closest literary relative is the romance rather than the exemplum. Defining just what constitutes a romance is notoriously difficult, but this definition by D. S. Brewer remains one of the most helpful:

[14] The *Fabula* may in some ways be seen as Lydgate's answer to The Knight's Tale. See Farvolden, "'Love Can No Frenship,'" p. 27. Stretter also takes up this idea, although his purpose and argument differs from mine; see "Rewriting Perfect Friendship," and Stretter's "Engendering Obligation" in which he elaborates on the relationship between the ideals of brotherhood and friendship in Middle English romance.

> Romances are idealistic in moral tone and physical setting; they are usually about noble love and brave adventure concerning knights and ladies in exotic settings and culminating in marriage; and they are often elaborately written.[15]

In the *Fabula,* Lydgate creates a highly idealized tone and setting, elevating his merchants to the status of courtly lovers and noble friends, and placing them into an explicitly romance setting. The poem is peopled with noble characters who move within a courtly landscape, in evidence from the opening stanza, which places us immediately into the exotic and faraway land of Egypt, and indeed recalls the opening of both Chaucer's Knight's and Squire's Tales:

In Egipt whilom as I reede and fynde,	*once (long ago)*
Ther dwellyd a marchaunt of hih and gret estat,	
Nat oonly riche but bounteuous and kynde,	*generous*
As of nature to hym it was innat.	
For alle vertues in hym wern aggregat,	*gathered together*
Of vices voyd, pitous, and merciable	*kind and merciful*
And of his woord as any centre stable.[16] (lines 1–7)	

The merchants themselves are immediately characterized in noble terms: the Egyptian is wealthy, generous, and kind, and the Syrian too is honest and worthy. Further, this friendship is also idealized in terms that remind us of romance, particularly romances of male friendship. The theme of male friendship had some currency in medieval continental and English romance literature,[17] as evinced by such works as *Amis and Amiloun* and its many

---

[15] D. S. Brewer, ed., *English Gothic Literature,* p. 77. Other useful discussions include H. Cooper, *English Romance in Time*; Finlayson, "Definitions of the Middle English Romance"; Pearsall, "Development of Middle English Romance"; and Strohm, "Origin and Meaning." Useful studies and collections of articles include (but are not limited to) Aertsen and MacDonald, ed., *Companion to Middle English Romance*; C. Brewer, ed., *Traditions and Innovations*; Fewster, *Traditionality and Genre*; Kreuger, ed., *Cambridge Companion to Medieval Romance*; Meale, ed., *Readings in Middle English Romance*; Mehl, *Middle English Romances of the Thirteenth and Fourteenth Centuries*; Purdie and Cichon, ed., *Medieval Romance, Medieval Contexts*; Radulescu and Rushton, ed., *A Companion to Medieval Popular Romance*; and Stevens, *Medieval Romance*.

[16] The Knight also refers to a time long past and a tale found in books: "Whilom, as olde stories tellen us, / Ther was a duc that highte Theseus" (*CT* I [A], 859–60). Compare also The Squire's Tale: the kyng of Tartarye was "hardy, wys, and riche, / And pitous and just, alwey yliche; / Sooth of his word, benigne, and honurable; / Of his corage as any centre stable" (*CT* V[F], 19–22).

[17] An excellent overview of the development of friendship ideals and a survey of recent scholarship can be found in the introduction to Lochman, Lopez, and Hutson's *Friendship in Early Modern Europe*. Two other particularly useful surveys of philosophical and literary traditions of friendship are Langer's *Perfect Friendship* and Hyatte's *Arts of Friendship*. Interestingly, neither Langer nor Hyatte mentions Lydgate's *Fabula,* though both take note of Boccaccio's tale, particularly Hyatte, who discusses *Titus and Gisippus* at some length (*Arts of Friendship*, pp. 146–63). See also Jaeger's *Ennobling Love*, in which he argues for a tradition of male friendship that was an ennobling, aristocratic, and social ideal long before the twelfth-century emergence of what is traditionally called courtly love. Also useful are Purdy's "Friendship Motif" and Mills's *One Soul in Bodies Twain*.

analogues,[18] *Sir Amadace, Eger and Grime,* and *Guy of Warwick,*[19] and by its popularity as a subject for discussion in such works as Gower's *Mirror de l'Omme* (13693–740) and de Meun's *Roman de la Rose* (lines 4680–4762 and 4865–4974).[20] The protagonists' relationships in the romances are based on chivalric ideals of knightly brotherhood as well as classical friendship ideals, and although Lydgate's merchants are hardly knights, they are nevertheless elevated beyond their bourgeois status by their virtue and innate nobility. They can be ideal friends because of their virtue, and the friendship in turn ennobles them. When this friendship is threatened first by a courtly love triangle and then by despair and imminent death, they choose friendship: each gives up that which is most valuable to save the life of the other.

Lydgate draws heavily on classical and medieval ideals to portray the relationship between the two merchants, invoking Aristotelian and especially Ciceronian ideals that emphasize virtue as the basis for friendship.[21] In the *Fabula,* virtue is immediately emphasized in the opening stanza. The Egyptian is entirely free of vice, innately generous and kind. The equally virtuous Syrian is worthy, beloved, and honest (lines 43–44). Virtue draws them together (line 47) and they become fast friends without ever having seen each other:[22]

> Withoute siht, ech is to othir deere
> Love hath her hertys so soore set affyre. (lines 90–91)

When they meet, it is as established friends: "Wolcom my feithful freend so deere!" (line 140) exclaims the Egyptian. In its development and subsequent testing, the two merchants' friendship demonstrates several key components of the ideal, summarized usefully by Reginald Hyatte:

[18] For a useful survey and discussion of these see Leach's introduction to his edition of *Amis and Amiloun*.

[19] But not, it must be noted, in Lydgate's *Guy*, which treats only the last part of the narrative. See the Introduction to Lydgate's *Guy* in this volume.

[20] For Gower, see *Mirour de l'Omme*. For *Rose*, see Dahlberg, ed., *Romance of the Rose*. This section, like so many others in the *Rose*, is heavily indebted to Boethius's *Consolation of Philosophy*. Lydgate himself wrote a short didactic poem on friendship built on the "friend at need" theme, drawing together a series of commonplaces and mentioning a number of famous friends, including Amis and Amiloun; it makes an interesting comparison with the *Fabula.* Chaucer's poem "Fortune" is also relevant. The connection between fortune and friendship — the idea that one only comes to know one's true friends when fortune turns against one — is fundamental to the *Fabula* and is discussed below. See Lydgate, "Freond at Neode" (MacCracken, *Minor Poems* 2:755), and Chaucer, "Fortune" (Bensen, *Riverside*, pp. 652–53).

[21] The connection between virtue and friendship was articulated in Aristotle's *Nichomachean Ethics* but Cicero's *De amicitia* was the *locus classicus* for the ideal. For articulations of classical friendship ideals and their transmission to the medieval period, see Jaeger, *Ennobling Love,* pp. 28–31; as well as Langer, *Perfect Friendship,* pp. 18–25; and Hyatte, *Arts of Friendship,* Chapter 1, especially pp. 16–21 on Aristotle and pp. 26–33 on Cicero. See also Mills, *One Soul in Bodies Twain,* especially Chapters 1 and 2; Purdy, "Friendship Motif," pp. 113–15; and Mathew, "Ideals." See also Mathew and Purdy, especially for a correlation of Ciceronian ideals with the writings of, for example, St. Augustine ("Friendship Motif," p. 120), St. Thomas Aquinas ("Ideals," pp. 47–48), St. Aelred of Rivaeaulx ("Friendship Motif," pp. 120–21), and Richard Rolle ("Friendship Motif," p. 127).

[22] That virtue can create friendship and love across a distance is a Ciceronian idea. See Explanatory Note to lines 48–49.

> [P]erfect friendship exists only between virtuous men who love virtue in one another for its own sake; *amici veri* [true friends] are like a single soul in two . . . bodies; they have all possessions in common, and their affection is reciprocal; their characters, tastes, and opinions are in complete agreement; while growing closer to one another in intimacy, they also grow in virtue and wisdom that benefit others besides themselves; *vera amicitia* [true friendship] . . . is worth pursuing and even dying for; it requires a long period of maturation and testing; it lasts for a lifetime or even beyond life; and finally, there are exceedingly few, if any, living examples to which to refer.[23]

The merchants' own virtues and their ennobling friendship[24] elevates them from their bourgeois status and fits them for courtly romance. Their manners, their speech, their behavior, and the world within which they move conform to all the conventions that govern this world of romance. They conduct themselves nobly and courteously at all times, enacting patterns of *gentil* behavior that govern, for example, greeting and leavetaking,[25] feasting and reveling, hawking and hunting — a particularly aristocratic pursuit — and, especially, falling sick with love.

AMOR HEREOS AND ITS SOURCES

The love-stricken Syrian merchant in Lydgate's poem suffers from an illness that Lydgate, drawing upon a long medical and literary tradition, identifies as "Amor Ereos" (line 336). Suffered perhaps most famously by Arcite in Chaucer's Knight's Tale, "the loveris maladye / Of Hereos" (*CT* I [A] 1373–74) is the medical condition of lovesickness, an acute melancholia brought about by excessive love that, if left untreated, could be life-threatening.[26] The conventional symptoms of lovesickness included a changed appearance, insomnia, and melancholy, and are well-illustrated by the love-stricken Arcite in Chaucer's Knight's Tale:

> His slep, his mete, his drynke, is hym biraft,
> That lene he wex and drye as is a shaft;
> His eyen holwe and grisly to biholde,

[23] Hyatte, *Arts of Friendship,* pp. 4–5. Hyatte's last point here, that this sort of friendship is rare, is also emphasized at the end of the *Fabula,* when the king marvels at the strength of the love that has saved not one but two lives, and wishes that there were more in his "regioun" who could display "an obligacioun / of such enteernesse" (lines 858–60) to one another.

[24] Some of what Jaeger points to in his study of the historical, literary, and philosophical tradition of passionate male friendship is relevant to the merchants' love for each other. For example, he characterizes this "ennobling love as 'primarily a way of behaving, only secondarily a way of feeling . . . Its social function is to show forth virtue in lovers, to raise their inner worth, to increase their honour and enhance their reputation'" (Jaeger, *Ennobling Love,* p. 6). He also points out that love both comes from and creates virtue as well as noble manners (p. 116).

[25] For example, compare the Egyptian's words to the Syrian when he arrives: "Wolcom my feithful freend so deere! / Now have I found that I so longe have souht" (lines 140–41), with those of Bertilak to Gawain in *Sir Gawain and the Green Knight*: "Ȝe ar welcum to welde as yow lykez / þat here is; al is yowre awen, to haue at yowre wylle and welde" (Tolkien, lines 836–37).

[26] See Wack, *Lovesickness,* p. 189. Wack's work is an essential source for medieval conceptions of love and lovesickness. Also essential is Wells, *Secret Wound,* especially pp. 1–51; and Lowes, "Loveres Maladye."

His hewe falow and pale as asshen colde,
And solitarie he was and evere allone,
And waillynge al the nyght, makynge his mone;
And if he herde song or instrument,
Thanne wolde he wepe, he myghte nat be stent. (*CT* I[A] 1361–68)

Like Arcite, the Syrian merchant suffers so acutely from melancholy that his life is in danger. The first part of the poem is replete with medical details concerning the Syrian's symptoms, the doctors' struggles to identify the causes of his illness, their diagnosis of lovesickness, and the causes of this disease. Lydgate draws so heavily on medical terminology and current medical knowledge to describe the symptoms and diagnosis of this illness that this abundance of medical detail threatens at times to derail the poem. However, these details, in combination with numerous allusions, both explicit and implicit, to Chaucer's Knight's Tale and *Troilus and Criseyde*, place the Syrian firmly in the company of other noble sufferers like Arcite and Troilus.

As both Marion A. Wells and Mary Wack explain, the term "Amor Hereos" and the idea of acute lovesickness seem to have their roots in Arabic medical lore, transmitted to Western Europe in the eleventh century by Constantine the African, whose chapter on lovesickness in the *Viaticum* "was the most widely-read text on the subject" until a translation of Avicenna's *Canon medicinae* became available in the late thirteenth century.[27] It is not known how Constantine's "amor qui et eros dicitur" became *amor hereos*, but the term seems to have arisen by a conflation of the words *eros*, erotic love, and *hero*. As Wells explains, "The conflation of [these] two distinct etymological lines . . . seems to have provided sufficient opportunity for the coining of the hybrid term *amor hereos*."[28] Wack notes that *eros* seems to have become *heros* very early in the tradition, and suggests that love and nobility were linked as early as the twelfth century.[29] Gerard of Berry's twelfth-century commentary on the *Viaticum*, the earliest to survive, explicitly links the medical and the social in his description of the sufferers of "amor qui heros": "Heroes are said to be noble men who, on account of riches and the softness of their lives, are more likely to suffer this disease. "[30] The association between nobility, love, and love-melancholy had become firmly established not only in medical treatises but also in such literary works as Andreas Capellanus's twelfth century *Art of Courtly Love*, in which Andreas describes love as "a certain inborn suffering" and takes as a given that it is both noble and ennobling.[31] At the same time, commentaries on the *Viaticum* as well as other numerous medical treatises[32] discuss the causes, symptoms and treatment of lovesickness as they would any other disease. By the fourteenth century, lovesickness as a specific medical condition that could be suffered only by the noble was well established.

---

[27] Wack, *Lovesickness*, p. xiii.

[28] Wells, *Secret Wound*, p. 22.

[29] See Wack, *Lovesickness*, p. 60.

[30] Wack, *Lovesickness*, p. 203. See also Wells, *Secret Wound*, pp. 22–23.

[31] See Andreas Capellanus, *Art of Courtly Love*, p. 28. For a comparison of Andreas's and Gerard of Berry's definitions of love, see Wack, *Lovesickness*, pp. 61–62.

[32] Some fourteenth and fifteenth century writers who treat of lovesickness are Jacques Despars, William of Corvi, Gerard de Solo, Arnald of Villanova, John of Gaddesden, and Bernard of Gordon. See Lowes, "Loveres Maladye"; Wack, *Lovesickness*; and Wells, *Secret Wound*.

THE CAUSES OF *AMOR HEREOS*

Lydgate provides an abundance of sometimes bewildering medical detail to establish the diagnosis of lovesickness, drawing heavily on contemporary medical knowledge and terminology to describe in detail the causes and effects of the particular illness known as *amor ereos*. Though it is difficult to say whether Lydgate had an exact source for his lengthy description of the process whereby a lover falls prey to the malady (see lines 330–50), one close contemporary description comes from the *Lilium Medicinae* of Bernard of Gordon, a well-known fourteenth-century physician.[33] This popular medical treatise contains a description of *amor hereos* which is very close to Lydgate's:

> The cause of this passion is a corruption of the *virtus aestimativa* on account of a firmly fixed form and figure. Thus when anyone is overcome by love [*philocaptus*], with reference to any woman, he so conceives her beauty and figure and manner that he thinks and believes that she is more beautiful, more venerable, more attractive, and more gifted in nature and conduct than any other; and thus he ardently desires her without method or measure, thinking if he could attain his end it would be his felicity and blessedness . . . .[34]

This description depends on our understanding of medieval theories of how the mind works. Mental activity was explained in terms of three main ventricles, or cells, in the brain, each given over to a particular task. According to John Trevisa, translating the work of the early encyclopedist Bartholomaeus Anglicus, the first cell is the *ymaginativa*, or imagination, which forms images delivered to it by sense impressions. The middle ventricle is where logic is found, wherein "Þe vertu *estimatiue* is maister"; and the third and last is *memoratiua*, memory.[35] The imaginative faculty[36] receives images which are examined and judged by the middle cell, the estimative, while the third ventricle "retains such forms as pass this examination and so is the seat of memory."[37]

Lovesickness is caused when the estimative faculty malfunctions, overestimating an excessively pleasing form and judging it to be better and more beautiful than any other. The *estimatyfe* then orders the imaginative faculty "to fix its gaze on the mental image of the

---

[33] Bernard appears in Chaucer's General Prologue (line 434) as part of a long list of medical writers with whose work the Physician is said to be well acquainted. See *CT* I[A] 429–34. For a brief but useful account of Bernard, see Demaitre, "Bernard de Gordon," pp. 84–85. Bernard was considered an authority on "various baffling diseases" including lovesickness. Seaton cautiously suggests that Lydgate's source was Bernard. See Seaton, *Roos*, p. 275.

[34] Translation by D. W. Robertson, *Preface to Chaucer,* p. 458. For the original Latin, see Lowes, "Loveres Maladye," p. 499. Gerard of Berry, the thirteenth-century glossator of Constantine, seems to have been the first to articulate this particular view of the causes of lovesickness. Bernard's description here can be profitably compared to Gerard's, quoted and translated by Wells, *Secret Wound*, pp. 38–39. See also Wack, *Lovesickness*, pp. 56–58, whose useful summary is also quoted in the Explanatory Notes to lines 338–43.

[35] See Seymour, ed., *Properties,* 1:98. See also Winny, "Chaucer's Science," pp. 177–78; Thorndike, *History,* 1:660; and the helpful diagram in Wack, *Lovesickness,* p. 57. For a detailed account of the physiology of lovesickness, see Ciavolella, "Medieval Medicine."

[36] Also known as the "fantastical" (line 56) or the "celle fantastik" (*CT* I [A], 1376).

[37] Thorndike, *History,* 1:660. Both Wells, *Secret Wound,* pp. 40–42, and Wack, *Lovesickness,* p. 56, point out that Avicenna is the ultimate source for this picture of the brain's physiology.

beloved" — it "ovirlordshipith / his imagynatif" (line 340) — and this faculty "in turn orders the concupiscible faculty to desire that person alone."[38] The process leads to melancholy solitude and can even result in madness ("manye," line 344) as the lover's soul becomes fixated on the object to the exclusion of all else.

AMOR HEREOS, FEVER, AND TROILUS

The Syrian's main symptom, a "brennyng fever" (line 202) is not usually the most prominent feature of the literary lover nor a well-attested symptom in medical treatises. But Lydgate may have found this detail in the work of Giles de Corbeil, or Aegidius Corboliensis, the "Gyles" of line 308.[39] Lydgate's description of the three different sorts of fevers the Syrian might have, Effymera, Putrida, and Etyk, closely resemble Giles's discussion.[40] An explanation for the connection between lovesickness and fever can be found in both the medical and literary traditions which fix the seat of emotions in the heart and not the brain.[41] According to medieval physiology, the heart was not an organ which pumps blood but a furnace "from which heat and vital spirits spread outwards along the arteries, to warm and vivify all the members."[42] A fever is the natural heat of the body gone out of control, as Bartholomaeus explains: "Feuer cometh of distemperaunce of the herte, for as Constantinus seith, a feuer is an vnkynde hete that cometh out of the herte."[43] And this is the source of the Syrian merchant's fever: Cupid's arrow has stricken him in his breast (line 225), and he feels it "hoolly" in his "herte" (line 232).

In literary tradition, love is also described in terms of fire and heat. In the Middle English *Romaunt of the Rose* and *Troilus and Criseyde*, fever is connected with the pains of love. In the *Romaunt*, the God of love warns the young lover about the many pains of love he is bound to suffer:

---

[38] Wack, *Lovesickness*, p. 58.

[39] Giles de Corbeil, sometimes called "the medical poet" (Thorndike, *History*, 1:737), was a twelfth-century medical scholar and teacher who produced medical texts in poetry. See Wallis, "Giles de Corbeil," pp. 198–99. Zupitza was at first unable to determine the source of Lydgate's lines on the various kinds of fever but he apparently later traced them to Giles. Neither Zupitza nor Schleich, however, note Giles' *Viaticus* as the source. See Schleich and Zupitza, ed., *Fabula Duorum Mercatorum*, pp. lxxxvii–viii and n1. Seaton, however, determined the source as Giles's *Viaticus: De signis et symptomatibus aegritudinum*, a compendium of symptoms and causes of illness. See Seaton, *Roos*, p. 275.

[40] For Giles's original, see Rose, ed., *Egidii Corboliensis*, lines 1919–24, 1950–60, 2185–90 (pp. 78, 80, 90). The remaining 168 lines of the *Viaticus* (there are 2358 in all) also provide a relevant background to Lydgate's discussion of Putrida.

[41] "Medical writers traditionally maintained that the brain was the seat of sensation and emotion, but Aristotle claimed that [emotions] . . . originated in the heart" (Wack, *Lovesickness*, p. 78). The commentaries on Constantine of "Giles" (probably, Giles of Santarem, says Wack, *Lovesickness*, p. 74) and Peter of Spain both question Constantine's view that love was a disease of the brain. See Wack, *Lovesickness*, pp. 78–79, 94–95.

[42] Winny, "Chaucer's Science," p. 177.

[43] See Seymour, ed., *Properties*, 1:379.

Thou shalt no whyle be in o stat
But whylom cold and whilom hat,[44]
Now reed as rose, now yelowe and fade.
Such sorowe, I trow, thou never hade;
Cotidien ne quarteyn,
It is nat so ful of peyne. (Frag. B, lines 2397–2402)[45]

The comparison of love's pains with those of "cotidien" or "quartan" fever is taken a step further in *Troilus*, when the young Trojan, in order to hide the pains of love by which he is suddenly smitten,

a title . . . gan him for to borwe
Of other siknesse, lest men of hym wende
That the hote fir of love hym brende,
And seyde he hadde a fevere and ferde amys. (*Troilus and Criseyde*, 1.488–91)

Troilus's choice of fever as an appropriate cover for his illness would be a natural one, since both fever and love are hot. It would have been a small leap from the consideration of fever as an appropriate disguise for lovesickness to the treatment of it as an actual manifestation of the disease.

Book 1 of *Troilus* may have provided Lydgate his inspiration for the *Fabula*'s explicit connection of lovesickness and fever. Lydgate would have recognized the similarity between the situations of Troilus and the merchant, who both suffer from a love which they feel compelled to keep secret. Both suffer alone and in agony, and both are wounded by the "fyr of love" (*Troilus*, 1.436), but while Troilus feigns fever to cover his symptoms, the Syrian merchant actually experiences a serious fever. In *Troilus*, the descriptive focus is on the general imagery of love's fire and heat: love's fire burns Troilus so that he loses his color "sexti tyme a day"; he wishes to see Criseyde, "his hote fir to cesse" (1.445) but the "ner he was, the more he brende" (1.448). In the *Fabula*, Lydgate converts the imagery of love's burning fire into the literal fact; his merchant becomes ill with a real, "brennyng fevere" (line 202) which threatens his life. In his employment and description of this fever, Lydgate skilfully synthesizes medical theory and literary convention.[46]

THE *FABULA* AND *THE CONSOLATION OF PHILOSOPHY* OF BOETHIUS

The *Consolation of Philosophy* of 6th-century philosopher Boethius provides a significant background for understanding the *Fabula*. In the *Consolation*, Lady Philosophy appears to

---

[44] Variations of this phrase appear in *Troilus and Criseyde*, 1.420, and the *Fabula*, line 222.

[45] Fragment B of the Middle English *Rose* cannot be attributed to Chaucer. See Benson's introduction to *The Romaunt of the Rose* (*Riverside*, pp. 685–86).

[46] The *Fabula* includes a number of other allusions to *Troilus and Criseyde*. Both Troilus and the Syrian give voice to their suffering in an artistic complaint, although the merchant's differs in content and quality from the "Canticus Troili," which Chaucer translated from Petrarch's Sonnet 88. See *Troilus*, 1.400–20. Lydgate probably also owes several turns of phrase to *Troilus;* like Troilus, the merchant has been stricken with love through "the castyng of an ye" (*Fabula*, lines 229–30, *Troilus*, 1.305–06), takes to his bed and begins to "sike and groone" (*Fabula*, line 205, *Troilus*, 1.360), and suffers from extremes of heat and cold (*Fabula*, line 222, *Troilus*, 1.420).

Boethius,[47] who, imprisoned and facing execution for treason, bewails the loss of his riches, position, and friends, blaming his present unwarranted adversity and the injustice of his situation on bad fortune. Through a series of dialogues, Lady Philosophy leads Boethius to an understanding of the nature of Fortune, happiness, free will, evil, and God's providence. One of her first lessons is that bad fortune is actually good fortune because it reveals that only things of true value — virtue, love, friendship — are not subject to the mutability characteristic of the sublunary world ruled by Fortune.[48] This is, of course, also the lesson learned by both merchants in the second part of the poem, which traces the Egyptian's fall from prosperity into poverty, his bitter complaints against Fortune, his despairing bid for death by confessing to a murder he did not commit, and his redemption, brought about by the same friendship he thought he had lost. Lydgate ties the Egyptian's losses to the theme of worldly instability and sharply contrasts the stability of friendship with the instability of the sublunary world. Only when the Egyptian is at his lowest point can he be rescued from despair and certain death by the Syrian's selfless act of friendship, which act in turn prompts the true murderer to confess his guilt, thereby saving the Syrian through the virtue of truth.

That Lydgate may have drawn on the *Consolation* to shape the *Fabula* is not surprising; this popular and enormously influential work was readily available in Latin and had been translated several times into both French and English by the fifteenth century.[49] Three of the most significant were the French translation of Jean de Meun, continuator of the *Romance of the Rose*, Chaucer's English prose translation, *Boece*, and John Walton's 1410 English verse translation.[50] Lydgate's own monastic library at Bury St. Edmund's had at least a partial Latin copy of the *Consolation*, British Library, MS Royal 8.B.4, as well as a copy of Nicholas Trevet's commentary.[51] This library, one of England's largest and best, almost certainly would have had a complete copy as well. Yet Lydgate seldom mentions Boethius. In the vast corpus of his work, Lydgate refers to Boethius only four times, just twice as the

[47] For the sake of clarity, I will refer to the first-person speaker in the *Consolation* as Boethius although as Frakes, for example, points out, the speaker should perhaps more properly be referred to as the Prisoner to ensure that we do not read the *Consolation* as autobiography. See Frakes, *Fate of Fortune*, p. 5n13.

[48] Fortune was often personified as a blind goddess who, in turning her wheel, threw down the high and sometimes raised the low. Perverse, mutable, and often hostile, she rules the sublunary world and assails those who place too much importance on the worldly and the material. For a useful introduction to the figure of Fortuna, see Frakes, *Fate of Fortune*. Also still useful is Patch, *Goddess Fortuna*. For recent discussion of Lydgate's treatment of fortune and tragedy, see Nolan, *John Lydgate and the Making of Public Culture*, especially pp. 120–83; and John Mortimer, *Narrative Tragedy*, especially pp. 153–216. Pearsall's chapter on the *Fall of Princes* (*John Lydgate*, pp. 223–54), is also still useful.

[49] On the medieval popularity of Boethius, see Richard Green, *Poets and Princepleasers*, pp. 145–49; Minnis, "Aspects"; and Minnis and Machan, "The *Boece*." See also Cropp, "*Livre de Boece*," who notes that there were "at least twelve distinguishable French translations" completed between the thirteenth and fifteenth centuries (p. 64).

[50] *Boece* survives in ten manuscripts and Walton's in twenty-one. See Minnis and Machan, "The *Boece* as Late-Medieval Translation," who point out that the *Boece* was one of Chaucer's most popular works (p. 167) and that Walton's superseded Chaucer's in popularity (p. 186).

[51] See James, *On the Abbey of St. Edmund*, p. 76, and Pearsall, *John Lydgate*, p. 37.

author of the *Consolation*.[52] And in the *Fall of Princes*, Lydgate shortens the tragedy of Boethius to only five stanzas and makes no reference to the *Consolation*, though he does mention Chaucer's *Boece* briefly in the Prologue to the work.[53] This led Henry Bergen, the *Fall of Princes*'s editor, to remark rather dryly that "Lydgate's knowledge of Boethius as a philosopher . . . does not seem to have been very profound. He must have known something about Chaucer's [*Boece*] . . . yet he may never have read it."[54] It may have been this comment to which Richard Dwyer refers in the only article of which I am aware on Lydgate's specific use of the *Consolation*.[55] The *Fabula* may now provide a similar example. Lydgate may have turned to the *Consolation* to provide gravitas to his romance, particularly in the light of its resemblances and persistent allusiveness to Chaucer's two great philosophical romances, The Knight's Tale and *Troilus and Criseyde*. Like these, the *Fabula* examines virtue, love, friendship, and human experience within a philosophical context provided by Boethius.

Echoes of Boethius lie behind the Egyptian merchant's plunge from prosperity to poverty. At the nadir of his fortunes, he resembles those figures whose falls from high to low form the *de casibus* tradition of which Lydgate's monumental *Fall of Princes* is the fullest (and lengthiest) fifteenth-century English expression.[56] *De casibus* narratives like Lydgate's *Fall of Princes* and Chaucer's Monk's Tale are based on a concept of tragedy that comes ultimately from Boethius: "What other thynge bywaylen the cryinges of tragedyes but oonly the dedes of Fortune, that with an unwar strook overturneth the realmes of greet nobleye."[57] The merchant is not a noble, though both friends have been presented as such over the course of the poem, but perhaps that is the point: all who live under the sway of the blind goddess are subject to the turning of her wheel. Like the eminent men whose falls are recorded by *de casibus* literature, he too has been blind-sided by the "unwar strook" of Fortune; and like them too he is an exemplar of those who think their positions can be

[52] These are in the *Troy Book* (Bergen, 4:652, lines 3008–13) and "A Thoroughfare of Woe"(MacCracken, ed., *Minor Poems* 2:822–23, lines 9–12). "Boys" is mentioned in connection with music in "A Pageant of Knowledge" (MacCracken, ed., *Minor Poems* 2:729, line 127) and in "Henry VI's Triumphal Entry into London" (MacCracken, ed., *Minor Poems* 2:638–39, lines 244–46).

[53] Prologue, line 291 (Bergen, ed., *Fall of Princes*, 1:9). The tragedy of Boethius is at 8:897, lines 2626–60.

[54] See Bergen, ed., *Fall of Princes*, 4:326. Eleanor Hammond, too, despite her identification of Lydgate's translation of the lines from Boethius, also doubted how much Lydgate had used or cared about Boethius. See "Boethius: Chaucer: Walton: Lydgate," p. 534.

[55] Robert Ayers noted some years ago that the *Siege of Thebes* is "essentially Boethian" ("Medieval History, Moral Purpose," p. 465) in connection with the more general "moral and philosophical framework" of the poem. David Lawton's important article on fifteenth-century Boethianism ("Dullness") includes several of Lydgate's major poems in his discussion. While the *Fabula* shares in a "pervasive Boethianism" (Lerer, *Chaucer and His Readers*, p. 14), in its attention to Fortune and its brush with the *de casibus* theme, it demonstrates beyond these a more specific influence from the *Consolation* itself. See also the General Introduction, n1.

[56] Duke Humphrey commissioned Lydgate's translation of Boccaccio's *De casibus virorum illustrium* probably in 1431. Working from Laurence de Premierfait's French translation of Boccaccio, Lydgate spent eight years on the 36,365-line work. See Pearsall, *John Lydgate*, p. 223; see also Mortimer, *Narrative Tragedy*, pp. 53–61, and Petrina, *Cultural Politics*, pp. 281–312.

[57] Chaucer, *Boece*, 2.pr2.67–70 (Bensen, ed., *Riverside*, p. 409). On the significance of the "unwar strook" and how it relates to Lydgate's conception of tragedy, see Nolan, *Making of Public Culture*, especially pp. 124–30, and Mortimer, *Narrative Tragedy*, especially pp. 165–68.

secure in a sublunary world. Lydgate spells this out for us: "Take heed, ye ryche, of what estat ye bee / For in this marchaunt your myrour ye may see" (lines 664–65). The merchant is a mirror as much as are those "pryncis" of the *Fall of Princes*, whose stories show "a merour how al the world shal faile / And how Fortune . . . Hath vpon [them] iurediccioun."[58]

But although the *Fabula* may gesture toward *de casibus* tragedy, the Egyptian merchant's story does not end at the bottom of Fortune's wheel. Unlike the unfortunates whose falls are permanent, and unlike Boethius himself, the merchant is restored to happiness. Paradoxically, it is in his redemption and the means by which it is achieved that the influence of the *Consolation* can most clearly be seen. The *Fabula* demonstrates in the Egyptian's downward plunge and restoration that when the illusory gifts of "worldly blisse" (line 565) are withdrawn, all that remains is friendship, a virtue which, existing outside of Fortune's domain, is the only thing each merchant has that is truly valuable. This is exactly what Lady Philosophy points out to Boethius in the *Consolation of Philosophy* at the end of Book 2: "Now pleyne the [thee] nat thanne of rychesse ylorn, syn thow hast fouwnden the moste precyous kynde of rychesses, that is to seyn, thi verray freendes."[59]

The Egyptian merchant's situation in particular recalls that of Boethius. Having lost his wealth, his position, and, most importantly, his friends, the Egyptian wanders alone and homeless in the wilderness, his misery made more acute by the remembrance of "oold prosperité" (line 533). Like Boethius, who explains to Philosophy that "in alle adversites of fortune the moost unzeely kynde of contrarious fortune is to han ben weleful [i.e. prosperous],"[60] the merchant blames fortune for his desperate condition, bewailing his situation in a long lament (lines 549–88) decrying the instability of the world. Both men at this stage understand their situations in terms of the "sodeyn turn" (line 566) of Fortune's wheel. Each is more acutely aware of his misery because he was formerly fortunate, and each blames fortune for his desperate condition.

Both Boethius and the merchant move toward enlightenment through wise philosophical counsel. Philosophy teaches Boethius that so-called bad fortune reveals what is truly worthwhile, and the *Fabula*'s narrator, addressing the merchant, counsels patience in adversity. Quoting Seneca,[61] the narrator explains that no one can be virtuous "withouten assay" (line 609), particularly if he has been weighed down by too much plenitude and "fals felicité" (line 614). The merchant now recognizes that the world is "ful unstable" (line 622). Having achieved this insight, he falls to his knees, putting himself under God's protection and praying for hope. Significantly, he does not ask for his riches to be restored. He receives immediate "consolacioun" (line 640) in the form of a new understanding about those fleeting gifts, and he determines to seek his friend's help. Like Boethius, the merchant has moved from misery and complaint to the beginnings of recognition that friendship is outside of Fortune's domain.

Yet the Egyptian suffers a further setback. Arriving in Baldac, he suddenly feels deeply ashamed and finds that he cannot, after all, forget his former wealth and position. Shrinking from the possibility that his friend might turn him away, he resolves to spend the night in a temple where he witnesses a murder. In deep despair, he confesses to the murder,

---

[58] Lydgate, Prologue, lines 159–61 (Bergen, ed. *Fall of Princes*, 1:5).

[59] Chaucer, *Boece*, 2.pr.8.45–48 (Bensen, ed. *Riverside*, p. 420).

[60] Chaucer, *Boece*, 2.pr.4.7–9 (Bensen, ed. *Riverside*, p. 411).

[61] See Explanatory Notes to lines 603–09 and 610–16.

hoping death will bring a final end to his suffering. Here we encounter a striking parallel between the *Fabula* and the *Consolation* in the words of the merchant as he is led to the gallows:

O deth, desyred in adversité,	*adversity*
Whan thu art callyd, why nylt thu wrecchys heere?	
And art so reedy in felicité	*happiness (prosperity)*
To come to them that thee nothyng desire?	
O com now, deth, and maak of me thy feere! (lines 743–47)	*partner*

As Eleanor Hammond recognized, these lines appear to be a "close and spirited translation"[62] of several lines from the opening meter of the *Consolation of Philosophy*.[63] Chaucer translated the lines in the *Boece*[64] and adapted them in the *Troilus*,[65] but Lydgate's lines are closer to the original than they are to either the literal prose of the *Boece* or the eloquence of *Troilus*. Lydgate's version captures, at a dramatically and contextually appropriate moment, the fervency and emotion of the original, drawing a contrast that emphasizes death's cruel irony: it too often comes unbidden but too seldom comes to those who desire it. The lines aptly parallel those of the *Consolation* in context and tone, and their appearance here is strongly suggestive.[66]

Striking imagery that seems rooted in the *Consolation* prepares for and underlines this turning point in the text. Just before the merchant witnesses the murder, the forward movement of the narrative is halted for a digression on Fortune and the movements of the stars. Fortune's assaults on both "free and bonde" (line 670) are vividly described, setting up two stanzas implicitly suggesting that Fortune does not, after all, rule the world. There is a plan, and the universe is orderly, despite our inability to maintain a constant awareness of this truth:

For by exaumplys Nature doth declare,	
Which is of God mynystir and vikeer,	*minister and vicar*
Withoute tonge she biddith us beware	*be aware*
By thylke sterrys that shynen briht and cleer,	*those*
Which, by her concours and mevyng circuleer	*their courses and circular motion*
In her discens, westyng undir wavys,	
Us to enfourmen by chaungyng of hir lawys.	*inform us*
And fewe of hem alway to us appeere,	
But yif it be the bere briht and sheene	*Unless it is the bear (the Big Dipper)*
In thilke plow that Arthow doth it steere;	*Arcturus*
For yit Boetes, that twynkelith wondir keene,	*In addition; Boötes; wonderfully bright*
Somwhile is dym that men may nat hym seene;	*Sometimes*

[62] Hammond, *English Verse*, p. 185. Hammond first made the observation in her short article "Boethius: Chaucer: Walton: Lydgate."

[63] "Mors hominum felix quae se nec dulcibus annis / Inserit et maestis saepe vocata venit," *The Consolation of Philosophy*, 1.m1.13–15 (Stewart, et al., trans. *Theological Tractates*, p. 130).

[64] "Thilke deth of men is weleful that ne comyth noght in yeeris that ben swete, but cometh to wrecches often yclepid," *Boece*, 1.m1.18–20 (Bensen, ed., *Riverside*, p. 397).

[65] See *Troilus* 4.501–04.

[66] Alessandra Petrina asserts without equivocation that Lydgate translated the lines *(Cultural Politics*, p. 310).

Eek Lucifeer, at morowhil prymycere, *the morning star*
By nyht hym hidith undir our empeere. *hides himself under the empyrean*
(lines 673–686)

In imagery and context, these stanzas are very close to Meters 5 and 6 of the *Consolation*'s Book 4, which reassure Boethius that the stars and constellations move according to God's plan. They are orderly, even if they do not always seem so: "Whoso that ne knowe nat the sterres of Arctour, ytorned neyghe to the sovereyne centre or poynt . . . and wot nat why the sterre Boetes passeth or gadreth his waynes and drencheth his late flaumbes in the see; and whi that Boetes, the sterre, unfooldeth his overswifte arysynges, thanne schal he wondryn of the lawe of the heie eyr."[67] The courses of the stars are designed to ensure concord: Ursa "nis nevere mo wasschen in the depe westrene see, ne coveyteth nat to deeyen his flaumbes in the see of the Occian, although it see othere sterres iplowngid in the see. And Hesperus the sterre bodith and telleth alwey the late nyghtes, and Lucyfer the sterre brygneth agein the clere day."[68] It is not just the striking similarity in image; in context, too, the references are appropriate. Philosophy is responding to Boethius's question of why the good are punished and the evil rewarded in what appears to be a random universe. The *Fabula*'s narrator is likewise signaling that Fortune's power is limited — and it is significant that Fortune is not mentioned again in the poem.

This cluster of images is immediately followed by an extended reference to Jupiter's two casks, one filled with honey and the other with gall, an image also found in the *Consolation*.[69] The figure is a medieval commonplace,[70] and Lydgate used it several times, most significantly for this discussion in his "Disguysing at London."[71] In her cogent analysis of how Lydgate's conception of tragedy is articulated in the "Disguysing,"[72] Maura Nolan shows how the topos of the two casks connects Fortune with Boethian tragedy. When Philosophy in the voice of Fortune asks Boethius somewhat mockingly what right he has to complain if he has consumed too much from the cask of sweetness, the question, Nolan notes, "is consistent with the providential vision of the *Consolation*, in which lament is repeatedly set aside in favor of a philosophy of world rejection, a turning away from earthly matters and toward the divine, toward a universe bound up by love."[73] In the *Fabula*, the two tuns are also intimately connected with worldly rejection and universal harmony. After hearing of the reassuringly orderly universe, we are urged to "despise . . . erthly lustys" (lines 691–92) and are reminded that we cannot have the sweet without the bitter: "who that wil swetnesse first abroche, / He

[67] Chaucer, *Boece*, 4.m5.1–9 (Bensen, *Riverside*, p. 450).

[68] Chaucer, *Boece*, 4.m6.11–18 (Bensen, *Riverside*, p. 454).

[69] See Chaucer, *Boece*, 2.pr2.73–76 (Bensen, *Riverside*, p. 410).

[70] Chaucer and Jean de Meun, for example, both borrowed it from Boethius. See Chaucer's Wife of Bath's Prologue (*CT* III (D), 170–71) and *Roman de la Rose* (lines 6813–29). Though Boethius is the medieval locus for this topos, the ultimate source is Homer's *Iliad* (Lattimore, trans., 24:527–533, p. 489).

[71] For a recent edition, see Sponsler, ed., *Mummings and Entertainments*. Also known as the "Mumming at London" (see MacCracken, ed., *Minor Poems* 2:682), this dramatic performance text demonstrates how Fortune can be overcome by the four cardinal virtues of Prudence, Justice, Fortitude, and Temperance.

[72] Nolan, *Making of Public Culture*, especially pp. 120–54.

[73] Nolan, *Making of Public Culture*, p. 187.

mot be war, or bittir wol approche" (lines 706–07). The Egyptian has drunk deeply from both (line 708) and is about to utter the despairing lament translated from Boethius. Thus both the "Disguysing" and the *Fabula* make use of the same cluster of Boethian images and to the same ends. Nolan recognizes Boethius as one of Lydgate's three main sources for the "Disguysing," along with Chaucer and Jean de Meun.[74] It is significant that Fortune, who no longer has any power over either merchant, disappears from the *Fabula* at this point. The Syrian's enduring friendship rescues the Egyptian from the gallows and prompts the true murderer to confess, causing the king, amazed at the willingness of one friend to die for another, to release all three men. The power of this friendship to redeem and remove the men from the unstable world governed by Fortune has been aptly demonstrated.

DATING THE *FABULA*

A date for the composition of the *Fabula* has not been satisfactorily established. The manuscript texts of the poem contain no headings, marginal glosses, or other notations that might indicate an occasion, a commission, or a patron for the poem. Only Pearsall and Schirmer address the question,[75] and Pearsall considers it a non-issue. Grouping the poem with Lydgate's "Fables and Didactic Poems,"[76] Pearsall says, "the moralistic and didactic preoccupations of these poems are the permanent preoccupations of Lydgate . . . and the manner in which he wrote changed little through the years."[77] Schirmer, treating the *Fabula* in the last chapter of his book on Lydgate's last works, clearly thought that the *Fabula* was a very late work, after 1440, but he offers little reliable support. His assessment of Lydgate's later style is clearly influenced by his interest in depicting Lydgate as a forerunner of humanism,[78] and his description of the poem itself is flawed by several inaccuracies.[79] Speculations about date on the basis of style and theme must be treated cautiously.

---

[74] See Nolan, *Making of Public Culture*, pp. 139, 141, and throughout her discussion. The "Disguysing" bears some interesting additional similarities to the *Fabula* in its treatment of Fortune, its *de casibus* section, and its promotion of virtue as a way to overcome Fortune's depredations.

[75] Ebin (*John Lydgate*), perhaps following Pearsall, does not address questions of date, nor does Stretter ("Rewriting Perfect Friendship"). L. Cooper mentions that the *Fabula* is "believed to have [been] composed in the same period" as the "Letter to Gloucester" but offers no evidence (L. Cooper, "His guttys wer out shake," p. 305).

[76] This is the title of the chapter in which Pearsall considers such works as *Isopes Fabules* and *The Churl and the Bird* as well as a number of Lydgate's shorter moral and didactic poems (*John Lydgate*).

[77] Pearsall, *John Lydgate*, p. 192.

[78] According to Schirmer, Lydgate's later work "is characterized by verbose dialogues and monologues that could almost be called humanistic, mysterious flourishes, and a delight in obscure language. Even where he introduces a simile drawn from nature he uses far-fetched phrases suggestive of the style of the sixteenth and seventeenth centuries" (*John Lydgate: A Study*, p. 238). Schirmer's example from the *Fabula* of one such simile is itself problematic and mis-contextualized. He tells us that lines 193–94 ("her ioiful somer is tapited al in greene / Of stable blew is her bothen hewe") illustrate the "meeting of the two friends" (p. 238). In fact, the merchants have already met and the lines depict the strength of their already established relationship.

[79] For example, Schirmer writes that the merchants become acquainted through a third person (*John Lydgate: A Study*, p. 237), that they "compete honorably" (p. 237) for the hand of the woman they both love, and that the poem "closes with a panegyric to divine justice" (p. 238).

It may, however, be reasonable to make some suggestions about audience and period of composition if the poem is seen, as the foregoing introduction has suggested, as a philosophical romance rather than a fable or purely didactic work. The treatment of love, the contextualizing of the merchants' behavior within a courtly setting, and the Boethian shape of the narrative all suggest connections with Lydgate's courtly poems such as "A Complaynt of a Lover's Life" and the *Temple of Glas* as well as his mummings, including the "Disguysing at London," works probably written before 1430.[80] Also belonging to this period are "The Mumming at Bishopswood," "The Mumming for the London Goldsmiths," and "The Mumming for the Mercers of London." Wealthy merchants would certainly have been part of the audience for these performances.[81] It might not be unreasonable to suggest a similar audience and date in the late 1420s for the *Fabula*, which, in its portrayal of merchants' noble, virtuous, and gentle behavior, might have spoken to the aspirations of the merchant class.

There is what seems to be a contemporary reference near the poem's end. The king, reflecting on the virtue and faith of the merchants, wishes

that thoruh his regioun
Were ful affermyd an obligacioun
Of such enteernesse fro man to man aboute; *complete loyalty*
Of tresoun than ful litil wer to doute.

Ful hard it were tacomplisshen his desyr, *It would be hard*
Or in his rewm such a bargeyn dryve, *realm*
The aeyer infect, the wedir is nat cleer, *is infected*
Ne nevir ne shal whil tresoun is so ryve. *nor will it be; rife*
For now, of trowthe, no man can contryve *produce (create)*
A verray seel, or thenpreent igrave, *A true seal or engraved imprint*
Withoute a label his armes hool to save.
(lines 858–68)

While the complaints about treason seem generalized[82] and could refer to any number of events during the reigns of Henry V or VI (including his minority), they are coupled here with some fairly specific concerns about creating and preserving seals, their imprints, and coats of arms. Seals were used to authenticate official letters and documents and were often engraved with armorial bearings or heraldic devices; and labels refer to marks of cadency on heraldic arms that usually indicated the bearer as the eldest son.[83] The use of seals and armorial bearings was not limited to kings, nobility, or the knightly classes; the merchant class and the

[80] See Pearsall, *Bio-Bibliography*, pp. 28–31. J. Alan Mitchell dates the *Temple of Glas* to between 1427 and 1432 ("Secret of Lydgate's Temple of Glas," p. 63). On the date of "A Complaynt of Lover's Life," see Symons, ed., *Dream Visions and Complaints*, p. 83.

[81] On the audience for these texts, see Pearsall, *Bio-bibliography*, pp. 28–31; Warren, "Lydgate, Lovelich," especially pp. 114–19; and Sponsler, "Lydgate and London's Public Culture," especially p. 19. Both Warren and Sponsler describe the intended audience of these public texts as including members of London's civic elite, including merchants and members of craft guilds. James Simpson suggests that the *Fabula* may have been written for the Goldsmiths ("Energies," p. 58).

[82] The word *treason* could mean anything from traitorous behavior to falseness, duplicity, or general wickedness (see *MED treisoun*).

[83] For the connection between seals and heraldry, see especially Keen, *Chivalry*, pp. 132–33 and Thrupp, *Merchant Class*, pp. 250–54.

newly emerging gentry had been increasingly adopting armorial bearings of their own volition throughout the fourteenth and early fifteenth centuries and imprinting these on their seals.[84] Whether the lines above refer to the upper or middle classes is not clear; nor is it clear whether the treason spoken of might refer to a case of counterfeiting or forging. At this point, no particular historical occurrence or set of circumstances can be identified that would help explain the context of these lines, though they would seem to point to something specific and current.

MANUSCRIPTS

The *Fabula* is indexed in IMEV 1481. The poem is found in seven fifteenth-century manuscripts: London, British Library, MS Harley 2251 (Ha); London, British Library, Additional MS 34360 (A); London, British Library, MS Lansdowne 699 (L); Leiden, University Library, MS Vossius Germ. Gall. Q.9 (V); Oxford, Bodleian Library, MS Rawlinson Poetry F. 32 (R); Cambridge, University Library, MS Hh.4.12 (C); and London, British Library, MS Harley 2255 (H). The text is complete in only three of the manuscripts, H, C, and V. L is missing eight stanzas, Ha and A are missing one each, and R is missing the final two. Five of these manuscripts (Ha, A, L, V, and H) are part of a larger group of interrelated fifteenth century English manuscripts. Many are Lydgate anthologies, a number are directly or indirectly connected with John Shirley, and several significantly overlap in terms of the number and order of their Lydgate items, which in some cases are also strikingly similar in text and textual variants.[85] With respect to our group, L and V, often called "sister manuscripts," share closely similar Lydgate texts and variants; Ha and A, both derived from Shirley manuscripts, share the same scribe and a number of Lydgate items; and H has twelve Lydgate poems in common with Ha.

London, British Library, MS Harley 2251 (Ha): 293 leaves, on paper, dated by Manly and Rickert after 1464 and by Hammond to "during or after the reign of Edward IV."[86] Both this volume and A belong to a group of manuscripts which in whole or in part were copied by the Hammond scribe, so called because he was first identified by Eleanor Hammond. This scribe was active in London between the 1460s and 1480s and copied a large variety of works,

[84] On the inter-connections between seals, heraldry, and social aspiration, see Keen, *Origins of the English Gentleman* (especially pp. 23–24, 99, 128–31, 155–58) and Thrupp, *Merchant Class*, pp. 249–309. See also Coss's *Origins of the English Gentry*, especially pp. 216–54, for a useful overview of the emergence of the gentry class.

[85] First discussed by Hammond in "Two British Museum Manuscripts" (pp. 1–28), these manuscripts are linked in a variety of ways in terms of content, scribe(s), and provenance. Many of the manuscripts containing one or both of the poems edited in this volume belong to this group; in addition to the five noted above, these include Cambridge, MA, Harvard University, Houghton Library MS Eng. 530; BL MS Harley 7333; Cambridge, Trinity College MS R.3.21; and Oxford, Bodleian Library MS Laud Misc. 683. There are a number of discussions and descriptions of the larger group and sub-groups: for Shirley-related manuscripts, see especially Linne Mooney, "John Shirley's Heirs" (pp. 182–98) and Margaret Connolly, *John Shirley*, pp. 173–89. Other useful discussions are those of Julia Boffey, "Short Texts in Manuscript Anthologies" (pp. 70–72) and A. S. G. Edwards, "Fifteenth-Century Middle English Verse Author Collections" (pp. 103–04).

[86] See Manly and Rickert, *Text of the Canterbury Tales*, 1:242; Hammond, "Two British Museum Manuscripts," p. 27; and M. C. Seymour, *Chaucer Bibliography*, 1:140–43.

including Chaucer's *Canterbury Tales*, Hoccleve's *Regiment of Princes*, Fortescue's *Governance*, Lydgate's and Burgh's *Secrees*, and many others.[87] Harley 2255 contains 133 religious and secular items, most of them Lydgate's. The *Fabula* appears on fols. 55r–70r and ends with this colophon: *Explicit ffabula duorum mercatorum De et super gestis Romanorum*. Lines 100, 171, 214, and 484–90 are missing, and stanza 17 appears after stanza 12.

British Library, MS Additional 34360 (A) (olim Phillips 9053): 116 leaves, on paper, with a *terminus ad quem* of 1485.[88] This MS, also copied by the Hammond scribe, contains 24 items in common with Ha, eleven of which appear in the same order in both. Like Ha too, it contains mostly Lydgatian works. The *Fabula* appears on fols. 4r–18v and ends with the same colophon as appears in Ha. The text is also missing the same lines, with the exception of 171, and stanza 17 is also misplaced.

London, British Library, MS Lansdowne 699 (L): 176 leaves, on paper, quarto, mid to late fifteenth century. The manuscript consists of two main parts, the first (fols. 1–94) containing Chaucer's "Fortune," "Truth," and sixteen Lydgate items (all of which also appear in V), and the second (fols. 96r–176r) containing Lydgate's *Life of Saint Albon and Saint Amphibalus*.[89] The *Fabula* appears on fols. 3r–18r. Stanzas 41–48 are missing, owing to a leaf lost between folios 7 and 8.

Leiden, University Library, MS Vossius Germ. Gall. Q.9 (V): 135 leaves, quarto, late fifteenth century. Like L, V consists of two parts, distinguishable on the basis of hand, paper, and gatherings. The first part of the manuscript (fols. 1–116) contains the same eighteen items as appear in L, ten of them in the same order. The second part contains Lydgate's *Testament* and eight anonymous short works. The parallels with L in the first part of this manuscript, not only in content but also in the frequently similar texts and variants, led Van Dorsten to posit a common ancestor.[90] The *Fabula* appears on fols. 49–65.

---

[87] See Hammond, "Two British Museum Manuscripts" and "A Scribe of Chaucer," pp. 27–33. Since Hammond's articles, a number of scholars have added to the list of manuscripts copied by this scribe. For excellent summaries of this scholarship and recent discoveries and discussion, see Linne Mooney, "More Manuscripts Written by a Chaucer Scribe," pp. 401–07; and Mooney, "A New Manuscript," pp. 113–23. See also Daniel Mosser, who suggests paper stocks as a way of sequencing and dating these manuscripts in "Dating the Manuscripts of the Hammond Scribe," pp. 31–70, especially pp. 31–45.

[88] See Pearsall, ed., *The Floure and the Leafe and The Assembly of Ladies*, p. 8.

[89] The two Chaucer poems are counted as one item by both Robinson ("On Two Manuscripts," p. 191) and the cataloguer of the Lansdowne manuscript. For good descriptions of this manuscript, see Hammond, *Bibliographical Manual*, pp. 331–32; Reinecke, ed., *Saint Albon and Saint Amphibalus* (pp. xi–xiii); and Withrington, "Arthurian Epitaph," pp. 232–33.

[90] See Van Dorsten, "The Leyden Lydgate Manuscript," p. 320; the entire article contains a good description of V. See also Robinson, "On Two Manuscripts," pp. 186–94. The texts of both the *Fabula* and *Guy* in L and V are very similar and often — but not always — share the same or similar variants. See the Textual Notes to both poems in this volume, which sometimes correct MacCracken's collation. (To compare, see MacCracken's textual apparatus for the *Fabula* and for *Guy* in *Minor Poems*, 2:486–516 and 516–38.)

Oxford, Bodleian Library, MS Rawlinson Poetry F. 32 (R): a small volume, on paper and parchment, dating from perhaps the mid to late fifteenth century.[91] Its contents are varied, including several shorter religious and didactic pieces, four by Lydgate, and two longer works, *Brut* and *Libelle of English Policy*. The *Fabula* appears on fols. 38r–53v, with the last two stanzas of the poem missing, owing to a lost leaf after fol. 53. (Folio 54r is blank, save for an indecipherable scribble; a new text, the "Prouerbis of Wysdom" (IMEV 3502) begins on fol. 54v.)

Cambridge, University Library, MS Hh.4.12 (C): a quarto volume on paper and parchment, dating from the late fifteenth century,[92] with many poems by Lydgate; it also includes Burgh's *Cato* and ends with an incomplete copy of Chaucer's *Parliament of Fowls*. The *Fabula* appears on fols. 61r–77r and is not titled. It ends simply with a scribal ffinit.

London, British Library, MS Harley 2255 (H): Harley 2255 is an illuminated volume of 157 leaves, on vellum, measuring 10 3/4 by 7 5/8 inches. Most of the forty-five items are religious and didactic poems; of these, twenty-five are specifically marked *explicit quod Lidgate*, and in two more Lydgate names himself as author. This is clearly a quality manuscript, with illuminated capitals flourished with green sprays and gold balls, blue or gold paraph marks, and a clear, well-proportioned fifteenth-century hand.[93] Formerly thought to have been produced for Lydgate's abbot, William Curteys, possibly under Lydgate's own direction, and thus dating to no later than the 1440s,[94] the manuscript can now with some confidence be placed in the group of manuscripts written by the "Edmund-Fremund scribe" and dated to the 1460s. It was certainly written at least in part and probably in whole by this scribe, who was responsible for at least ten other manuscripts (including four of Lydgate's *Lives of SS Edmund and Fremund*) characterized by hand, decorative program, primarily Lydgatean contents, and

---

[91] Madan, *Summary Catalogue,* 3:290. For more information on R, see my unpublished dissertation, *A Critical Edition of John Lydgate's* Fabula Duorum Mercatorum, University of Alberta, 1993, pp. 27–31. (This dissertation contains fuller descriptions of all the *Fabula* manuscripts, though some have been superceded since then, notably that of Harley 2255.)

[92] For a description and discussion of this manuscript, see Boffey, "Short Texts in Manuscript Anthologies," pp. 76–81. See also Mooney, Horobin, and Stubbs, "Cambridge Hh 4.12," *Late Medieval English Scribes*. Available online at http://www.medievalscribes.com/index.php?browse=manuscripts&id=20&nav=off.

[93] For a complete description of this manuscript, see Reimer and Farvolden, "Of Arms and the Manuscript," especially pp. 241–43. Eleanor Hammond was the first to describe the manuscript, briefly, and dated the hand to the early fifteenth century. See Hammond, "Two British Museum Manuscripts," p. 24. For two excellent studies of the contents and themes of Harley 2255, see Joseph Gross, "Where Ioye is ay Lasting" and "Cloistered Lydgate, Commercial Scribe."

[94] This idea, based on Eleanor Hammond's suggestion in "Two Manuscripts," (pp. 24–25) that the coat of arms in the first capital of the manuscript might represent a combination of the Bury coat of arms and those of Curteys, was accepted for a number of years. However, as Steven Reimer and I have shown, we can no longer accept without question either this interpretation of the coat of arms or the dating of the manuscript to the early 1440s. See Reimer and Farvolden, "Of Arms and the Manuscript."

probable location in Suffolk, perhaps even in the town of Bury St. Edmunds.[95] The text of this edition is based on Harley 2255, the earliest of the seven and one of the best authorities for Lydgate's work. This is also the text upon which the Schleich and Zupitza (1897) and MacCracken (1934) editions are based. However, neither edition takes account of all seven manuscripts, Schleich and Zupitza omitting V and MacCracken C.

NOTE ON THE TEXT

As outlined in the General Introduction, I have followed METS guidelines in preparing this edition of the *Fabula*. I have based the edition on the text in Harley 2255, emending very little and only when not to do so would cause confusion. I have silently expanded scribal abbreviations, taking the macron to indicate *m* or *n*. Strokes ignored as otiose are those occasionally appearing on final *r* or penultimate *r* with *s*, and *h* with a cross-stroke, which appears frequently but entirely inconsistently. (MacCracken ignores flourished *r* and generally the crossed *h*, though not consistently; Schleich and Zupitza are also inconsistent in both cases). I have also silently separated words written as one word where clarity dictates there be two; for example *acerteyn* (line 26) becomes *a certeyn*. On the other hand, two-word phrases beginning with *for* when *for* is used as an intensifying prefix (see *MED for-* (pref. 1)) have been joined: *forwar* (line 389), *forpossyd* (line 532), *forblowe* (line 563), *forwhirlyd* (line 574), *format* (line 662), and *fordempt* (line 755) on the model of scribal *forfareth* (line 445), *fordoo* (line 483) and *forwandryd* (line 662). *For astonyd* (line 729), however, as it often appears as a set phrase (see *MED astonyd,* (ppl.)) has been left unaltered. Where the scribe writes the *I/i* of the past participle signifier as a separate word, I have silently joined these words as well; for example, *I fet* becomes *ifet* (line 58). I have also inserted stanza numbers for ease of reference. The textual notes include substantive variants that record significant differences in meaning or form as well as any emendations I have made. I have not included variations in spelling or grammatical form (for example, *no/noon, thankyth/thankid*), though on occasion I have included an interesting or unusual example. Where the meaning is the same but the form significantly different, I have also included the variant (for example, *eke/also*). I have ignored spelling differences between variants, including only one form, usually from the sigla that comes first alphabetically. If it is uncertain whether the variant records a different word or simply a different spelling (for example, *dool/dulle*), I have also included it. I do not make a special point of indicating where my text or collation differs from MacCracken's or Schleich and Zupitza's. I have not usually noted whether variants are scribal corrections nor have I included marginalia unless it is of particular interest.

---

[95] The latest addition to the Edmund-Fremund group is a manuscript in two fragments of Chaucer's *Canterbury Tales*, identified by Simon Horobin. See Horobin, "The Edmund-Fremund Scribe Copying Chaucer." Horobin here also provides an excellent summary of scholarship to date on the Edmund-Fremund scribe, including such essential articles as Kathleen Scott's "Lydgate's Lives of Saints Edmund and Fremund" and A. S. G. Edwards' "The McGill Fragment of Lydgate's *Fall of Princes*." For Harley 2255 specifically and its relationship to the E-F group, see Reimer and Farvolden, "Of Arms and the Manuscript."

Fabula Duorum Mercatorum

1

In Egipt whilom as I reede and fynde, *once (long ago)*
Ther dwellyd a marchaunt of hih and gret estat,
Nat oonly riche but bounteuous and kynde, *generous*
As of nature to hym it was innat.
For alle vertues in hym wern aggregat, *gathered together*
Of vices voyd, pitous, and merciable *benevolent and merciful*
And of his woord as any centre stable.

2

But as me thynkith it were convenient
Or in this tale I any ferther passe, *Before*
For to descryve to you that be present
Wher that this contré stant and in what place,
And if I erre I put me in your grace;
Forberith me now and heerith paciently, *listen*
For as myn auctour seith, riht so sey I.

3

This riche lond, moost passaunt of plenté,
With Surry marchith toward thorient, *Syria; the Orient (East)*
On which syde is eek the Rede Se *also the Red Sea*
And Libye stant ful in the Occident. *Libya; West*
Who castith the coostys of the firmament, *calculates (see note)*
The Grete Se northward shal he fynde,
And ferre by south, Ethiope and Ynde. *far toward the south*

4

As auctours witnesse, this lond is desolat
Of cloude and reynes aboute in every yle,
But yeer by yeer the soil is irrigat
And ovyrflowyd with the flood of Nyle,
The which endurith but a certeyn whyle,

As for a norshyng her frutys to fecunde, *to make fertile*
With corn and greyn to make the lond habounde.[1] *abundant*

5

Of sondry frutys and of marchaundise, *various*
Thoruhout envyroun it is so plenteuous, *the region*
What mercymony that men list devise *goods; wish for*
Is ther ful reedy and ful copious.
I hold it best to be compendious:
Of al richesse ther is such habundaunce
That every wiht hath ther suffisaunce. *man has enough*

6

This worthy marchaunt, this Egipcien
Which I of spak, was named ferre and wyde, *Of whom I have spoken; renowned*
For many oon that hym had seen *a person*
Spak of his name which gladly wol nat hyde; *would not like to*
And in a contré cald Baldac ther besyde *Syria*
Anothir marchaunt, as by relacioun, *by word of mouth*
Of hym hadde herd and of his hih renoun.

7

This latter marchaunt was eek a worthy man, *other; also*
Ful weel belovid also in his contré.
In trouthe he hadde al that evyr he wan, *he had looked after all of his profits*
And hym governyd evirmore in honesté. *himself*
From ech to othir the name began to fle,
That by report and by noon othir mene
Of her two lovys was maad a stable chene. *their*

8

Revolvyth ech by contemplacioun,
Al of his freend the lyknesse and ymage,
Thynkyng hath grave with deep impressioun *engraved a deep impression [of]*
Ech othris fourme, stature, and visage. *face*
Her hertys eye did alwey her message, *imagination; carried their messages*
And mynde medleth in the memorial, *intermingled*
And fet his foode in the fantastical. *found its emotional satisfaction*

9

Thoruhout her erys, wellyd of memorye, *ears; resounding with (filled with)*
The soun of fame of hem so ferre ifet *from far and wide*
Hath past and wonne the castel of victorye;
Forgetilnesse ne may it nat unshet. *Forgetfulness*

[1] Lines 24–29: *The yearly overflowing of the Nile makes the land fertile and abundant with corn and grain*

Love berith the keye and also the cliket — *lock*
As trewe porteer, that they mot needys dwelle; — *must necessarily*
So ar they loke withyne myndys selle. — *Thus are they locked (see note)*

10

Vertu goth ferre; he may nat hyde his liht.
Withoute feet, a gret paas doth he renne, — *great pace; run*
And wher he shyneth, no dirknesse of the nyht
His beemys dymmen, nor no cloude of synne.
Withoute smoke, fire ne may nat brenne, — *burn*
And gladly vertu wil into vertu trace
To seeke his feer in every coost or place. — *peer; region*

11

For riht as falsnesse anoon fyndith out his feere, — *soon; its*
So trouthe and trouthe as faste been at accorde. — *quickly*
Tweyne of o kynde togidre drawe neere, — *one*
So strong of nature is the myhty corde.
Kynde is in werkyng a ful myhty lorde, — *Nature*
In love he lynketh hem that be vertuous — *those*
Riht as dissolven thynges that be contrarious. — *Just as*

12

For lich of lich is serchyd and enqueerid:[1]
To merthe longith to fynden out gladnesse, — *mirth*
And wo can weepe thouh he be nat leryd, — *educated*
And dool eek drawith unto drerynesse, — *sorrow draws towards*
Honour is weddyd unto worthynesse.
Unto his semblable thus every thyng can drawe, — *Toward that which is similar*
And nothyng bynde hem but natur by hir lawe.

13

Repoort of vertu, oonly by audience, — *by word of mouth*
From ech to othir hath brouht the blisful soun — *report*
Of thes two marchauntis disseveryd by absence, — *severed*
That they been oon as by affeccioun; — *one*
Ther may be maad no divisioun.
Withoute siht, ech is to othir deere,
Love hath her hertys so soore set affyre. — *keenly*

14

By lond or se the good her chapmen carye — *goods; agents*
Was entircomownyd by her bothys assent. — *intermingled; their common*
Yif oon hadde ouht plesaunt or necessarye, — *If; anything*

---

[1] *Things that are alike seek each other out*

Unto the tothir anoon he hath it sent, *immediately*
So ful they were of oon accordement.
As oon in two and two in oon forevere,
That nouht but deth her love may dissevere. *nothing; sever*

15

Ferthere to telle how it fel of thes two,
As fortune wolde and eek necessité, *willed (required)*
That he of Baldac to Egipt must goo
For marchaundise that was in that contré.
Ful glad he was that he his freend shal see.
A blisful wynd into his seyl hath blowe,
His ship to dryve theras he may hym knowe. *to the place where*

16

And whan that he was arryved unto londe,
For joye hym thouhte he was in Paradys,
For every lovere may weel undirstonde,
That of frenship the moost sovereyn blys
Is for to be, withouten any mys, *without exception*
In thilke place where rootid is his herte, *that*
For to relese of love his peynes smerte. *alleviate; sharp*

17

For, riht as aftir the blake nyht of sorwe *just as*
Gladnesse folwith thoruh suyng of the day, *because of the ensuing day*
And fressh flourys displayen by the morwe
That wern toforn in dirknesse and affray,
And aftir wyntir sueth greene May, *follows*
Riht so of freendys, her tristesse for to fyne, *Just so; their sadness; end*
Is liht of presence whan it to them may shyne.

18

O out on absence of hem that loven trewe! *away with (fie on)*
O out on partyng by disseveraunce!
O ground of woo of her fevere newe!
I meene of freendys that langour in distaunce.
O bittir bale hangyng in ballaunce, *fate*
On thee a clamour now I wil begynne,
That causist lovers assondir for to twynne!

19

But as to them that han itastyd galle, *have; bitterness*
Mor aggreable is the hoony soote, *sweet*
Riht so to them that wern in myscheef falle *have fallen into trouble*
Is whan they heryn kalendys of her boote. *news of a remedy*
Of lovers art ful bittir is the roote,

But weel is hym that may the frute atteyne,
As whilom diden thes noble marchauntis tweyne.

20

For whan that he of Egipt herde seye
How that his freend was entryd into the londe,
For verray joye he felte his herte pleye,
And hym tencontre he seyde he wolde fonde. *he said he would meet him*
And whan they mette, he took hym by the honde
And kist hym aftir, and with unfeyned cheere *sincere*
He seide, "Wolcom my feithful freend so deere!

21

Now have I found that I so longe have souht! *what*
Wolcom!" he seide, by rowe an hundryd sithe. *a hundred times in a row*
And to his place anoon he hath hym brouht,
And hym receyved with herte glad and blithe.
He maad his menee her deveer doon as swithe *servants do their duty; quickly*
That al wer reedy that myht be to hym ese,
So fayn he was his freend to queeme and plese. *eager; make comfortable*

22

Unto a chaunbre ful riche and weel arrayed *well-appointed*
Anoon he lad hym, which stood somwhat on heihte, *rather high*
And seide, "Freend, I am ful weel appayed *well satisfied*
That I be grace of you have cauht a sihte,
For nothyng moore myn herte myht lihte.[1]
Wherfore wolcom, also, God me save,
Unto your owne and to al that I have." *You are welcome to whatever I have*

23

Of mete and drynk, deyntees and vitaille, *delicacies, meat*
Of divers wynes, ther was no skarseté;
Of straunge viaundys in sondry apparaille, *exotic foods presented elaborately*
That nevir aforn was seen such roialté.
To moore and lasse it snowyd doun plenté.
To rekken the fare and cours in thrifty wyse,
A somerys day ne myht nat suffise.[2]

24

The riche beddyng of sute so weel beseyne, *suite; well furnished*
Passaunt and plesyng, eek the roial paramentis *Excellent; decorations*
That for his freend this marchaunt did ordeyne,

[1] *Nothing could lighten my heart more*; (i.e., *I have nothing more to wish for now that I have seen you*)

[2] Lines 160–61: *A summer's day would not be enough time to count up all the courses and variety of food*

With al the soun of dyvers instrumentys, *sound, music*
Revel disguysed with chaung of garnementis, *costumed revels*
Of song and musyk, the merthe and melodye,
Al to reherse my witt I can nat plye.[1]

25

They ryde aboute with hauk and eek with houndys,
He shewith hym maneers, castellis, and eek tours;[2]
Thoruh al his lordship he lat hym in the boundys, *property (lands)*
By park, by forest, by meedwys fressh of flowrs. *meadows*
And list he were pryked with paramours, *lest; aroused by the desire to love*
Ful many a lady and maiden by his side
On white palfreys he made for to ryde.

26

Of al his tresour withyne and withoute,
Nothyng he hidith; of al he hadde a siht.
He saide, "Freend, withouten any doute,
What so I have is platly in your myht, *Whatever I have is all yours*
I feffe you fully in al my good and riht. *endow*
Beth glad and wolcom! I can sey you no more,
Have her myn hand for now and evirmore."

27

This straunge marchaunt thankyth hym with herte, *foreign*
Nay, straunge nat; allas, why seid I soo?
I spak amys; this woord now me asterte,[3]
Sith in accord confederat been they two, *united*
The boond is maad bothe for wele and woo. *for good and bad (for wealth or misfortune)*
I erryd foule to speke of straungenesse, *erred badly*
Of tweyne allyed so kneet in stabilnesse. *two; knit*

28

But as I seyde, with al herte entieer *wholeheartedly*
His freend he thankith of entent ful cleene. *very sincerely*
For now presence hath maad the wedir cleer,
Of absence chacyd the mystis ful of teene, *troubles*
Her joiful somer is tapited al in greene. *decorated (as with tapestry)*
Of stable blew is her bothen hewe, *Both take on the stable color of blue*
To shewe that two in love wer nevir so trewe.

---

[1] *I cannot shape my wit to describe all of it*

[2] *He shows him manors, castles, and also towers*

[3] *I spoke in error; the word slipped out inadvertently*

29

This blisful lyf from day to day they leede,
Tyl that fortune to them had enmyté;
Allas, for dool myn herte I feele bleede, *sorrow*
For evir unwarly cometh adversité. *Always unexpectedly*
This straunge marchaunt hath cauht infirmyté,
A brennyng fevere so soore did hym shake, *burning*
That fro the deth he trowith nat to skape. *from; he believed he could not*

30

A bed in haste was maad ful softely,
In which he cowchyd and gan to sike and groone; *lay; sigh and groan*
His prayeer was to alle pitously
That by hymsilf he myhte been alloone,
So kowde he best geven issu to his moone. *give issue to*
But than his freend for woo began to melte,
That al his peynes he seemyd that he felte.

31

Thus longith it to freendys entirparte *it is appropriate for friends to share*
Nat oonly merthe, but wo and hevynesse;
Yif oon hath peyne, bothe hertis it doth thoruh darte,
Yif that her love be set in sikirnesse; *stability*
And yif oon drye, bothe they have distresse. *shrivels*
This is the ballaunce oonly of freendys riht,
Evenly to deele wher they be glad or liht. *share whether*

32

And for tassaye yif it myht ese, *to test (try)*
The chaunbre is voyded and he is left al sool. *chamber; emptied; alone*
Than to hymselven he spak in his disese,
And seid, "Allas! My langour and my dool!
Now hoot, now coold, I erre as doth a fool,
Allas, and yit the cheffest of my peyne *worst*
Is that I dar to no wiht weel compleyne. *no one*

33

I am hurt but closyd is my wounde, *closed (i.e., secret, hidden)*
My dethis spere strykith in my brest.
My bollyng festrith that it may nat sounde, *morbid swelling festers; heal*
And yit no cicatrice shewith at the lest. *scar*
Cupidis darte on me hath maad arrest, *has rested on me*
The cleer streemys of castyng of an ye, *eye*
This is tharwe me causith for to dye. *the arrow*

34

And at myn herte is hoolly that I feele, — *I feel it entirely in my heart*
But aftir cure, God wot, I dar nat seche, — *God knows; seek*
My sweete fo is hard as any steele, — *foe*
Allas, unmercy doth to cruel wreche. — *the cruelty to a poor wretch*
For thilke flour that myhte be my leche, — *doctor (cure)*
She wot rihtnouht what wo that I endure,
And to be ded I dar me nat discure.[1]

35

And eek my freend, whom I love moost of al,
Yif that he knewh my secre maladye, — *secret ailment*
Ful cruel vengaunce shuld upon me fal
For myn outrage, despiht, and velanye, — *effrontery; disobedience*
That I durst evir clymbyn up so hihe — *dared*
To love that maiden kept for his owne stoor, — *treasury*
Thus must I deyen: what shuld I pleynen mor?[2]

36

I sauh ful many ladyes in the rowte, — *company*
So fayr, so fressh, ibrouht for my plesaunce,
But now for oon my liff lith al in dowte, — *my life is in doubt*
That of my deth ther is noon avoidaunce.
And yit the thyng that doth me moost grevaunce
Is that I shulde to hym I am so bounde,
Disnatural or traitour been ifounde.

37

For thilke goodly that he lovyd moost, — *that lovely [one]*
I am abowte falsly hym to reve. — *rob*
Love can no frenship, I se weel in no coost. — *knows*
Allas, Cupide, disseyvable for to leve! — *deceitful to trust*
Love rechchith nat his freend wrath and greve. — *cares not*
Allas of love! Such is the fervent heete
That litil chargith his freend for to leete."[3]

38

And whil he lay in langour thus musyng, — *wretchedness; fretting*
His freend wol besy was with al his myht — *fully occupied*
To serche aboute the lond environnyng;
His menee riden bothe day and niht — *retainers*
To founden som man that wer expert arriht, — *To find someone who was indeed expert*

---

[1] Lines 237–38: *She does not know the woe that I endure, / And for fear of my life, I dare not disclose my love*

[2] *Thus must I die: what is the use of further complaining?*

[3] *That cares little about [forcing someone to] forsake his friend*

Or phisicien, for no cost wold he spare
To have restoored the sike to weelfare. *sick man; well-being*

39

Assemblyd been of leechis many oon, *doctors*
The beste and wisest that he coude fynde;
Unto the sike they been icomen echoon,
To taste his poorys and for to deeme his kynde;[1]
They were ful besy to fynd out roote and rynde *completely*
Of what humour was causyd his dissese,
And theron werke his accesse to appese. *work to alleviate his illness*

40

With hem they brouhte, yif they sey neede, *saw*
Ful goode siropys to make dygestyves;
And therwithal the sonnere for to speede, *furthermore; the more quickly to heal*
Pelotes expert for evacuatyves, *Pills appropriate*
Ful precious poudrys and confortatives,
That whan they knew of maladyes the roote, *the root of the illness*
Nouht were behynden to werken for his boote. *Were not slow to work for his cure*

41

Whan they have serchid by signes his estat, *condition*
They merveyle gretly what it myht be,
That his fevere was nat interpollat, *intermittent*
But ay contynueth hoot and in oo degre.[2]
They seide certeyn it was noon of the thre,
But yif it were oonly Effymora *Except (i.e., Unless it were)*
For neithir Etyk it was ne Putrida.[3]

42

Effymera hath his original *originates*
Whan mannys spiritys been in distemperaunce,[4]
Or into excesse yif a wiht be fal, *or if a man has fallen into excess*
Of mete and drynk thoruh mysgovernaunce,
Of accidentis, of thouht, of perturbaunce,
Of hoot, of cold, or greef in any maneer,
This fevere cometh as auctours tellen heer.

---

[1] *To examine his urine* (or *to test his pulse*; see note) *and to determine the category of his illness*

[2] *But it continued hot and at a consistently high temperature*

[3] Lines 285–87: *They were certain it was none of the three* [*types of fevers*], / *unless it were* (i.e., *if it were, it could only be) Effymora; not Etyk or Putrida* (See note)

[4] *When the humours are imbalanced*

43

And Putrida is causyd gladly thus: *as a rule*
Whan any humour synneth in quantité,[1]
Or whan his flowyng is too plenteuous *its*
That he excedith mesoure in qualité; *it*
Yif by blood anoon ye may it see.
Yif quantité ouht erre, espyeth it thus: *If it errs in quantity, note it thus*
The fevere in phisyk is callyd Sinochus. *medical science*

44

And yif the humour in qualité exceedith,
Or heete or blood passe his temperament,[2]
Into a fevere anoon a man it leedith
Clepid Synocha, by putrefaccioun shent. *corrupted by putrifying*
And yif of Colre he take his groundement, *if bile is the cause [of the fever]*
Pure or unpure, citryn or vitellyne, *pale yellow or deep yellow*
Gyles you techith to juge it by uryne.

45

Also of Étikes ther be kyndes thre, *recurrent wasting fevers*
But oon ther is pereilous in special, *particularly perilous*
The which is whan, by degré,
Deeply profoundid is heete natural *The body's natural heat deeply penetrates*
In thilke humydité icallyd radical; *Into the primary moisture of the body*
The which fevere is gladly incurable, *as a rule*
For drye tisyk is withal partable. *severe cough; tolerable*

46

Of othir humours han thes leechys eek
Ful deepe enqueeryd to serchen out the trouthe
By every weye that they cowde seek;
In hem was founde defawte noon nor slouthe. *no fault or laziness*
But atte laste of o thyng ha they routhe, *had; pity (compassion)*
That he were falle, for ouht they cowd espye,
For thouht or love into malencolye.[3]

47

His uryne was remys, attenuat *watery thin*
By resoun gendryd of frigidité, *caused by*
The veyne ryveers for they wern oppilat, *blocked*
It was ful thynne and wannyssh for to see.

---

[1] *When there is too much of any one humor*

[2] *Or heat or blood exceeds a moderate or intermediate level*

[3] Lines 321–22: *That he had fallen, as near as they could tell / Because of [distorted] thinking or because of love*

The streihte passage causyd aquosité, *narrow; too much fluid*
Withoute substaunce to voyde hym of colour,
That they dispeired been to be his socour. *help*

48

For whan nature of vertu regitiff *controlling virtue*
Thoruh malencolye is pressyd and bordoun, *borne down*
It is to dreede gretly of the lif, *The life is in danger*
But soone be ordeyned opposicioun; *Unless an antidote can be prescribed quickly*
For it was likly that this passioun
Was eithir thouht, or love that men calle *anxiety (mental distress)*
Amor ereos, that he was in falle; *The disease of lovesickness*

49

The roote wherof and the corrupcioun *origin; misfunctioning*
Is of thilke vertu callid estimatiff, *the faculty of reason*
As yif a man have deep impressioun
That ovirlordshipith his imagynatif; *overpowers the faculty of imagination*
And that the cours be forth successyf, *as the course of the disease progresses*
To trowe a wiht for love mor fayr or pure, *believe*
Than evir hym ordeyned hath God or nature.

50

This causith man to fallen in manye, *mania*
So arn his spiritis vexid by travayle. *are; troubled by suffering*
Allas, that man shuld fallen in frenesye *frenzy*
For love of woman; that litil may avayle.
For now thes leechys, as by supposayle, *conjecture*
Konne of this man noon othir fevir espye, *Could*
But that for love was hool his malladye.

51

And whan his freend the sothe gan undirgrope *truth; began to grasp*
Of this myscheef, he nat ne wolde abide,
But into the chaunbyr anoon he is ilope, *arrived*
And kneelyd adoun by his beddys syde.
He seyd, "Freend, to me nothyng thu hyde; *you*
Telle me your herte, telle me your hevynesse,
And lat no thouht causen your drerynesse.

52

Yif loves fevere do yow ouht to quake, *makes you quake*
Telle me the soth and rake nat in the fyre; *truth; suffer*
Out of your slombre for shame why nyl ye wake? *why won't you wake up*
To me uncloose the somme of your desyre!
Be what she be, I shal do my deveere. *utmost*

Allas, mystrust, to lokke it up fro me, *from*
Telle on, for shame! Com of and lat me see. *Come on*

53

Your freend mystruste it is an hih repreeff, *reproof*
Or to concele from hym your privyté, *secrets*
Paraventure he may to your myscheeff *Perhaps*
Fynde remedye sonnere than may ye.
And sith in feith so deepe isworn be we, *since*
I wol it weten withouten mor delay *know*
What may you helpyn, by God and by my fay." *faith (i.e., most certainly, truly)*

54

And alle the ladyes and maydenys of his hous,
Bothe oold and yong, were brouht to his presence.
And oon ther was so fair and vertuous,
That for hir wysdam and hir excellence
Was moost of alle had in reverence,
The which this marchaunt for oon the beste alyve,
Kept in his hous in purpoos hir to wyve. *to marry*

55

Ful wys she was of so tendir age,
Prudent and war and ful of honesté, *capable (wise)*
Devoyde cleene of vices and outrage, *Completely free; sin*
Whos beauté flouryd and virginité,
Plesaunt of poort, roote of humylité, *demeanour*
Of maneer myrour and welle of womanheede, *source of womanliness*
Goodly abayssht and femynyn of dreede. *modest and shy*

56

Hool of hir herte, benygne and immutable, *Sincere; benign; calm*
Nat frel fadyng, but ful of affiaunce; *not fragile or frail; confidence*
In moral vertu mesuryd and tretable, *reasonable*
Housoold to guye forwar of governaunce; *guide; very careful*
To been exaunple Kynde hir lyst avaunce,[1]
That yif I shal hir shortly comprehende, *briefly describe*
In hir was nothyng that Nature myht amende.

57

The sike marchaunt, whan he hir beheeld, *when he saw her*
With dreedful herte and voys ful tymerous, *a heart full of dread*
He seide, "Certis, but mercy be my sheeld! *Indeed, may mercy protect me*
To you, my freend, that ye be gracious,

---

[1] *Nature wanted to promote her as an example*

That on my trespas ye be nat rigerous
To take vengaunce on myn hih folye,
That I was boold to sette myn herte so hihe.

58

O mercy, freend, and rewe upon my lif! — *have pity on my life*
Deth fro my gilt I wot is resounable, — *for; know*
Love is gynnere and ground of al my strif, — *the origin of*
But in o thyng I am inexcusable, — *one*
That I so love that fayr incomperable,
Which is to you so plesaunt and so meete,
And to be slayn, to love I can nat leete.[1]

59

Do what yow list, for tyl myn herte ryve, — *wish; break*
I may nat chesyn that I am hir man; — *choose*
For with mysilf thouh I evirmor stryve,
Ther is noon othir that I love can.
For hir in syknesse I am so pale and wan,
Thus I me confesse and put me in your grace,
My liff, my deeth, is portrayed in hir face."

60

This freendly marchaunt of this nat dysmayed,
But with good herte saide as ye may heere:
"Allas, my freend, why art thu so dismayed
For love, anoon, sith thu maist han hir heere?[2]
With al hir beauté and cristal eyen cleere, — *eyes*
Betwix yow two in love to make a boond,
I gyf hir thee; have, tak hir by the hond.

61

And ful and hool, as I have any riht,
I give hir thee, which is so wys and sage.
Rys up anoon, and be riht glad and liht,
For I wil makyn between yow the maryage,
And bere thexpence fully and costage — *bear the expense and costs*
Of your weddyng"; and hath a day iset — *has set a day*
Of hir spousayl, to see the knotte iknet. — *their marriage; knot knit*

62

Anoon he ros, supportyd by gladnesse,
And doun he fel lowly on his kne,

---

[1] *At the risk of being slain, I cannot stop loving her*

[2] Lines 416–17: *Why are you so dismayed about your love, since you may immediately have her here?*

And hym he thankyd for his gentillesse, *noble behavior*
That fro the deth hath maad hym skapid fre. *completely escape*
"Allas," he seide, "Whan shal I thanken thee,
That hast so freely thyn owne love forsake,
Thy freend to save hool and sound to make?"

63

The passaunt costys, the feeste of her weddyng, *surpassing; their*
Justys and revel and al the purveiaunce, *Jousts; revelry; provisions*
The grete giftys, the cheer so surmountyng, *the great cheer*
I wante witt to telle the circumstaunce; *lack*
For Ymeneus that hath the governaunce *(see note)*
Of such feestys to make accordement, *feasts to create accord*
I trowe that Fortune was therat present. *believe*

64

Thus is the syke of his langour lissyd, *sick [man]; relieved of his suffering*
The blosme of bounté by frenshipe hath he wonne,
For hertly merthe to hym is now nat myssyd,
No shadwe of sorwe forfarith nat his sonne; *disfigures*
His freend to hym abrochyd hath the tonne *has tapped the cask*
Of freendly triacle, for nevir I radde yit, *triacle [i.e., a remedy]; read*
O freend to anothir that so weel hath hym quyt.[1]

65

To hym relesyd he hath his hertly glorye,
Hymsilf dismyttid of his inward joye,[2] *divested*
The briht myrour, the liht of his memorye,
Which al his rancour by refut cowde coye;[3] *refuge [i.e. comfort]; soothe*
He hath forsake the guyere of his joye, *guide*
His lives lanterne, staff of his crokyd age, *life's*
To bryng his freend in quiete out of rage.

66

Of this mateer what shuld I write mor?
I wil entrete this processe forth in pleyn: *plainly give an account*
Hir and hir jowellys, hir richesse and hir stor, *jewels, riches, and goods*
He hath hym yoven, the stoory seith certeyn, *given; as the story says*
And hom with al repayred is ageyn, *everything is returned*
And lad hir with hym, as was his freendys wyl, *led*
Which cowde nat feyne his plesaunce to fulfyl.[4]

---

[1] Lines 447–48: *I have never yet read / of one friend rewarding another one so well*

[2] Lines 449–50: *He has released the glory of his heart / and divested himself of his inward joy*

[3] *Who could soothe him when he was irritated by providing comfort*

[4] *Who could not refrain from fulfilling his [friend's] pleasure*

67

At ther departyng, the moornyng that is for to wite, *mourning; know*
The wooful teerys, dolour, and hevynesse, *sadness*
Myn herte bleedith whan I therof endite, *write*
To knowe her trouble, turment, and distresse. *torment*
But of this marchaunt, lyst the kyndenesse: *listen [to]*
His freendys partyng did hym mor to smerte *hurt him more*
Than love of hir that sat so nyh his herte.

68

Moornyng for absence he is left allone,
The tothir streiht to Baldoc, his contré, *other straight*
With wyf and catel the riht weye is gone, *chattels*
And ther receyved with gret solennyté.
Her lyf they ledde in gret prosperité, *Their*
His wif and he of oon herte in quyete, *peacefully*
For with a bettir no man ne myht mete.

69

Ther was no stryf between hem, nor debate, *them*
But ful accordid they be bothe nyht and day.
She hym obeyeth in al, erlich and late, *early*
Whan he seid "ya," she coud nat sey "nay";
A bettir wyf was nevir at al assay.[1]
Joyned in oon, thus been her hertys two
That nouht but deth her love may fordoo. *destroy*

70

For alle wyves, as ferre as evir I kneuh, *as far as I ever knew*
Withyne her brest hath growyng pacience,
Suffryng and meeke they been ilich new. *ever constant*
But yif so be that men hem doon offence,
They love nat men make experience *(see note)*
Of her lownesse; but lyst I hem displese *obedience (humility) lest I displease them*
Ye gete no more; passe ovir is an ese. *it is better to pass over this matter*

71

Thus leve I hem in her jolité, *Thus I leave them in their happiness*
I meene thes two, ech lykyng othir weel,
I speke no mor of her felicité,
For no man may such joye and merthe feel,
But he were expert to telle it everydeel. *Unless; entirely*
For to the marchaunt of Egipt wil I turne,
Which for his freend in woo I lefte moorne. *mourning*

---

[1] *There was never, under any circumstances, a better wife.*

72

But now, allas, who shal my stile guye? — *guide*
Or hensforth who shall be my muse? — *henceforth*
For verray dool I stond in jupartye, — *jeopardy*
Al merthe of makyng my mateer mot refuse,[1]
Me into stoon transmued hath Meduse, — *transformed*
For verray stonyng of Fortunys fikylnesse, — *astonishment*
That for the merveyle no woord I can expresse. — *because of this wonderment*

73

Allas, Meggera, I mot now unto thee — *must*
Of herte calle to helpe me compleyne,
And to thy sustir eek Thesiphone,
That aftir joye Goddessys been of peyne.
O weepyng Mirre, now lat thy teerys reyne — *let your tears rain*
Into myn ynke, so clubbyd in my penne, — *ink; clogged; pen*
That rowthe in swaggyng abrood make it renne. — *assuaging; flow*

74

It sitt thee nat enlumyned for to be — *befits*
Of othir colour, but oonly al of sable. — *black*
O doolful mateer! Who so now reede thee, — *Whoever reads you*
He may weel seyn this world is ful chaungable!
For how this marchaunt, whilom so worshipable, — *honorable (noble)*
I meene of Egipt, Fortune did avale, — *treat*
Mot be as now remenaunt of my tale. — *Must; the remainder*

75

To hym Fortune hir falsnesse hath overt, — *revealed*
Hir swift wheel turned up so doun, — *upside down*
For he is fallen and plonget in povert, — *poverty*
Thoruh vanysshyng of his possessioun.
Now al is brouht into destruccioun,
Rychesse and freendys been alle ifeere goon, — *Riches; together*
And he in myscheef is sool ilefft aloon.

76

This newe Job, icast in indigence,
He weepith, wayleth, soleyn and solitarye,
Allone he drouh hym, fleeyng al presence, — *drew himself*
And evir his lif he gan to curse and warye. — *angrily lament*
"O out on neede, of malys multipharye!" — *malice of many kinds*
He gan to crye in his ire and woo,
Lych a man in furye forpoosyd to and froo. — *agitated (severely troubled)*

---

[1] *My [subject] matter precludes all joy in [poetic] creation*

77

For remembraunce of oold prosperité
Hath with a darte hym woundid to the herte.
Mor unkouth was to hym adversité,
That nevir toforn no trouble did hym smerte. *cause him pain*
For mor despeyred he was for a sterte, *for a time*
That he ne hadde of woo noon excersise,
Hym thouhte it was to hym a newe emprise. *undertaking*

78

Thus is the sweete of his tranquyllité,
Ful neewly turned into bittirnesse;
Thus is he valyd adoun from hih degré *fallen down*
Ful many a steiher lowe into wrechydnesse.[1] *stair*
His lyf he leedith al in werynesse,
For now Fortune hath chaungid newe his weede, *clothing*
Freend nor foo ne took of hym noon heede.

79

Out by hymsilf, walkyng in wildirnesse,
He gan to pleyne his sodeyn poore estaat, *complain; condition*
And seide, "Allas, wher is the kyndenesse
Of alle my freendys to me, disconsolaat? *disconsolate*
I pley sool; I am almoost chekmaat, *alone; checkmated*
That whilom hadde my menee me aboute, *once; household*
Now destitut, I am beshet withoute. *shut out*

80

Now am I repreef to my freendys alle, *reproof*
Markyd of many and of the peeple fable, *subject of gossip*
Now wot I nat to whom for helpe calle, *know; not*
That sat so glorious somtyme at my table.
And they that than wer to me servisable, *willing to serve*
Han by despit at myscheef me forsake,[2]
Gret cause have I an outcry for to make.

81

O out on shame, of hauhtesse plongid lowe! *pride*
O out on dolour, of lordship brouht to nouht! *nothing*
O out on richesse, with vanyté forblowe, *puffed-up*
Forsakyng soone and with gret travayle souht!
O worldly blisse of me ful dere abouht, *dearly bought*

---

[1] Lines 542–43: *Thus has he fallen down many a stair from his high degree into wretchedness*

[2] *Have by contempt at my need forsaken me*

Thy sodeyn turn now doublith my grevaunce,
Mor than of it I nevir hadde had plesaunce.

82

Now hongir, thrust, unkouth sueth to me, *(see note)*
Unwarly sueth my passyd habundaunce;[1]
Now cold, now nakyd in necessité,
I walke aboute for my sustenaunce,
Whilom in plenté and now al in grevaunce.
Allas! My fulle is derkyd into wane, *My full moon is waning*
With wynd forwhirlyd as is a muaunt fane. *whirled about; shifting weathervane*

83

O, in this world what woo and werynesse!
What mortal torment assaileth al aboute!
What grevous molest and what besynesse, *affliction; anxiety*
With many assaut in dreed doth us to doute! *assault; puts us into doubt*
Now up, now doun as doth a curraunt goute, *running gout*
So ar we travailed with solicitude! *troubled with care*
The world with mowhes so weel can us delude *mockery (deceptions) well*

84

But I knowe weel, who trustith on thee moost, *whoever*
Shal be deceyved whan he to thee hath neede.
Wher is the clarioun of thy cry and boost,
That to skyes my fame did beede? *proclaim*
Who servyth thee, what shal be his meede, *Whoever serves; reward*
Whan that he wenyth thu maist hym most availe, *thinks you will most help him*
Than in the hand rathest thu wilt hym fayle?"[2]

85

O seely marchaunt, myn hand I feele quake, *wretched*
To write thy woo in my translacioun,
Ful ofte I weepe also for thy sake
For to beholde the revolucioun *overturning*
Of thy degree and transmutacioun. *position and great change*
Allas, to thee I can no bet diffence, *know no better defense*
Than thee to arme strongly in pacience.

86

Nat oonly thu, but every man on lyve, *alive*
How hih in throne he sittith exaltat, *However*
Lat hym nat tempte ageyns God to stryve,

---

[1] *Without warning follows my former abundance*

[2] *Then, shortly, you will most readily fail him*

But take His sonde meekly withoute debat, *ordinance*
For who so do, he is infortunat; *who does so (i.e., debates)*
No wele is worthy that may no woo endure, *prosperity; misfortune*
Wherfor ech man tak paciently his ewre. *destiny*

87

For Senek seith with ful hih sentence, *Seneca; with great wisdom*
Of preef in povert, who so that hym reede *experience*
In thylke book he made of providence, *that*
That he unhappy is, withouten dreede,
Which nevir ne hadde adversité nor neede.
Of whom the goddys dempten pleynly thus: *judge*
"Withouten assay no man is vertuous." *testing*

88

And yif a tre with frut be ovirlade, *laden*
In his Epistles he seith as ye may see:
Both braunche and bouh wol enclyne and fade, *incline and fade*
And greyne oppressith too moche uberté.[1]
Riht so it farith of fals felicité, *It is the same way with false happiness*
That yif his weihte mesure do exceede,
Than of a fal gretly is to dreede. *is likely*

89

But why that God this marchaunt list visite,[2]
As I suppose, it was hym for to preeve; *to test him*
Thouh he were wooful, he was the lasse wite, *the less to blame*
Sith nevir afforn Fortune did hym greeve.
From his wantrust he was brouht in beleeve, *lack of confidence; to believe*
That he weel kneuh this world was ful unstable, *knew*
And nat abydyng, but evirmor variable.

90

And whan he kneuh the grete unsikyrnesse *instability*
Of worldly lust, by preef in special, *pleasure; particular experience*
On knees he fel with devout humblesse,
Ful lowe of herte, and thankyd God of al,
And sayde, "Lord, thouh I have had a fal,
Ne put me nat fro thy proteccioun,
Sith I it take for my probacioun. *testing (trial by adversity)*

---

[1] *Grain (as in fruit or produce) overburdens too much fruitfulness*

[2] *But why God wanted to visit [trials] on the merchant*

91

But, goode Lord, lat me thy grace fynde,
And guye my wittis that I be nat despeyred; *guide*
But me enspeere, puttyng in my mynde
Som hoope of refut that am so soore appeyred. *relief; sorely diminished (damaged)*
And thouh to richesse ther be no grees isteyred *steps arranged in the form of stairs*
Tascenden up, as I was wont to doone, *as I used to do*
Yit, goode Lord, do confort to my boone." *please grant my prayer*

92

And whil he lay thus in his orisoun, *prayer*
Ful poorly clad in ful symple weede, *garments*
His herte was brouht in consolacioun,
Which into lissyng his langour did leede. *relief; distress*
He thouhte he wolde preeve his freend at neede,[1]
And unto Baldac, for to make assay, *to make trial (i.e., to test his friendship)*
In pilgrym wise he took the rihte way. *Like a pilgrim*

93

And whan he was comen to that londe,
Ful soore afferd he was for to compleyne.
"Allas!" he seide, "Myn herte dar nat fonde *attempt*
Unto my freend to shewen out my peyne, *expose; pain*
That whiloom was in richesse so hauhteyne; *proud*
For to be ded, I dar nat for shamfastnesse
Nat shewe a poynt to hym of my distresse."[2]

94

And eek that it was somwhat late *also*
Whan he was entryd into that cité,
Hym liked nat to knocken at the gate,
And namly in so poore degré, *particularly in so low a rank*
And it was nyht; therfor he lefte be,
List of his freend he were anoon refusyd *Lest his friend refused him*
As man unknowe, or for som spye accusyd. *As a stranger; spy*

95

Into a temple foundid by dayes olde, *ancient temple*
He is ientryd a place al desolat, *has entered*
And leyd hym doun by the wallys colde,
So weyk, so wery, forwandryd, and format.[3] *dejected*
O pompe unporisshyd, whilom so elat! *impoverished, formerly so exalted*

---

[1] *He thought he would prove his friend by testing at [this] time of distress*

[2] Lines 650–651: *To save my life, I dare not, for shame, show him one bit of my distress*

[3] *So weak, so weary, exhausted with wandering, and thoroughly dejected and discouraged*

Take heed, ye ryche, of what estat ye bee, *rank (position)*
For in this marchaunt your myrour ye may see.

96

How many a man hath fortune assayled *tested*
With sleihte icast, whan he best wende ha stonde,
Her habiriownys of steel also unmayled;
For al her trust she nolde the lasse wonde[1]
To pleye this pleye bothe with free and bonde. *game; free and bound (i.e., everyone)*
For who stood evir yit in sureté, *security*
That in som siht infect was his degré?[2]

97

For by exaumplys Nature doth declare,
Which is of God mynystir and vikeer, *minister and vicar*
Withoute tonge she biddith us beware *be aware*
By thylke sterrys that shynen briht and cleer, *those*
Which, by her concours and mevyng circuleer *their courses and circular motion*
In her discens, westyng undir wavys,[3]
Us to enfourmen by chaungyng of hir lawys. *inform us*

98

And fewe of hem alway to us appeere,[4]
But yif it be the bere briht and sheene *Unless it is the bear (the Big Dipper)*
In thilke plow that Arthow doth it steere; *Arcturus*
For yit Boetes, that twynkelith wondir keene, *In addition; Boötes; wonderfully bright*
Somwhile is dym that men may nat hym seene; *Sometimes*
Eek Lucifeer, at morowhil prymycere, *the morning star (see note)*
By nyht hym hidith undir our empeere. *hides himself under the empyrean*

99

The day doth passe of vanité and glorye,
And nyht approchith whan Titan is gon doun, *the sun*
But who list wynne the palme by victorye,
The world to venquyssh ful of elacioun, *vanquish; elation*
Lat hym despise as a chaunpioun *champion*

---

[1] Lines 667–69: *With planned slyness and deceit [just] when a man might most expect to [be able to] withstand [her] / [Fortune] has also dismantled their habergeons [mail jacket armor] / For all their trust [in her], she would not hesitate in the least*

[2] *For who has ever been so secure / that his rank could not be questioned by some*

[3] *In their descent, moving westward to set beneath the waves*

[4] *Few of them are always apparent to us* (see note)

Al erthly lustys that shynen but in dreede,[1] — *as a warning*
And of this marchaunt evir among tak heede. — *always*

100

Evir entirmedlyd is merthe and hevynesse, — *intermingled*
Now liht, now soory, now joiful, now in woo,
Now cleer aloffte, now lowe in dirknesse;
As Jubiter hath couchyd tonnes two — *put down two casks*
Withyne his ceeleer, platly and no moo, — *cellar; precisely; more*
That oon is ful of joye and gladnesse,
That othir ful of sorwe and bittirnesse.

101

Who that wil entren to tamen of the sweete — *broach (i.e., open)*
He must as weel taken his aventure — *chance*
To taste in bittir, or he the vessel leete, — *before; relinquish*
And bothe ilich of strong herte endure. — *equally*
He may nat clense the thykke from the pure; — *separate the impurities*
For who that wil swetnesse first abroche, — *tap*
He mot be war or bittir wol approche. — *be careful*

102

Of thes two idronken at the fulle
Hath this marchaunt that I of spak erwhyle. — *formerly*
The laste bevere so maad his hed to dulle — *beverage made his head so dazed*
That he ne lest but litil lawh or smyle. — *cared little for laughing or smiling*
Expert he was bothe of trust and guyle, — *Well-informed*
For wher that he his beddyng whilom chees, — *Whereas; formerly chose*
Slept on the ground now nakyd herberwelees. — *without shelter*

103

And whil that he lay sleepyng in this wise, — *in this way*
An hap befel of two men in the toun, — *chance event*
Betwix the which a contek gan to ryse — *Between whom conflict arose*
Riht ther besyde, with gret noyse and soun; — *sound*
That oon his felawe hath slayn and boredoun, — *overcome*
Undir the temple wher as this marchaunt lay, — *behind*
And left hym ther and fled anoon his way. — *immediately*

104

The toun was reised with rumour riht anoon,
And to the temple faste gonne renne, — *ran very quickly*
Now heer, now ther, ful swyftly they goon,
To taken hym that hadde wrouht this synne; — *committed*

---

[1] Lines 689–92: *But whoever wishes to win the palm of victory / must despise earthly pleasures that shine only to warn us*

Tyl atte laste they souhte han hym withynne,	*they have sought him within*
And with the noyse, as they gonne in threste,	*thrust in*
The poore marchaunt abrayd out of his reste.	*awoke suddenly*
105	
Riht for astonyd, palen gan his hewe	*Completely astonished, he turned pale*
Whan they hym asken what mystirman he were,	*what kind of person he was*
Or yif that he thomycide knewe	*the murderer*
That hadde slayn the man that liggith there.	*lay*
And he anoon withouten dreed or fere	
Seyde, "Certeynly, thouh ye me hange and drawe,	
No wiht but I hath this man islawe."	*person; slain*
106	
His covetise was to ha be ded,	*wish; have*
That he by deth hys myserye myht fyne;	*end*
His woo heeng on hym hevyere than led,	*hung; lead*
And poverté did hym so moche pyne,	*gave him so much pain*
He wolde that deth had leyd hook and lyne	*wished*
Tacacchyd hym into his bittir las.	*To have caught him in his bitter noose*
Therfor on hym he took this hih trespas.	*on himself; serious transgression*
107	
"O deth, desyred in adversité,	*adversity*
Whan thu art callyd, why nylt thu wrecchys heere?	
And art so reedy in felicité	*happiness (prosperity)*
To come to them that thee nothyng desire?	
O com now, deth, and maak of me thy feere!"	*partner*
This marchaunt crieth in his wooful herte,	
So ful he was of inward peynes smerte.	*sharp inner pains*
108	
Anoon he was itaken and ibounde,	*taken and bound*
And cast in prisoun, tyl on the nexte morwe,	
And than itaken and brouht as they hym founde,	
Aforn the justice for no man wold hym borwe;	*Before; give surety (i.e., bail)*
To seen a fyn he hopith of his sorwe,	*end*
Fordempt he was thoruh his owne speche,	*Convicted*
By jugement to han for deth the wreche.	*to have death as punishment*
109	
And than as faste as he to deth was lad,	*just as; led*
His oold freend happyd forby passe,	*happened to pass nearby*
The which beheeld hym with cheer demure and sad,[1]	
And kneuh the feturys and signes of his face;	

[1] *Who beheld him with a grave and sober face*

And anoon he prayeth leyseer to hym, and space, — *leisure*
For to been herd of hem in pacience, — *to be heard by them patiently*
And stynt awhyle to give hym audience. — *pause*

110

"Sires," he seith, "So it nat yow displese,
This man is dampned, so ful of innocence, — *condemned*
And giltles ye don hym this disese. — *guiltless; you wrong him*
For I mysilf have wrouht this gret offence,
To me it fallith tencurren the sentence — *to incur*
Of deth, the trouthe weel to founde, — *to pursue the truth*
For with myn hand I gaff his dedly wounde." — *gave*

111

His herte was meevyd of oold naturesse — *fellow-feeling*
To save his freend, and for hym for to deye,
And he was hent anoon and pullyd by duresse; — *seized*
With sure arrest they handys on hym leye — *secure (firm); lay*
And al her lust meekly he did obeye. — *will*
Tofore the juge he was ilad and drawe, — *Before; led and dragged*
Wher he was dampned by concours of the lawe.[1]

112

Thoo was he lad with weepyng and pité — *Thereupon*
Toward his deth, of many hym besyde; — *with many beside him*
His poore freend was loos at liberté,
Which thouhte for woo deth thoruh his herte glyde. — *Who*
Whyls in the prees, the verray homycide, — *crowd; true murderer*
That sothfastly that deede hadde iwrouht, — *Who had truly done the deed*
Spak to hymsylf thus in his owne thouht: — *Spoke*

113

"Allas, myn herte, hard as the dyamaunt! — *diamond*
How maist thu suffre this cruelté to seen? — *allow; see*
Allas, thoruh remors, why ne were I repentaunt, — *am I not repentant*
The southfast trouthe to be confessyd cleen? — *To be confessed of the genuine truth*
Allas this wrong! How may I thus susteen
To see afore me ungilté thus itake, — *[the] unguilty [one] taken thus*
And lad to dethward oonly for my sake?

114

O rihtwys God, to whom ech pryvyté — *secret*
Is pleyn and open to Thy magnyficence,
O Lord that knowyst myn hyd iniquité, — *hidden iniquity*
Beholdyng al, O Sonne of Sapience, — *(see note)*

---

[1] *Where he was convicted in accordance with the law*

Ne take no vengaunce of myn hih offence,
That I so longe concelyd have the trouthe, *concealed*
But of thy mercy, Lord, have on me routhe! *pity*

115

For weel I wot that of thy rihtwysnesse, *know; justice (precepts)*
Thu must me punysshen at thy jugement,
And thouh thu suffre awhile in esynesse, *you will allow mercy sometimes*
Blood wil have wreche that wrongfully is spent. *vengeance*
O blood ungilté! O blood so innocent!
How canst thu gon to deth and nat compleyne,
To wreke thee aftir on me with cruel peyne?[1]

116

To the hih God, eternal in His see, *seat (throne)*
Blood crieth out that is ishad in wronge, *wrongly shed*
And seith, 'O lord, whan wilt Thu vengyd bee
Upon our deth? Why bydist Thu so longe?' *Why do you wait so long?*
Of innocentys, this is the noote and songe. *innocent people; note*
Wherfor I wol, whil I have lif and space, *Therefore I will*
The sothe be knowe, and put me in Thy grace. *truth*

117

It is too moche that I have slayn oon, *too much*
And but I speke, toward is anothir, *unless; imminent [is the death of] another*
The which is domb and stille as ony stoon, *dumb; quiet*
For verray love for to save his brothir; *true*
Everych is reedy to fonge deth for othir. *Each one; undergo*
Now wyl I goon and pleynly me confesse,
And for my gilt receyven the redresse." *punishment*

118

With open mouth, lowde he gan to crye:
"O ye disceyved peeple by errour, *deceived*
That innocent, allas, why shal he dye,
Which nevir ne was his lyve trespasour?
Turneth ageyn and let be this clamour, *leave off*
And let to me her doom been hool reserved,[2]
For I am he that hath the deth disserved.

119

Let hym go loos, sith he of gilt is fre; *since*
It is mysilf that hath the deede ido! *who has done the deed*

---

[1] *To inflict vengeance upon me afterward*

[2] *let their sentence be wholly reserved for me*

Why wyl ye erren and punysshen verité, *err and punish truth*
And let falsnesse at his large go?" *and let falseness go free?*
The peeple of this gan for to wondren tho, *then began to marvel*
And eek the justices, of this sodeyn chaunce, *also; at this sudden occurrence*
That alle here wittis wer hangid in ballaunce.

120

Yit nevirtheles thus they iwrouhte: *this is what they did*
The firste they unbounde, and this othir take,
And by assent hem everychon ibrouhte *brought all three of them*
Tofore the kyng, and ther a processe make: *related the tale*
How ech of thes hath don for othrys sake,
And prayn hym good juge for to bee
To fynde a wey the trouthe for to see.

121

This worthy kyng, to serchyn out the riht, *to search out the truth*
Shewith hymsilf bothe wys and eek tretable, *wise and reasonable*
And made mercy to goon aforn his myht *put mercy before might*
Shapyng a mene ful just and resonable. *solution very*
To alle thre he shewyd hym merciable *himself merciful*
Of al the crym; withyne woordys fewe, *in a few words*
Pardon he grauntith so they the trouthe shewe. *as long as they told the truth*

122

Of al the cas they have no poynt isparyd: *spared no detail*
First of her frenship, joye, and adversité,
But woord by woord, the stoory hool declaryd,
Bothe of thes tweyne the love and unyté —
Ye han that herd; ye gete no mor of me — *have*
And how the thrydde hadde a conscience
For his trespace so dampned innocence. *for his sin of condemning innocence*

123

With gret merveile they wondryn on this thyng,
To seen in frenship so hool affeccioun; *such complete affection*
And specially this wise, worthy kyng
Gan wisshe of herte that thoruh his regioun
Were ful affermyd an obligacioun
Of such enteernesse fro man to man aboute; *complete loyalty*
Of tresoun than ful litil wer to doute.[1]

124

Ful hard it were tacomplisshen his desyr, *It would be hard*
Or in his rewm such a bargeyn dryve, *realm*

---

[1] *There would be little reason to fear treason*

The aeyer infect, the wedir is nat cleer, *is infected*
Ne nevir ne shal whil tresoun is so ryve. *nor will it be; rife*
For now, of trowthe, no man can contryve *contrive (produce)*
A verray seel, or thenpreent igrave,
Withoute a label his armes hool to save.[1]

125

But whan thys kyng hath thus doon hem grace, *granted them mercy*
He let hem goo at her eleccioun; *free will*
And he of Baldac hath lad hoom to his place
His poore freend with gret processioun, *procession (with the sense of celebration)*
He rayeth hym newe with good affeccioun, *arrayed*
And seide, "Freend, your pensiffheed asswage, *be relieved of your vexation (anxiety)*
And for povert ne beeth no more in rage. *distress*

126

But here anoon, as ferre as it may laste,
Of al my good, halvendeel is youre. *half is yours*
I wyl that it departyd be as faste *will have it divided immediately*
At your devise, your povert to socoure. *at your discretion (i.e., as you like); cure*
For our frenship shal every sesoun floure,
And in short tyme, I telle it you in pleyn,
Ye shul to richesse restooryd be ageyn.

127

And than, at erst avised, ye may telle, *having first considered [the matter]*
Unto your contré whedir ye wil returne,
Or heer with me al your lyff dwelle.
The choys is your; look no more ye moorne.
And whersobe ye goon, or heer sojourne, *wherever*
Have heer my trouthe: our hertys shul been oon *pledge*
Whil breeth may laste, and nevir unsondir goon." *asunder*

128

By egal witt his goodys everychon *equal judgment (wisdom)*
Wer tho departyd betwix thes freendys two, *divided*
Bycause this marchaunt wold algatys gon *particularly wanted to go*
Hom to his contré that he lovyd soo.
The stoory tellith withoute woordys moo,
Riht into Egipt he is goon ageyn.
Of her frenship what shuld I you moor seyn?

[1] Lines 867–68: *A true seal [as in heraldry] or engrave the imprint / Without a band on his coat of arms to save them*

129

I say you platly, so as it seemyth me, — *plainly to you*
Of thyng weel preevyd to maken rehersayl — *made evident*
Too oftyn sith it were but vanyté,[1]
Lest tediousté your erys did assayl;
Sith ye it knowe, it may nothyng avayl — *Since*
Of her frenship ferther more divyne, — *describe*
For as they gonne, so in love they fyne. — *as they began, so they end in love*

130

L'envoye

Thus of this tale to you I make an eende.
On my rewde tellyng of curtesye ye rewe. — *unsophisticated; have pity*
And God I prey that He His grace sende
That every freend to othir be as trewe
As were thes marchauntis, alway ilich newe. — *always unchanging (i.e., constant)*
This my desyr in al degrees of men.
That it so be, I pray you seith "Amen."

[1] *Too many times it is just vanity [to rehearse something already well-proven]*

 Explanatory Notes to *Fabula duorum mercatorum*

Abbreviations: ***CP***: Boethius, *Consolation of Philosophy*; ***CT***: Chaucer, *The Canterbury Tales*; ***FP***: Lydgate, *Fall of Princes*; **Ha**: London, British Library, MS Harley 2251; ***KnT***: Chaucer, The Knight's Tale; ***MED***: *Middle English Dictionary*; ***OED***: *Oxford English Dictionary*; ***TB***: Lydgate, *Troy Book*; ***TC***: Chaucer, *Troilus and Criseyde*; **Trevisa**: Trevisa, *On the Properties of Things*; ***TG***: Lydgate, *Temple of Glas*; **Whiting**: Whiting, *Proverbs, Sentences, and Proverbial Phrases*.

7 *of his woord as any centre stable*. Compare The Squire's Tale: "sooth of his word, benigne, and honurable; / Of his corage as any centre stable" (*CT* V[F] 21–22). For Lydgate's use of the phrase elsewhere, see also Reinecke, ed., *Saint Albon and Amphibalus* (2.1012), and *FP* (4.1310).

14 *as myn auctour seith, riht so sey I*. A common topos and a favorite saying of Lydgate's.

15–35 Lydgate's source for this geographical description may have been a version of Mandeville's *Travels*, as Seaton suggests (*Roos*, p. 275); the Cotton (British Library, MS Cotton Titus c. xvi) and Egerton (British Library, MS Egerton 1982) versions are closest. However, the description in Trevisa, book 15, chapter 53 (ed. Seymour, 2:755–56) seems closer to *Fabula* than the Mandeville does:

> In þe eeste syde vnder þe Reede See þis londe ioyneth to Siria, and hath Libia in þe west syde, and þe Grete See in þe norþe syde, and passeth inwarde in þe southe syde and streccheþ anoone to þe Ethiopes. . . . And is a cuntre vnvsynge to dewe and vnknowynge to reyne. And oneliche Nilus moisteþ þat londe and renneþ þere aboute and makith it plenteuous with risynge and wexinge. And hath plente of wylde bestees and fedeþ a grete dele of þe worlde with whete and with other corne and fruyte; and is so plenteuous of oþer marchaundises and chaffare, þat it filleþ ny3e alle þe worlde with nedeful marchaundises.

To compare, see Mandeville, ch. 7 (Hamelius, ed., *Mandeville*, pp. 28–29). Perhaps Lydgate also drew on Mandeville for the very similar geographical description in lines 5–7 and lines 35–44 of his *Mumming for the Mercers of London* (MacCracken, ed., *Minor Poems* 2:695–98).

19 *Who castith the coostys of the firmament*. Whoever reckons or calculates the divisions of the heavens into quarters (in order to ascertain direction). Compare Chaucer's *Treatise on the Astrolabe* (Benson, *Riverside*, 1.19.8–9, p. 667).

39 *Spak of his name which gladly wol nat hyde*. The phrase *gladly wol* is defined in the *MED* (*gladlī* (adv.), sense 2) as "would like to," though the word *gladly* also frequently means "willingly," "with pleasure," or "customarily" (senses 2a, b, c). The general sense of the line seems to be that the merchant's name is well known and that people speak of him with approval. Part of the difficulty in rendering a literal sense for the line rests on determining the referent for *which*. It seems to refer to *name*, yielding an implied reflexive sense: "the name did not wish to hide [itself]." It could also refer to or stand in for *many oon* (line 38), yielding the only slightly less awkward "they spoke his name which they did not like to hide." Both, however, convey the same general sense that his name was well known and spoken with approval.

48–49 *by report and by noon othir mene / Of her two lovys was maad a stable chene*. According to Cicero, falling in love from a distance is enabled by virtue: "on account of their virtue and uprightness we can in some sense love even those whom we have never seen" (quoted in Jaeger, *Ennobling Love*, p. 124). Jaeger goes on to note that "For Cicero, presence is not necessary." Compare also line 85, which reiterates that it was the "Repoort of vertu oonly by audience," that is, it was only by hearsay that the two merchants came to love each other.

stable chene. One of the several references in the first part of the poem to the chain of nature which binds all things in harmony, also known as the Great Chain of Being or the golden chain. See also line 74, the *myhty cord* of nature, and line 84: *nothyng bynde hem but natur by hir lawe*. The idea has a long literary history which seems to have started with Homer's *Iliad* (Lattimore, trans., 8.19). For some well-known medieval examples, see *Romance of the Rose* (lines 16785–87) and *KnT* (*CT* I[A] 2987–94). For the golden chain in English literature, see A. O. Lovejoy, *The Great Chain of Being*. For Lydgate's use of the chain metaphor in *TG*, see Norton-Smith's edition (*Poems*, p. 190), and his article "Lydgate's Metaphors."

50–53 These lines and those following depend on medieval theories of perception. See the Introduction to *Fabula*, pp. 15–16, for further explanation.

54 *hertys eye*. This striking phrase may have been suggested by *TC:* "His herte, which that is his brestez yë / Was ay on hire" (1.453–54). Compare also Ephesians 1:18: "The eyes of your heart enlightened . . ." The *MED (herte,* sense 2a) glosses this phrase as meaning "mind," but here the phrase has a stronger meaning. The idea of enlightenment and intuitive knowledge is contextually appropriate as Lydgate describes the merchants' ability to perceive and love each other without having met.

did alwey her message. To "do message" is to deliver a message or carry out a command or wish (*MED message* n. 1, sense 2b). "Do" is a causative aspect of "don."

55–56 *memorial . . . fantastical*. The third and first cells in the brain. The other is the *estimatyf* (see note to line 338 below). The *fantasticall* is the cell of imagination, sometimes defined as phantasm; *memorial* that of memory. Here and in the following stanza Lydgate is using the imagery of perception to describe the

growth of affection between the two merchants. For more on this imagery, see the Introduction to *Fabula*, pp. 15–16.

63 *myndys selle*. The "memorial" cell.

64 The connection of virtue with friendship is ultimately a classical idea. The fullest and most influential expression of the association is found throughout Cicero's *De Amicitia*, particularly in the book's final section:

> Virtue . . . Virtue, I say, both creates the bond of friendship and preserves it. For in Virtue is complete harmony, in her is permanence, in her is fidelity; and when she has raised her head and shown her own light and has seen and recognized the same light in another, she moves towards it and in return receives its beams; as a result love or friendship leaps into flame. . . . I exhort you both so to esteem virtue (without which friendship cannot exist), that, excepting virtue, you will think nothing more excellent than friendship. (*De Amicitia*, chapters 26–27; see Falconer, *Cicero*, pp. 206–11)

See also the Introduction to *Fabula*, pp. 12–13, for more on classical ideals of friendship.

69–84 That "like draws to like" is proverbial; see Whiting L272. The ultimate source is Cicero, *De Amicitia*. The notion was a familiar one and would have been well known from Boethius' *CP*; see Chaucer's *Boece* 3.pr11.130–40. Pearsall (*John Lydgate*, p. 202) remarks that the sentiment was one of Lydgate's "favorite themes"; compare line 260 of the "Churl and the Bird" (MacCracken, ed., *Minor Poems* 2:468) and the short poem "Every Thing to his Semblable" (MacCracken, ed., *Minor Poems* 2:801). Purdy notes that the principle of similarity, "like attracts to like," is a "logical outgrowth" of the association of virtue and friendship ("Friendship Motif," p. 114).

97–98 *As oon in two and two in oon*. Lydgate makes use of the classical idea of two friends having but one soul between them. Purdy provides a useful overview, noting Plato (Aristophanes' myth of the divided soul in Plato's *Symposium* 192a–193a 4.301), Aristotle ("a friend is another self," *Nicomachean Ethics* 9.4), Cicero (man seeks out "another whose soul he may so mingle with his own as almost to make one out of two," *De Amicitia* chapter 21; see Falconer, *Cicero*, pp. 188–89), and Plutarch ("Two friends, though severed in body, yet have their souls joined and as it were melted together, and neither desire to be two nor believe themselves to be separate persons"; *Morals* 4.301). See Purdy, "Friendship Motif," pp. 116–18. As Purdy explains, the idea could also be applied to the love between man and woman (p. 117), and Lydgate does so in much the same language at lines 482–83, describing the love between the Syrian merchant and his new wife. For a verbal similarity to line 483, see *TG*, line 1270.

100 *fortune . . . and . . . necessité*. In philosophical terms, *necessité* refers to something which must happen. The idea is central to Boethius's discussion of predestination and free will in 5.pr6, where Lady Philosophy makes a distinction between "symple" and "condicionel" necessity to explain how, even given God's foreknowledge, free will can still operate. Chaucer uses the distinction in *TC*

(4.958–1078) and the Nun's Priest's Tale (*CT* VII[B²] 3245–250). Here, Lydgate links fortune and "necessité," implying that fortune is working in accordance with God's will. While "fortune" here seems simply to be a conventional reference to the normal events of everyday experience, it will become an increasingly important idea as the poem unfolds. Lady Fortune, whose turning wheel can suddenly turn happiness into misery — or vice versa — is a familiar personage in medieval literature. Her main features are her fickleness, unpredictability, and instability. This is the first of many references to Fortune in the poem. For more on the development of the medieval personage of Fortune, whose roots lie in the ancient Roman goddess Fortuna, see H. R. Patch, *Goddess Fortuna*, and Frankes, *Fate of Fortune*.

104 *wynd into his seyl*. The connection between Fortune and wind is a "favourite medieval metaphor" (Stevens, "Winds of Fortune," p. 286). Chaucer makes frequent use of this metaphor in *TC*; see especially 2.1–7. See also *TB* 2:241, lines 3387–92 and 5:791, lines 631–35.

113–18 *riht as . . . Riht so*. A correlative construction, "just as . . . so also." See also lines 127–29, *But as . . . Riht so*, "just as . . . likewise, in that same way." The construction is similar to an epic simile, a comparison that extends across several lines. Note here as well the presence of the "doctrine of contraries," a way of defining something according to its opposite. Compare *TG* lines 394–416, 1250–56 and Norton-Smith's helpful explanatory notes to the *Temple of Glas*, (Norton-Smith, *Poems*, pp. 185, 190–91).

120 *out on*: a curse on, fie on, somebody or something. See *MED out(e* (interj.).

124 *hangyng in ballaunce*. Lydgate frequently uses the image of the balance to describe risk or danger, as he does here, or uncertainty, as in line 833. See, for example, *TG*: "Atwixen two so hang I in balaunce" (line 348) and "Hanging in balaunce bitwix hope and drede" (line 641). Compare *TB* 4:720, lines 5348–49 and *FP* 1:86, lines 3123–24. See also Schleich and Zupitza (eds., *Fabula Duorum Mercatorum*, p. 73) for other examples in Lydgate, and Whiting B17 for other writers' uses of the figure.

127–28 *itastyd galle . . . hoony soote*. The "doctrine of contraries" again. The use of juxtapositional imagery such as *galle* and *hoony*, bitter and sweet, is found throughout the poem; compare lines 446–47, 540–41, and especially lines 697–700. See the note below to lines 697–707.

159 *it snowyd doun plenté*. Compare Chaucer's Franklin's hospitality: "It snewed in his hous of mete and drynke" (*CT* I[A] 345).

171 *lat hym in the boundys*. All other MSS have *lad*. There is really only a slight difference either way. The Egyptian is allowing his guest the freedom of his territory, or he led him throughout his land. Either way, he is showing his guest everything within the boundaries of his land, and his generosity is clear.

184 *Nay, straunge nat; allas, why seid I soo?* Although Pearsall (*John Lydgate*, p. 203) considers this to be the rhetorical figure of *dubitatio*, or feigned hesitation, it more nearly resembles *correctio*, "the retraction of what has just been said." See

Geoffrey of Vinsauf, pp. 58–59, 105. Since "straunge" can mean both "foreign, other" and "unfriendly, hostile" (*MED straunge*, (adj.), senses 1, 3), Lydgate wants to clarify that only the former sense applies to the Syrian merchant.

187 *wele and woo*. Proverbial. See Whiting W132–W140. For good and bad; for welfare or misfortune.

190 *with al herte entieer*. Perhaps a conflation of two common phrases, "with hert enter," sincerely, devotedly, devoutly (*MED enter*, (adj.), sense 1); and "with al herte," without dissimulation, unaffectedly, sincerely, fervently (*MED herte*, (n.), sense 2b). The phrase means, then, something like "with the greatest sincerity and fervour."

191 *of entent ful cleene*. Literally, the phrase means that the merchant thanked his friend with very pure wishes or intentions. Taken as a whole, the phrase probably means "wholeheartedly, sincerely." "Entent(e)" is often used in adverbial phrases to modify action; for example, "in his entente" means "at his will" Specifically, "of hol entente" means "wholeheartedly, without reservation" (*MED entente*, (n.), senses 3a, b). And "ful cleene" as an adverbial phrase means "fully, completely" (*MED clene* (adv.), sense 3a). We should probably take *entent ful cleene*, then, to mean "altogether and totally sincerely."

193 *mystis ful of teene*. Note here and in the rest of the stanza the continuation of weather and seasonal imagery as well as the familiar device of contrast, here between presence and absence, to describe the emotional state of the two merchants. The mists of irritability are banished by the clear weather brought on by the presence together of the two friends. The sense in this line is that absence, signified by the "mystis full of tene," has been chased away by the clear weather, the sunny presence of the friends. Compare Chaucer's *Boece*, 1.m7.

194 *tapited*. To be hung with tapestry. This striking and unusual word conveys a sense of richness and freshness to the merchants' "joyful summer." It is used in a similar sense by Lydgate in *TB* to describe Medea's ability to transform winter, to "araye þe erþe and tapite hym in grene" (1:61, line 1659); and it also appears in line 2766 of *Resoun and Sensuallyte*, a work attributed to Lydgate (ed. Sieper, p. 73). In *Book of the Duchess*, Chaucer uses the word in a non-figurative sense: "al hys halles / I wol . . . tapite hem ful many fold" (lines 258–60).

195 *stable blew*. According to medieval color symbolism, blue signified constancy and fidelity, as in accord with the Virgin Mary. See Ferguson, *Signs and Symbols*, p. 151.

198 *Tyl that fortune to them had enmyté*. Though fortune is often figured as blind and disinterested, turning her wheel randomly, she can also be presented as a persecuting figure who actively seeks the destruction of happiness, as she is here.

200 *unwarly cometh adversité*. Misfortune comes without warning. No doubt proverbial. Compare "Death comes without warning" (Whiting D92) and numerous proverbs about the changeability of Fortune. Compare also lines 666–67, which express the similar idea that fortune assails those who feel on sure ground. See Whiting F507 ("Fortune assails many a man"). See Whiting for other proverbs expressing similar sentiments, for example, F514 ("Fortune fails

at the most need"), F530 ("Fortune is uncertain to all mortal folk"), F531 ("Fortune makes a man (soonest) to fall when he is most on height"), S669 ("He that weens to stand stithest"), and so on.

205 *gan to sike and groone*. Compare the description of Troilus's lovesickness: "And first he gan to sike, and eft to grone" (*TC* 1.360).

209 *for woo began to melte*. Compare Pandarus, "that neigh malt for wo and routhe" (*TC* 1.582).

211 *to freendys entirparte*. Compare Pandarus's words on friends: "I wol parten with the al thi peyne / . . . As it is frendes right, soth for to seyne / To entreparten wo as glad desport" (*TC* 1.589–92); see also line 216 in *Fabula* for repetition of the same sentiment.

222 *Now hoot, now coold*. Compare Troilus's symptoms: "For hote of cold, for cold of hote, I dye" (*TC* 1.420).

225 *but closyd is my wounde*. Compare *TG*: "That hatter brenne [th]at closid is my wounde" (line 362). Lines 356–62 of the *TG* contain several close verbal similarities to *Fabula* at this point.

230–31 *cleer streemys . . . of an ye . . . causith for to dye*. Compare the "subtile stremes" of Criseyde's eyes, which have a similar effect on Troilus (*TC* 1.305–06). See also *TG*, lines 582, 815. Also note the implicit allusion to Cupid, who strikes with his arrows to make us fall in love.

237–38 In a letter to John Paston, Marjery Brews (later Paston) uses similar phrasing: "And there wotteth no creature what pain I endure; / And for to be dead, I dare it not discure" (See Davis, ed. *Paston Letters*, 1:662). Compare also *TB* 1:73, line 2057.

255 *Love can no frenship*. Love knows no friendship. Proverbial; see Whiting L501; see L495 ("Love and lordship will have no fellowship") for other examples. The sense is that love and friendship cannot exist simultaneously, being totally incompatible. Compare *KnT* (*CT* I[A] 1625–26): "Ful sooth is seyd that love ne lordshipe / Wol noght, his thankes, have no felaweshipe." The *MED* gloss, "love ignores friendship," does not quite convey the sense that there is no possibility of love and friendship can co-exist. See *MED connen* (v.), sense 8c.

270 *poorys*. Internal channels for bodily fluids such as blood or urine (*MED pore* (n.1), sense 2a). This may, however, be a scribal error for *pouse*, "pulse"; C reads *pulse*, A and Ha *pounce*. To "tasten pulse" is a common phrase for testing the pulse, a way for doctors to diagnose lovesickness. See Wack, *Lovesickness*, pp. 135–39. In Peter Alfonsi's tale, Lydgate's narrative source, the doctors test the sick man's pulse. Nevertheless, *poorys* may have been what Lydgate intended; the doctors could be testing the merchant's urine. Since the word can make sense as it is, it has been left unemended.

271 *roote and rynde*. Proverbial, *completely*. See Whiting R193.

272 *humour*. Bodily fluid. The belief that there were four bodily fluids, blood, phlegm, bile (also choler, or red or yellow bile) and black bile, had been dominant in medieval medical theory since Galen. The proportion in which these humors were present in the body determined physical type and temperament: the dominance of blood (hot and moist) engendered a sanguine personality; that of phlegm (cold and moist) made one phlegmatic; bile (hot and dry) gave one a choleric disposition, and black bile (cold and dry) rendered one melancholic. To make a proper diagnosis, physicians had first to determine the patient's dominant humor.

286–87 *Effymora . . . Etyk . . . Putrida*. Three different kinds of fevers. *Effymora* is ephemeral, lasting just a day or so. An *Etyk* fever is caused by emotional disturbance, and *Putrida*, by putrefaction of the humors, though Lydgate goes on to tell us that a putrid fever is caused by excess or disproportion in the humor. The physicians are agreed that the fever, if it is any of the three, is *Effymora*, not *Etyk* or *Putrida*. Bartholomaeus explains the three types of fever as corresponding to each of the three things which make up the body: "sotile þinges as of spirits and fletinge þinges [Effymora, stanza 42], and of humours [Putrida, stanzas 43–44], and more bodiliche þinges and of þe membres [Etyk, stanza 45]" (Trevisa, book 7, chapter 33, ed. Seymour, 1:379). See also *MED*, *effimera* (n.), quoting Bartholomaeus: "Þe firste maner feuere is whan þe spiritis beþ distempred in hete, and hatte effimera, one daies feuere. . . Alway if [sic] failleþ sone aftir a day oþir turneþ in to feuere putrida or Etik."

288–301 The description of the three kinds of fever and their causes is based on Giles de Corbeil's *Viaticus: De signis et symptomatiubs aegritudinum* (Rose, ed., *Viaticus*, p. 275). See Introduction to *Fabula*, p. 16n40. Bartholomaeus's chapter on fevers also contains much relevant information. See Trevisa, book 7, chapters 33–43 (ed. Seymour, 1:379–91).

295–305 This passage distinguishes between the two causes and types of *putrida*, which can be caused when the *quantity* of any humor or its *quality*, that is, its property (wetness, coldness, dryness, or heat), is out of proportion. If there is an excess, particularly of blood, the variety of putrid fever that results is *sinochus*; if, on the other hand, the problem is of quality, again particularly in the case of blood or heat, *synocha* is the result.

306–08 *Colre*: choler, yellow bile, one of the four humors.

citryn: Yellowish, sallow; "colre citrine," a variety of unnatural choler resulting from mixture of the humor choler with thin phlegm.

vitellyne: colored like egg yolk; deep yellow. "Colre citrina" and "Colre vitellina" were two kinds of "vnkindly colre" (each humour had two manifestations, kind and unkind). "Vnkindeliche colera comeþ of kynde by somme strange humour imedled þerwith. For if rede colera is imedled with wattry fleume [phlegm], þan is ibred *citrina colera*. . . . If þe fleume is gret and þicke, þan is bred ȝelewȝ [vitellyne] colera." See Trevisa, book 4, chapter 10 (ed. Seymour, 1:158). On the relationship between choler and fever, Bartholomaeus is again enlightening, even if his terminology is slightly different:

> And somtyme colera and blood rotiþ togedres in veines and pipis, and if þe more partie of blood rotiþ þan he hatte *sinochides,* and if þe more partie of colera rotieþ þe feuir hatte *causonides.* . . . And in *causon* . . . þe vreyne semeþ rede and sotile and þinne . . . if colera haþ a defaute in qualite. And if colra haue defaute in quantite, þan comeþ flux of þe wombe and colerik spuynge. And þe same signes and tokenes semeþ in *causonide* and *sinochide,* and þe diuersite þerof is iknowe most by vreyne. (Trevisa, book 7, chapter 41, ed. Seymour, 1:389–90)

308 *Gyles.* Aegidius Corboliensis, or Giles de Corbeil, French humanist and physician to Philip Augustus, d. c. 1220. See Wallis, "Gilles de Corbeil," p. 198. In addition to *Viaticus* (see note 288–301 above), Giles also wrote a treatise entitled *De urinis et de pulsibus,* but Lydgate seems not to have borrowed from this.

309–15 When the natural heat of the body (*heete natural)* is deeply immersed in the vital, primary moisture of the body (*radical humidity),* the fuel of the fire of life, the heat burns or uses up this moisture. "And whanne hit is iwastid hit may not be restorid, and herof comeþ þe þridde maner of etik, þat is incurable" (Trevisa, book 7, chapter 35, ed. Seymour, 1:382). The consequent drying out of the body's vital moisture may explain the reference to *drye Tisyk,* which is tolerable (*partable*), as opposed to life-threatening.

322 *malencolye.* The physicians have determined that the merchant suffers, on account either of thought or of love, from *melancholia.* See also Introduction to *Fabula,* pp. 13–15. The note by Vincent J. DiMarco in the *Riverside Chaucer* (ed. Benson, p. 832) to lines 1374–76 of the *KnT* is helpful:

> The *humour malencolik,* . . . engendered in some cases by passions of the soul such as "grete thoughtes of sorwe, and of to grete studie and of drede" . . . could lead to melancholia, which affects the middle cell and deprives one of judgment and reason; or to mania, which deprives one of the imagination (i.e., he can perceive no new images but thinks continually of his beloved); see Bartholomaeus Anglicus 7.6, tr. Trevisa [ed. Seymour] 1:349.

323 *uryne.* Compare Bartholomaeus: "ȝif it [urine] is þynne in substaunce, it tokeneþ drines of humour þat haþ þe maistrie" (Trevisa, book 5, chapter 45, ed. Seymour, 1:258). Melancholy, caused by or engendering an excess of black bile, is cold and dry; this would explain the reference to "frigidite" and the "thin urine." Rawcliffe also notes the connection between urine's thinness, its pale color, and melancholy (*Medicine and Society,* p. 48).

325 *veyne ryveers*: An unusual combination; the only other comparable Middle English phrase is "veyne-blood" (*CT* I[A] 2747), but this refers to the drawing off of blood (See Vincent J. DiMarco, on his notes to *KnT* in Benson, *Riverside,* p. 839n2747). The *OED* gives the compound *vein-riveret* as an example, but this is from 1656 and is descriptive of a river (*OED vein,* sense C2). Perhaps the original exemplar read *reyne* (kidney) for *veyne,* yielding the reading that the passages leading to or from the kidneys were *oppilat* (obstructed). Contextually, this would

make sense, but there is no MS support for such a reading. The only MS variant is *vryn*, C.

330 *vertu regitiff.* Although Lygate may be thinking of one of the three main virtues that operated the body — "*virtus naturalis*, whose seat of action is primarily in the liver; the *virtus spiritualis*, or *vitalis*, which functions chiefly in the heart; and the *virtus animata*, or *animalis*, working through the brain" (Curry, *Chaucer and the Mediaeval Sciences*, p. 140) — it is more likely that *vertu* is here a more general term meaning "power" or "faculty." The sense is, then, that the basic, controlling faculty of one's nature can be so greatly oppressed by melancholy that one's life can be in danger unless a remedy is found. Bartholomaeus writes that "melancolia . . . is a suspeccioun þat haþ maistrie of þe soule . . ." (Trevisa, book 7, chapter 6, ed. Seymour, 1:349).

336 *Amor ereos*: the disease of lovesickness. See the Introduction to *Fabula*, pp. 13–17.

338–43 *estimatiff*: The estimative virtue or faculty, located in the second cerebral ventricle or cell. See note to lines 55–56 above, and the Introduction to *Fabula*, pp. 15–16. Wack also explains succinctly:

> [L]ovesickness was caused by a misfunctioning of the estimative faculty, which is responsible for judgement: [it misfunctions] because it is misled by an excessively pleasing sense perception, so strong that it eclipses other sense impressions that might contradict it. Hence the estimation judges a form to be better, more noble, and more desirable than all the others: it has 'overestimated' the object (*Lovesickness*, p. 56).

344 *manye*. Mania is often associated with melancholy. See Trevisa, book 4, chapter 11 (ed. Seymour, 1:161–62), book 7, chapter 6 (ed. Seymour, 1:349–50), and note to line 322 above.

351–71 The Egyptian's liveliness and persistence may be compared to that of Pandarus; see *TC* 1.617ff. Compare also *Fabula*, line 360 with *TC* 1.730ff. and *Fabula*, lines 367–68 with *TC* 1.619–20.

413 *My liff, my deeth, is portrayed in hir face*. The line is almost directly translated from Peter Alfonsi: "Ex hac est mihi mors et ex hac mea vita" (quoted in Schleich and Zupitza, ed., *Fabula Duorum Mercatorum*, p. 18). Compare *TG:* "my life, my deþ and eke my cure / Is in hir hond . . ." (lines 590–91) and "al vertues be portreid in hir face" (line 678).

438 *I wante witt* . . . The rhetorical figure of *occupatio*, an apparent refusal or inability to describe something which, by its very presence, draws attention to the description.

439 *Ymeneus*. Hymen, god of marriage. See also Chaucer's Merchant's Tale for a reference to Hymen's presence at a wedding, though the tone there is markedly different (*CT* IV[E] 1730).

446–47 *His freend to hym abrochyd hath the tonne / Of freendly triacle* . . . See note to lines 697–707 below.

456 *what shuld I write mor?* The figure of *occupatio* again.

472 *the riht weye*. On this phrase, see *Guy*, Explanatory Note to line 328.

480 Compare Chaucer's Merchant's fanciful definition of a good wife (*CT* IV[E] 1345).

484–86 The lines are antiphrastic. For woman as the target of this satirical device, see Lydgate's "Ballade per antiphrasim" (MacCracken, ed., *Minor Poems* 2:432) and "Beware of doubleness" *(Minor Poems* 2:438). Lydgate also employs standard antifeminist criticisms in, for example, "Ballade on an Ale Seller" (*Minor Poems* 2:429), "Examples Against women" (*Minor Poems* 2:442), "The Pain and Sorrow of an Evil Marriage" (*Minor Poems* 2:456), and parts of the *FP*, some of them excerpted in Ha. For an analysis of these excerpts, see A. S. G. Edwards, "Medieval Antifeminism." For an excellent overview of the medieval antifeminist tradition, see Alcuin Blamires, ed. *Woman Defamed and Woman Defended,* particularly Blamires's introduction. Another useful discussion of medieval antifeminism as it pertains to Chaucer is Jill Mann, *Geoffrey Chaucer,* pp. 48–86.

488–89 *make experience / Of her lownesse*. The *MED* glosses the phrase *maken experience* as "to make an investigation or experiment of" (*MED experience* (n.), sense 2a), but a more appropriate interpretation is provided by the third meaning, "personal or practical experience, practice" (sense 3) for which lines 488–89 are given as illustration. To paraphrase, "women do not love for men to experience their meekness." The line is clearly an ironic understatement continuing the antiphrastic thrust of lines 484–86 above. Compare these antiphrastic lines in *Resoun and Sensuallyte*: "Recorde I take of her husbondys / That knowe best experience / Of her mekenesse and pacience" (quoted in Pearsall, *John Lydgate*, p. 118).

498–501 Compare Lydgate's *Complaint of a Lover's Life* (Norton-Smith, *Poems*, p. 47): "But who shal helpe me now to compleyn? / Or who shal now my stile guy or lede?" (lines 176–77). Norton-Smith notes this as "the rhetorical figure *invocatio*" (*Poems*, p. 168); it is also helpful to see these and the following lines as a kind of "modesty topos," whereby the author confesses his trepidation regarding the task which lies ahead (Curtius, *European Literature*, pp. 83–84).

502–03 *Me into stoon transmued hath Meduse / For verray stonyng*. In Greek mythology, Medusa was one of the three Gorgons who had serpents for hair and eyes that turned onlookers into stone. There is a pun here on *stoon* and the two meanings of *stonyng* as astonishment and stupefaction or paralysis. The modern English word "stunned" nicely illustrates both meanings. Fortune's fickleness and instability will play a central thematic role over the next 150 lines detailing the downfall of the Egyptian merchant.

505–11 *Meggera . . . Thesiphone . . . Mirre*. In Greek mythology, Megaera and Tisiphone are two of the three vengeful *Erinys* or *Furies* (the other is Alecto), sent from the underworld to punish crime. Myrrha was cursed by Aphrodite with an incestuous love for her father; fleeing his anger, she was changed into a myrrh tree. Compare *TG*, lines 956–63, especially line 961: "Nou lete [y]oure teris into myn inke reyne," and *Complaint of a Lover's Life* lines 178–82, especially lines 178–79: "O Nyobe, let now thi teres reyn / Into my pen" (Norton-Smith, *Poems*, p. 52).

Compare also *TC* 1.6–10 and 4.22–24 for invocations to the Furies; in the first instance Thesiphone specifically is singled out. For Alecto, Lydgate substitutes Myrrha, whose tears are also used in *TC* 4.1134–41 to illustrate bitter sorrow. Here, the poet asks Myrrha to let her tears rain into the ink clogging his pen so that it may flow freely and both help him complain and assuage his sorrow. The quaking pen is a commonplace. Compare *TC* 4.13–14.

516–525 *For how this . . . is sool ilefft aloon.* These stanzas neatly articulate the medieval idea of Fortune as well as underline the Egyptian merchant's desolation. Fortune is here figured as the active agent of the Egyptian merchant's loss; the turning of her wheel has plunged the merchant into poverty and left him entirely alone, without riches or friends. The dichotomy is important: the merchant will discover that only material riches are actually subject to the turn of fortune's wheel; friendship, on the other hand, always remains outside the world of fortune, the only stability in an unstable world ruled by Fortune.

526 *Job.* The biblical *Book of Job* describes the variety of misfortunes God visits upon Job, a sinless and upright man, as a way of testing his faith.

533–36 *For remembraunce . . . did hym smerte.* Compare *Boece,* 2.pr4.7–9: "For in alle adversites of fortune the moost unzeely kynde of contrarious fortune is to han ben weleful." See also *TC* 3.1625–28 and Dante, *Inferno* canto 5, lines 121–23 (ed. Grandgent, p. 50). Compare also *Fabula,* lines 566–67.

542–43 *Thus is he valyd adoun from hih degré / Ful many a steiher lowe into wrechydnesse.* The metaphor of stairs climbing up to prosperity or down to lowliness embeds an implicit comparison to the random turnings of Fortune's wheel. See also *TC,* where the image brilliantly suggests both Troilus's culpability and his ultimate powerlessness in the face of life's vicissitudes: "This Troilus is clomben on the staire, / And litel weneth that he moot descenden" (1.215–16). In *Fabula,* lines 635–36, the image reappears to underline the merchant's sense of helplessness.

545 *For now Fortune hath chaungid newe his weede.* The literal meaning is that Fortune has changed the merchant's clothes (*weede*). A change in garb often signifies an inner change in outlook, attitude, or intention, and/or a corresponding change in status. Here, it is both literal and metaphorical, reflecting the merchant's changed outward social status and inner emotional state. Lydgate also makes use of this clothing metaphor in *Guy of Warwyk*; see *Guy* in this volume, lines 190–91 and line 203. For another striking example, see Chaucer's Clerk's Tale, in which Griselda must be stripped of her clothes twice to reify her change in status. Initially, her peasant rags are exchanged for the grand gown of a Marquess after Walter chooses her for his wife (*CT* IV[E] 374–85). Later, poignantly, she must put off her fine garments and return to her hovel in only her shift when Walter apparently discards her (*CT* IV[E] 890–96).

555 *of the peeple fable.* According to the *MED* (*fable* (n.), sense 3b), "the subject of idle talk or chatter." Lydgate's use of the word in this way seems to be unique.

565–66 *O worldly blisse . . . / Thy sodeyn turn.* Here, *worldly blisse* seems to be a synonym for fortune, as evidenced by the direct address and the verb *turn*.

568 *Now hongir, thrust . . . to me*. According to the *OED*, from 1200–1590 the metathetic *thrist, thrust* was interchangeable with *thirst, thurst*. See the headnote to OED, *thirst*.

sueth. Both previous editors emend this word (see Textual Note), probably because it is possible that scribal error accounts for its appearance here and immediately again in line 569. However, the sense of the line as it appears in the MS is perfectly appropriate: hunger and thirst, formerly unknown to the merchant, now pursue him.

574 *forwhirlyd*. According to the *MED*, the prefix *for* with past participles usually has intensive force (*MED for-* (pref. 1)). The effect here is thus of an intense, vigorous revolution, like that of a weathervane, an appropriate metaphor for the merchant's confusion and dismay. Although *forwhirlyd* technically modifies *fulle*, we are clearly meant to understand that it is the merchant, not the *fulle* [moon], that is being spun madly like a weathervane.

muaunt: From Old French *muant*, present participle of *muer* (*MED muaunt* (adj.)). Another unique word, although the noun, *muaunce* (change, mutation) is found in Barbour's *Bruce* 1.134 and Caxton's *Ovid's Metamorphoses* xiv.xii (as quoted in *OED, muance*).

fane: the weather vane was often used as a symbol of fickleness or mutability (*MED fane* (n.1), sense 3).

579–80 *Now up, now doun . . . travailed with solicitude*. Compare *TG* for similarities in phrasing: "Now vp now dovne with wind it is so blowe / So am I possid and almost ouer[th]rowe" (lines 607–08). These lines in turn echo *Fabula*, lines 532 and 563.

579 *curraunt goute*. A running gout; i.e., a type of gout that passes from one part of the body to another.

582 *thee*. The pronoun may refer either to *worldly blisse*, a synonym for fortune, whom the merchant has directly addressed in line 565, or the world in general, the subject of the immediately preceding stanza.

589–90 *O seely marchaunt, myn hand I feele quake, / To write thy woo in my translacioun*. A modesty topos. See note to lines 497–501 above.

601 *No wele is worthy*. Prosperity and good fortune are meaningless if they cannot withstand misfortune. Proverbial. See Whiting W143 for a similar sentiment: "He knows not what weal is that never suffered woe." See also Whiting W134, W144, and S141.

603–609 The reference is to Seneca's *Dialogue on Providence*. In his dialogue, the speaker explains to one Lucilius just why and how misfortune is good for us. The whole essay is relevant but see especially 3.3: "Nothing . . . seems to me more unhappy than the man who has no experience of adversity" (Davie, trans., *Dialogues and Essays*, p. 7, and Reynolds, *Dialogorum Libri Duodecim*, 3.3, p. 6).

610–15 The reference is to Seneca's 39th letter to Lucilius, in which Seneca explains that too much of a good thing is bad for us: in excess there can be harm. Soil that is too rich will cause a plant to grow too quickly, overburdening it and preventing the fruit from ripening. In the same way, too much prosperity is detrimental to a man's soul. See Gummere, ed. and trans., *Moral Letters*, p. 260–61.

622 *this world was ful unstable, / And nat abydyng, but evirmor variable*. The instability of the world is a commonplace. See Whiting W671. That the world under the sphere of the moon is unstable, subject to variance under the dominion of Fortune, is a central premise in Boethius's *CP* and a significant theme in the poem. As Lady Philosophy explains to Boethius, all material goods and riches — the gifts of fortune — are fleeting and unstable. Stability can be found only by transcending fortune in placing one's reliance in virtue, love, and friendship. The stability of the merchants' friendship has been stressed several times in the first part of the poem (see, for example, lines 7, 49, 189, 195, 214), and the merchant must learn to acknowledge that this is what is truly of value.

635 *ther be no grees isteyred / Tascenden up*. There are no stairs upon which to climb up and out of despair. See also note to lines 542–43.

642 *preeve his freend at neede*. This is a variant of two well-known proverbial ideas: that one should prove, or test, his friends before he has need; and the more commonplace "friend at need" proverb; that is, adversity, or need, brings out the true friend. See Whiting F625 ("Assay your friend ere you have need"), and F634 ("A friend in need").

664–65 *Take heed . . . your myrour ye may see*. The merchant's position is here offered as a *myrour*, that is, as an example, illustration, and warning to those who might consider themselves exempt from fortune's machinations. Lydgate uses the mirror in exactly the same way in his prologue to *FP*, whose exemplary and "noble stories" will show "a merour how al the world shal faile, / And how Fortune, for al ther hih renoun, / Hath vpon pryncis iurediccioun [jurisdiction]" (*FP* 1:5, lines 159–61). The use of the mirror as exemplary and/or admonitory has a long history; see Grabes's *The Mutable Glass*, especially Chapters 3 and 4, for examples. The full title of *The Mirror for Magistrates*, the sixteenth-century continuation of Lydgate's *FP*, illustrates this conception of the mirror: "*A Myrroure for Magistrates. Wherein may be seen by example of other, with howe greuous plages vices are punished: and howe frayle and vnstable worldly prosperitie is founde, even of those, whom Fortune seemeth most highly to fauour. Fœlix quem faciunt aliena pericula cautum*" (original italicization; Farnham, *Medieval Heritage*, p. 281).

673–74 *Nature . . . Which is of God mynystir and vikeer*. For nature as God's vicar on earth, see, for example, Chaucer's *Parliament of Fowls* (line 379) and Physician's Tale (line 20), and the *Romance of the Rose* (lines 16782–87, 19505–12). The main source is Alain de Lille's *De Planctu Naturae*, especially Pr. 4. On the goddess Natura, see Economou, *The Goddess Natura in Medieval Literature*.

675 *beware*. Interestingly, the *MED* says that there are very few occurrences in Middle English in which *be* and *ware* are written together as one word. However, the force of the single word here rather paradoxically is the one we would expect

were they written as two words. That is, the sense here is indeed *be aware of, be cognizant of,* rather than the expected *beware* as warning. See *MED ware* (adj.), sense 1a. Note that at line 707, the phrase rather than the word appears.

678 *westyng undir wavys*. A striking and evocative image of the stars setting below the waves on the western horizon. Schleich and Zupitza unnecessarily emend to *westyn* (ed., *Fabula Duorum Mercatorum*). This image may have been suggested by Boethius, *CP*, 4.m6, as well as 1.m2. See Introduction to *Fabula*, pp. 21–22 for further discussion.

680 *hem*. Perhaps a deliberate ambiguity referring to both the stars and to Nature's laws. Nature's laws and thus God's order declare themselves in the movements of the stars. These lines and those following show a strong connection to Boethius, *CP*, 4.m5 and 4.m6, as well as perhaps to 1.m2 and 1.m5. See Introduction to *Fabula*, pp. 21–22 for further discussion.

681–82 *the bere . . . Arthow*. Ursa Major, or the Big Dipper, also known as the plow. Arthow, or Arcturus, is the brightest star in the constellation Boetes, or Boötes, "which is also known as . . . Bear-keeper because the wagon it drives [here the plow] is the constellation of the Great Bear." Both constellations are high in the sky, hugging the North Pole. See Walsh, ed. *Consolation*, p. 151n7.

685 *Lucifeer*. Lucifer is the name often given to the planet Venus, which appears just before sunrise. The word Lucifer quite literally means "light-bearer" (Latin *lux*, meaning "light"; *fero*, meaning "to carry").

morowhil. The period of time around or before sunrise.

prymycere. "First candle-bearer," a bishop's chief official. See *OED primicery* (n.). Figuratively, the word is particularly appropriate to describe Lucifer, the morning star. The double metaphor is strikingly effective: Lucifer, the light bringer, is first candle-bearer at dawn.

686 *empeere*. The empyrean. In medieval cosmology, the highest part of heaven, the exalted realm of God and the angels. See *MED empiri* (n.) and *OED empyrean, empyre,* and *empyreal* for the etymology and history of this interesting word. Here Lydgate reinforces the theme of this cluster of stanzas, that celestial movements are evidence of a celestial plan.

694 *Evir entirmedlyd is merthe and hevynesse*. Proverbial. See Whiting J59.

697–707 *As Jubiter . . . wol approche*. The story that Jupiter placed two tuns (casks), one of joy and one of sorrow, in his cellar, is in *CP*, 2.pr2. The ultimate source is Homer's *Iliad*. Here and in the following stanza note also the commonplace that one cannot have sweet without sour or bitterness; see Whiting, S942, S947.

743–46 *"O deth, desyred . . . that thee nothyng desire?"* The source for these lines is probably Boethius, *CP*. See the Introduction, p. 18–23 for a discussion of the *CP*'s influence on *Fabula*.

747 *feere*. In some counties, including Suffolk, *feer(e)* is a variant spelling of *fire*. See McIntosh, *Linguistic Atlas*, 4:170. The scribe may have seen *feere* in his exemplar

and written *fire*. On the other hand, he may simply have changed the word to rhyme with *desire* in line 746, forgetting momentarily that it needed to rhyme with *heere* in line 744.

795 *O Sonne of Sapience*. The second person of the Trinity, the Son, is sometimes referred to as the son of wisdom or Sapience, a trait associated with the Father.

802–07 *Blood wil have wreche . . . in wronge*. An expansion of the proverbial "mordre wol out." See Whiting M806, Chaucer's Prioress's Tale (*CT* VII[B^2] 576), and the Nun's Priest's Tale (*CT* VII[B^2] 3050). The idea of innocent blood crying out is found in Genesis 4:10.

808–10 *And seith, 'O lord . . . noote and songe.'* See Habakkuk 1:2–4 for a close verbal parallel. Nor is the context entirely inappropriate, the idea being that wrong judgement might prevail without God's help:

> How long, O Lord, shall I cry, and thou wilt not hear? shall I cry out to thee suffering violence, and thou wilt not save? / Why hast thou shewn me iniquity and grievance, to see rapine and injustice before me? and there is a judgment, but opposition is more powerful. / Therefore the law is torn in pieces, and judgment cometh not to the end: because the wicked prevaileth against the just, therefore wrong judgment goeth forth.

852 *ye gete no mor of me*. A familiar filler line. See also line 896: "what shuld I you moor seyn?"

888–89 *Have heer my trouthe . . . unsondir goon*. Compare Dorigen's words to her husband in the Franklin's Tale: "have heer my trouthe — til that myn herte breste" (*CT* V[F] 759).

TEXTUAL NOTES TO *FABULA DUORUM MERCATORUM*

ABBREVIATIONS: A: British Library, MS Additional 34360; **C**: Cambridge, University Library, MS Hh 4.12; **Ha**: London, British Library, MS Harley 2251; **L**: London, British Library, MS Lansdowne 699; **M**: H. N. MacCracken, ed., *Lydgate's Minor Poems*; **MS**: London, British Library, MS Harley 2255 (base text); **R**: Oxford, Bodleian Library, MS Rawlinson Poetry F. 32; **SZ**: Schleich and Zupitza, eds., *Fabula Duorum Mercatorum*; **V**: Leiden, University Library, MS Vossius Germ. Gall. Q.9.

Incipit V: *Incipit de fideli amore duorum marcatorum*. R: (in a later hand): *An historye of two marchants*.

1 *whilom*. V: *whilon*.

3 *riche*. C: *wyse*.

4 *to hym it was*. A, Ha: *it was to hym*.

5 *in*. C, R: *to*.
in hym wern. A, Ha: *were to hym*.

6 *Of*. V: *Fro*.

8 *convenient*. MS, A, C, L, R, V: *inconvenient*. Ha, M, SZ: *convenient*. I emend for clarity.

9 *Or in this tale I*. Ha: *On this tale or I*. V: *I in this tale*.

11 *and*. C: *or*.

13 *heerith*. A, Ha: *here me*. C: *here*.

16 *With*. A, Ha: *Whiche*.

19 *the coostys*. R: *this cooistis*.

26 *which*. R: *while*.
but. L: *with*.

31 *list*. A, Ha: *list to*.

38 *had*. C: *had neuer*. L, M: *had neuer*. V: *had nevir*.

39 *gladly wol nat*. A, Ha: *wold nat gladly*.

44 *also*. A, Ha: *eke*.

45 *wan*. R: *whan*.

47 *began to*. A: *gonne*. C, Ha, L, R, V: *gan*.

49 *two*. MS: *too*. I make the same emendation for clarity at lines 87, 97, 99, 186, 196, 419, 482, 492, 697, 708, 716, and 891.

50 *ech*. Ha: *ech other*.

51 *freend*. A, Ha: *friendes*.

52 *grave*. A: *grate*. Ha: *grated*.

53 *othris*. C: *other*.

56 *fet his foode*. A, Ha: *sette his foote*.
the. A, Ha: *theyr*. R: *her*.

57 *of*. A: *a*. Ha: *amemory*.

58 *ifet*. A: *I sette*.

59 *of*. A, Ha: *and*.

60 *Forgetilnesse*. V: *for yentilnesse*.

63 *ar*. MS: *as ar*. V: *as*. A, C, Ha, L, R, M, SZ: *ar*. In emending for clarity, I follow the majority of manuscript readings as well as previous editions.
loke. A: *loken*. C: *loked*. Ha, L, V: *lokyn*. R: *loke*. The scribes may have had some difficulty in determining whether the verb is *lock, locked*, or *look, looked*. Both are possible (see *MED loken*, v.1 and v.2), but *lock* is consistent with the sense. The V scribe in particular seems to have taken the verb as *look*: *So as they lokyn*.
myndys. A, Ha: *mydes*.
selle. A, Ha: *welle*.

65 *feet*. Ha: *swte*.
he. A, Ha: omitted.

66 *shyneth*. C: *shewyth*.
of the. A, Ha: *is of*. L: *of*.

68 *fire*. C: *a gret fire*.
ne. A, Ha: omitted.

69 *into*. Ha: *in*.

70 *feer*. V: *frend*.

or. V: *and*.

72 *as faste been*. R: *be as fast*.

75 *is in werkyng*. A, Ha: *in werkyng is*.

76 *lynketh*. A, Ha: *thynkkyth*. V: *likneth*.

77 *as*. So A, C, Ha, L, R, V, M, SZ. MS: *has*.

dissolven. C: he *dissolueth*.

contrarious. V: *gracious*.

80. *wo*. C: *who*.

81 *dool*. A, Ha: *dulle*.

83 *can*. Ha, L, V: *gan*. C: omitted.

84 *hem*. Ha: omitted. A and Ha insert stanza 17 here.

85 *by*. A, Ha: omitted.

86–87 *From ech to . . . disseveryd by absence*. A and Ha transpose.

88 *as by*. Ha: *of*.

91 *affyre*. A: *on fyre*.

92 *or*. A, Ha, V: *and*.

the good her chapmen. A, Ha: *theyr goode chapmen*.

the. C: *her*.

her. C, L: *ther*. V: *the*.

95 *Unto*. A, R: *one to*.

tothir. A, Ha: *that other*.

he hath. A, Ha: omitted.

98 *her love may*. L: *may her loue*.

100 *As fortune wolde and eek necessité*. A, Ha: omitted.

104 *blisful*. V: *blissid*.

into. A: *in*.

105 *theras*. L: *wher as*.

106 *And*. A, C, Ha, L, R, V, M, SZ: omitted.

that. R: omitted.

unto londe. A: *vnto the lande*. Ha: *to the land*.

110 *any*. Ha: omitted.

111 *where*. A, Ha: *there*.

his. L: *her*.

112 *his*. V: *the*.

113 *aftir*. A, Ha: *a sterre*.

114 *suyng*. A, Ha: *shyneng*.

the. V: omitted.

115 *displayen*. A, Ha: *sprynggen*.

116 *dirknesse*. R: *dris[?t]resse*. Damage and very light ink make it difficult to discern the missing letter, but it is possible that it is *t*, yielding *dristresse*.

117 *sueth*. MS: *sweth*. A, Ha, V: *shewith*.

118 *fyne*. V: *fynde*.

119 *to them may*. A, Ha: *may to hem*.

120 *O*. A, Ha: omitted.

on. So A, C, Ha, R, V, M, SZ. MS, L: *of*.

absence. V: *presence*.

of. C: *to*.

122 *her*. A: *the*.

123 *of*. C: *on*.

125 *a*. A, Ha: omitted.

127 *that*. A: *than*.

129 *that wern*. A, Ha: omitted.

myscheef. A, Ha: *myscheffes*.

134 *that*. A, Ha, V: omitted.

135 *was*. V: *was was*.

into. C: omitted.

137 *hym tencontre*. A, Ha: *to encountre hym*.

hym. C, R: omitted.

fonde. V: *fong*.

138 *he*. Ha: *the*.

139 *and*. A, C, Ha: omitted.

140 *He*. A, C, Ha: *And*.

141 I_2. V: omitted.

142 *rowe*. C: *ȝow*.

144 *And*. R: *An*.

146 *al wer*. A, Ha: *was*.

be to. C: *done*. Ha: *do*.

148 *chaunbre*. I have supplied *n* rather than *m* on the basis of *chaunbyr* (lines 219, 353) and *chaunpion* (line 691).

149 *lad*. Ha: *hadde*.

somwhat. A, Ha: *sumdel*.

on. R: *in*. Ha: *~~aloft~~, o*.

151 *of you have cauht*. A, Ha: *have caught of yow*.

152 *myht*. R: *myht be*.

154 *Unto*. C, SZ: *as to*.

and to. C, SZ: *vnto*.

and to al that I have. V: *and that ever y haue*.

156 *skarseté*. C: *skaste*.

157 *viaundys*. R: *wiandis*.
apparaille. C: *appaill*.
158 *aforn*. R: *toforne*.
159 *it*. C: *ther*.
snowyd. A: *sowned*.
161 *myht*. A: *myht it*.
162 *so*. Ha: omitted.
163 *plesyng*. C, Ha: *plesant*.
paramentis. A, Ha: *paiement*.
166 *disguysed*. A: *disguysyng*.
167 *and*$_1$. A, Ha: *of*.
168 *plye*. C, R: *applye*.
169 *ryde*. V: *rode*.
hauk. A: *hawkes*. C: *haukys*. Ha: *havkys*. R, V, SZ: *haukis*.
eek. R: omitted.
170 *He*. A, C, Ha, R: *And*.
eek. A, C, Ha, SZ: omitted.
171 *Thoruh al his lordship he lat hym in the boundys*. Ha: omitted.
lat. A: *ladde*. C, L, R, V, SZ: *lad*.
172 *fressh*. R: *ful*.
174 *and*. V: omitted.
175 *made*. A, Ha: *made hem*.
176 *his*. V: omitted.
and. A, Ha: *and eke*.
181 *wolcom*. C: *blyth*.
183 *with*. L: *of*.
186 *confederat*. R: *feith plith*. V: *confident*.
187 *for*. V: *of*.
and. V: *and of*.
191 *of*. R: *with*.
194 *tapited*. C: *trappyd*.
in. Ha: *with*.
195 *her*. C: omitted.
bothen. A, Ha: *bothern*. C: *both ther*.
196 *that*. Ha: *in*.
in love wer nevir. Ha: *in love were neuer non*. L: *wer neuyr in love*.
197 *leede*. R: *dede leede*.
198 *enmyté*. A, Ha: *envie*.
201 *cauht*. C: *cawght an*.
202 *did hym*. L: *that hym doth*. V: *doth hym*.
204 *in haste was maad*. A, Ha: *was made in hast*.
205 *In*. L: *I*.
sike. V: *seke*.
206 *pitously*. A, Ha: *ful pitously*.
211 *Thus*. R: *This*.
to freendys. A, C, Ha, R, SZ: *for friendis to*.
212 *merthe*. A, Ha: *might*.
214 *Yif that her love be set in sikirnesse*. A, Ha: omitted.
215 *yif oon*. C: *if that oone*.
drye. C, R, V: *dye*.
216 *is*. V: *to*.
217 *wher*. A, Ha: *whether*. C: *whedyr*.
they. A, Ha: *it*.
218 *tassaye*. A: *assaye*.
yif. R: *where*.
myht. A, Ha, L, R, V, M, SZ: *myht hym*. C: *myght don hym*.
219 *he*. A, Ha: omitted.
220 *Than*. A, Ha: *That*.
223 *and yit*. A, Ha: omitted.
cheffest. A, Ha: *chevest part*.
my. R: omitted.
224 *weel*. C: omitted.
225 *hurt*. A, C, L, V, M, SZ: *I hurt*.
226 *dethis spere*. R: *deth is speke*.
strykith. C, SZ: *stykkyth*.
in. R: *at*. V: *on*.
227 *it*. A, Ha: *I*.
sounde. A, Ha: *founde*.
228 *the*. L, V: omitted.
229 *arrest*. L, R, V: *a rest*.
230 *of*$_1$. L: *and*. V: *off*.
231 *me causith*. C: *that causyth me*.
232 *hoolly*. A, Ha: *only*. R: *hole*.
235 *to*. A, L: omitted.
cruel. C: *cruelly*.
237 *that*. R, V: omitted.
238 *me nat*. L, R: *nat me*.
239 *moost of al*. V: *so well*.
241 *Ful*. A, V: *ffor*.
243 *I*. R: omitted.
246 *ladyes*. A, Ha: *maydens*.
247 *for*. L: *to*.
248 *al in dowte*. L: *in a doute*.
251 *hym*. C, V: *whom*. R: *him that*.
so. R: *most*.
253 *he*. C: omitted. Ha: *I*.
lovyd. A: *lovith*.

255 *no*. A: omitted.
257 *wrathe*. A, C, Ha, R, M, SZ: *to wrath*.
259 *his*. A: *he his*.
260 *lay in langour*. A, Ha: *in langoure lay*.
261 *wol*. A, Ha, R: *ful*.
262 *serche*. A, Ha, R: *seche*.
aboute the lond. A, Ha: *the lande aboute*.
263 *menee*. V: *men*.
267 *been*. R: *ther ben*.
270 *poorys*. C: *pulse*. A, Ha: *pounce*. R, V, L: *poris*. See also explanatory note.
271 *They*. So A, C, Ha, R. MS: *The*. L, V, M, SZ: *Thei*. I emend for clarity.
fynd. Ha: *serche*.
272 *his*. V: *al his*.
273 *thereon*. Ha: *therupon*.
werke. A, C, R: *to werke*.
274 *yif*. A, Ha: *if that*.
sey. A: *sye*. C: *se*. Ha: *sy*. L, V: *sey*. R: *had sei*.
275 *Ful*. Ha: *fful many*.
276 *the*. V: omitted.
277 *Pelotes*. A, Ha: *Pellettis*.
278 *poudrys*. A, Ha, R, SZ: omitted. C: *thynges*.
and. A, C, Ha, L, R, V: *for*.
279 *maladyes*. A, Ha: *malice*. C: *hys maladyes*.
280 *Nouht were beyhynden to*. R: *nouht behynden were but to*.
281–336 *Whan they have . . . was in falle*. Omitted in L, owing to a missing leaf.
284 *contynueth*. V: *conteyned*.
hoot. C: omitted.
and. C, V: omitted.
286–87 *But yif it . . . was ne Putrida*. A and Ha transpose.
286 *yif*. A, Ha: omitted.
289 *distemperaunce*. A, Ha: *desperaunce*.
290 *excesse*. Ha: *excessyf*.
with. A, C, Ha, R, SZ: *man*.
293 *of*$_2$. V: *or*.
or. A, Ha: *or*. V: omitted.
maneer. A, C, Ha, R, SZ: *tyme*.
in any maneer. V: *or metis crude*.
294 *tellen here*. A, Ha: *doth termyne*. C, R: *determyne*. V: *do conclude*.
297 *flowyng*. V: *folwyng*.
too. MS, A, C, R, V, M, SZ: *to*. Ha: *so*. I make the same emendation at lines 813 and 899.
plenteuous. A: *pletivous*.
299 *Yif by*. A, Ha: *If it be*.
ye. MS, C, Ha: *he*.
it. A: omitted.
304 *anoon a man*. C: *a man anon*.
leedith. A, Ha: *bedith*.
306 *of*. Ha: omitted.
Colre. A, Ha: *Colera*. C: *colour*. M: *Colra*.
his. R: *hir*.
308 *to juge*. R: *deme ye*.
309 *Also*. Ha: *And also*.
311 *degré*. A, C, Ha, R, M, SZ: *any degre*. V: *Auicenys degre*.
312 *is*. V: *his*.
314 *incurable*. V: *Inrecurable*.
315 *withal partable*. A, Ha: *therwith portabil*.
316 *othir*. A, Ha: omitted.
thes. A, Ha: *the*. C: *ther*.
318 *that*. R: *that that*.
319 *defawte noon*. V: *no defaute*.
321 *ouht they*. C: *owght þat they*.
325 *veyne*. C: *vryn*. See Explanatory Note.
326 *It was ful thynne and wannyssh for to see*. Ha: omitted but added in the margin by the scribe.
328 *voyde*. A: *avoyde*.
329 *to be*. So A, C, Ha, R, SZ. MS: *by*.
333 *soone be*. A, Ha: *som*.
334 *this*. A, Ha, V: *this*.
336 *Ereos*. A, Ha: *Ereas*.
he. R: *this man*.
337 *and*. A, C, Ha, R, V, SZ: omitted.
338 *Is*. A, C, Ha, L, R, V, SZ: omitted.
estimatiff. So M, SZ. MS: *estiantiff*. A, Ha, R, V, L: *estiantif*. C: *estimatyfe*. I emend for clarity, following M and SZ.
340 *ovirlordshipith*. A, Ha: *ouerbede shippith*.
341 *be forth*. A, Ha: *byfore the*. C: *by fore*.
successyf. So A, Ha, V, M, SZ. MS: *succesfyf*. C: *successyfe*. L, R: *successiff*.

342 *for love*. A, Ha: *more for love*. V: omitted.
for love mor fayr. R: *more fair for loue*.
343 *hath God*. A, Ha: *god hath*.
or. V: *of*.
344 *This*. A: *Thus*.
man. R: *a man*.
in. A, C, Ha, R, SZ: *in siknes*.
345 *by*. C: *with*.
346 *man*. A: *he*. Ha: omitted.
frenesye. C: *a frenesye*.
347 *woman*. C: *women*.
349 *of*. A, Ha: *on*.
othir. A, Ha: omitted.
350 *was hool*. Ha: *hole was*.
352 *this*. A, Ha: *his*.
nat ne wolde. C: *wold nat*.
353 *the*. Ha: *this*.
he is. V: *is he*.
355 *to*. L: *fro*.
thu. A, Ha: omitted. C: *ȝe*. L, R, V, SZ: *ne*.
357 *lat*. V: omitted.
thouht. L: *thyng*.
dreryness. A, Ha, V: *distresse*.
358 *Yif*. Ha: *Of*.
359 *rake*. MS, Ha: *Reke*. C: *stake*.
nat. A: *it nat*.
361 *uncloose*. A, Ha: *ye vncloose*.
363 *mystrust*. R: *mystrust ye*.
to lokke it up. C: *why lokȝe it*.
365 *mystruste*. A, C, Ha: *to mystrust*.
366 *concele*. A, Ha: *counsaile*.
372 *alle*. A, Ha: omitted.
375 *hir*$_2$. A, Ha: omitted. R: *his*.
377 *The*. A, Ha: *ffor*.
379 *Ful*. R: *ffor*.
of so tendir. A, Ha: *and tendre of*. L: *and of so tendre*.
380 *war*. L, V: *wis*.
of. R: omitted.
381 *Devoyde*. C: *deuote*.
383 *Plesaunt*. V: *plesance*.
384 *and*. Ha: omitted.
welle. R: *weel*.
386 *hir*. L: omitted.
387 *ful*. L: *filll*.
389 *forwar*. MS: *for war*. A, C, Ha, R, V, M, SZ: *ful war*.
390 *hir lyst*. A, C, Ha: *list hir*.
avaunce. A: *to avaunce*.
422 *so*. C: omitted.
423 *liht*. C: *blith*.
425 *fully the costage*. Ha: *and fully the costage*.
426 *spousayl*. C: *spousage*.
iknet. L: *be kneet*.
428 *supportyd*. A: *supprised*.
429 *on*. C: *upon*.
431 *the*. A, Ha: omitted.
hath. L: *he*.
432 *whan*. A, Ha: *what*.
433 *freely*. V: *frendly*.
434 *hool*. A, Ha, L, R, V, M, SZ: *and hool*.
hool and sound. C: *sownd and hool*.
437 *giftys, the cheer*. V: *cheer the yefftis*.
the$_2$. A, Ha: *and*.
439 *Ymeneus*. MS: *yineneus*. A, Ha: *Imeyne*. C: *Imeneus*. L, R, V, M, SZ: *Ymeneus*.
the. A, Ha: omitted.
441 *I trowe that*. A, Ha, M, SZ: *Therto*. C, R: *ther to*. L, V: *And ther to*.
therat. A: *there*. Ha: *theyrto*.
443 *bounté*. V: *beute*.
444 *hertly*. C, L: *erthly*.
is. Ha: *now is*. L: *as*.
445 *nat*. C: omitted.
446 *the*. L: *a*.
448 *weel*. A, Ha: omitted.
449 *hath*. V: *hartly*.
hertly. L: *hertis*.
450 *Hymsilf*. L: *his silf*.
451 *liht*. V: *lyffe*.
452 *refut*. V: *rancour*.
coye. A: *akoye*.
453 *his*. A, Ha: omitted.
454 *lives*. Ha: *lightes*.
457 *this*. L: *the*.
processe. So A, C, Ha, R, L, V, M, SZ. MS: *mateer*. I emend on the basis of all other manuscripts. This is very likely the scribal error of eyeskip; note the phrase "this mateer" in line 456 immediately above.

462 *feyne*. Ha: *steyne*.
plesaunce. C: *plesure*. R: *wil*.
463 *ther*. A: *the*.
is. V: *was*.
that is. M: omitted.
for. A, L: omitted.
467 *lyst*. C: *listȝe*.
469 *love*. Ha: *the love*.
nyh. R: *nyht*. V: *ner*.
476 *For with a bettir no man ne myht mete*. A, Ha: *For noman myght with a better mete*.
ne. C: omitted.
478 *nyht and day*. L: *day & nyht*.
479 *erlich*. A, Ha, V: *both erly*.
480 *he*. C: *she*.
481 *was*. L: omitted.
483 *her love may fordoo*. C: *love may for doo*. R: *may her hertis for doo*.
484–90 *For alle wyves . . . is an ese*. A, Ha: omitted.
486 *new*. R: *now*.
487 *hem doon*. C: *don hem*. R: *hem do*.
488 *men*. C: *that men*.
489 *lownesse*. V: *lovnesse*.
490 *pass ovir*. C: *of me as now it*.
491 *leve*. V: *love*. A, Ha: *I leve*.
492 *ech lykyng othir*. A, C: *eche lovyng other*. Ha: *eche other lykyng*.
495 *But*. A: *But if*.
were. A: *wore*. R: omitted.
496 *For*. C: *and*.
wil I. A: *I wil*.
497 *I lefte*. Ha: *left I*.
499 *Or*. A, Ha: *ffrom*.
501 *mateer*. L: *makyng*.
502 *stoon*. A, Ha: *astowne*. C: *a stone*. V: *astone*.
503 *stonyng*. Ha: *sykenes*.
fikylnesse. A, Ha: *sikenes*.
506 *compleyne*. A, C, Ha, R, SZ: *to compleyne*.
507 *eek*. V: omitted.
Thesiphone. MS: *the Siphone*. A, Ha: *Tysophone*. L: *Tessiphone*. V: *the sophye*. M, SZ: *Thesiphone*.
508 *goddessys*. L: *goddesse*.
510 *clubbyd*. MS: *cubbed*.
511 *swaggyng*. A, Ha: *swagenyng*.
renne. V: *kenne*.
513 *al*. Ha: omitted.
of. C: *on*.
516 *whilom*. A, Ha: *somtyme*.
517 *meene*. V: *me*.
518 *remenaunt*. A, Ha, C, L, M, SZ: *the remenaunt*.
519 *To*. C: *from*.
hir. V: omitted.
falsnesse. C: *face*. L, R: *falnesse*.
hath. Ha: *doth*.
overt. C: *auert*.
520 *turned*. A, Ha: *hath tourned*.
522 *possessioun*. V: *procession*.
523 *al*. A, Ha: omitted.
into. A, Ha: *vnto*.
524 *ifeere*. A, Ha: *in feere*. C: *ferre*.
525 *in mischeef is*. A: *is in mischef*.
sole. Ha: *foule*.
527 *wayleth*. L: *& wailith*.
528 *Allone*. C: omitted.
drouh hym. C: *withdrawith hymself*.
530 *on*. C: *of*.
534 *with a darte hym woundid*. A, Ha: *withouten darte wounded hym*.
535 *was to hym*. Ha: *to hym was*.
537 *For*. So M, SZ. A, C, Ha, L, R, V: *ffor*. MS: *ffo*.
for. C: *and*.
sterte. C: *stret*.
538 *ne hadde*. C: *had*.
540 *Thus*. A, Ha, V: *This*.
542 *Thus*. R: *This*.
543 *into*. A, Ha: *vnto*.
545 *hath*. V: *hat hath*.
weede. Ha: *nede*.
546 *Freend nor foo ne took of hym noon heede*. Ha: an interesting gloss by a later hand in the left hand margin reads *3 Negatives used in our Language, even by this Author*.
547 *Out*. A, C, Ha, L, R, V, M, SZ: *But*.
walkyng. C: *now walkyng*.
wildirnesse. R: *wildenesse*.
548 *poore*. V: *pleyn*.
551 *sool*. A, Ha: *the foole*.

556 *calle*. C, V: *to call*.
557 *so glorious somtyme*. R: *somtyme so glorious*.
558 *than wer to me*. A: *to me than were*. Ha: *to me than were so*. C: *than to me wer*.
servisable. R: *seruyable*.
559 *by*. C: *in*. V: omitted.
560 *for*. A: omitted.
561 *O*. A, Ha: omitted.
on. So A, C, Ha, L, R, V, M, SZ. MS: *of*.
hauhtesse. A, Ha, L: *hauntesse*. C: *hertys*.
562 *O*. A, Ha: omitted.
on. V: *of*.
lordship. V: *worschip*.
563 *O*. A, Ha: omitted.
out. R: *out out*.
565–66 *O worldly blisse . . . doublith my grevaunce*. L transposes these lines.
566 *Thy*. A, Ha: *The*.
sodeyn. Ha: *souerayne*.
567 *nevir hadde had*. A: *neuer hadde*. C: *had had neuer*.
568 *thrust*. A, Ha, L, R, V: *thurst*. C: *now thrust*. See Explanatory Note.
unkouth. R: *vnknouht*.
sueth to. A, Ha, SZ: *swete to*. C: *vnto*. L: *seweth*. M: *as vnto*.
572 *grevaunce*. A, Ha, SZ: *penaunce*. C, L, R, V: *penaunce*.
574 *is*. A, C: omitted.
muaunt. A: *a mevand*. Ha: *amevand*. V: *ajant*.
fane. A: *vaane*. C: *fan*. V: *fame*.
575 *werynesse*. C: *heuynes*.
576 *torment*. Ha: *tournement*.
577 *besynesse*. A, Ha, C, R, SZ: *hevynesse*. V: *besimesse*.
581 *so weel can us*. R: *can vs so weel*.
582 *weel*. A, C, Ha, L, R, V, SZ: omitted.
583 *he to thee*. C: *to the he*.
to. Ha: *of*.
neede. V: *most neede*.
584 *the*. V: *thy*.
cry. C: *crak*.
585 *skyes*. A, C, Ha, L, R, V, M, SZ: *the skyes*.
beede. C: *bete*.
586 *Who servyth thee*. A: *What servith he*.
587 *most*. C: omitted.
588 *the hand*. V: *thi handes*.
rathest thu. L: *thou rathest*.
594 *bet diffence*. V: *better fense*.
595 *thee*. A, Ha: omitted.
601 *is*. A, C: *is he*. Ha: *is hym*.
603 *seith*. C: omitted.
605 *thylke*. C: *thik*.
made. L: *may*.
of. A, C, Ha, R: omitted.
607 *ne*. L, V: omitted.
nor. A: *and*. C, Ha: *ne*.
608 *Of*. A, Ha: *on*.
pleynly. V: *privily*.
610 *ovirlade*. Ha: *lade*.
613 *And*. C: *and of*.
615 *yif*. A, Ha, SZ: *of*.
616 *Than*. Ha: *That*.
is. A, Ha: *it is*.
619 *he was the lasse*. A, Ha: *the lasse he was*.
wite. A, C, Ha, V, SZ: *to wite*.
621 *wantrust*. C: *vayn trust*.
623 *And*. A, Ha: omitted.
626 *devout*. C: *full gret*.
627 *and*. A: omitted.
628 *had*. A, Ha: omitted.
634 *am*. A, Ha: *I am*.
so. A: omitted.
635 *thouh*. L: omitted.
636 *I*. R: omitted.
doone. R: *doune*.
638 *his*. A, C, Ha, R, SZ: *this*.
639 *in*. C: *and in*.
642 *freend*. V: *friendis*.
644 *rihte*. C: omitted.
645 *And whan he was comen to that londe*. A: ~~*Vnto my friende to shew out my peyne*~~. This mistakenly copied and canceled text is at line 648. The correct text appears the next line down.
And. C: omitted.
646 *for*. A, C, Ha, L, V, SZ: omitted.

647 *dar*. V: *I dar*.
nat. L: *nar*.
fonde. A, Ha: *founde*.
650 *nat*. A, C, Ha, L, R, V, SZ, M: omitted.
651 *shew a poynt to hym*. A: *shew to hym oone poynt*. C: *shew to hym oo poynt*. Ha: *shew to hym on poynt*.
a. V: *o*.
654 *the*. V: omitted.
656 *therfor he lefte be*. C: *and therfor left he*.
658 *man*. R: *a man*.
spye. Ha: *man*.
659 *by*. A: *be*. Ha: *of*.
660 *al*. L: *full*. R: omitted.
662 *forwandryd and format*. C: *for wandryng and for wate*. L: *so wandred & so mat*.
663 *elat*. A, Ha: *late*.
665 *this*. L: *the*.
your myrour ye may see. A, Ha: *ye may your myrrour*.
666 *hath fortune*. A: *fortune hath*. V: *fortune had*.
667 *sleihte*. R: *fleihte*.
icast. C: *I cast doun*.
he. C: *they*.
whan he best wende ha stonde. A, Ha: *he wenyth best to stonde*.
ha stonde. L: *astonde*. R: *a stond*.
668 *also unmayled*. C: *and also mailed*.
669 *nolde*. A, Ha: *wold*.
670 *bothe*. A, Ha: omitted.
bonde. A: *with bonde*.
671 *who*. R: omitted.
yit. C: omitted.
sureté. C: *suchue suerte*.
672 *That*. C, SZ: *But that*.
in. A, Ha: omitted.
siht. A, C, Ha, R, SZ: *tyme*. L, V: *sithe*.
675 *beware*. A: *by ware*.
676 *that*. C: *there*.
677 *concours*. L: *cours*.
678 *westyng*. A, Ha: *wastyng*. V: *wassyng*. SZ: *westyn*. See Explanatory Note.
679 *chaungyng*. C: *tokynnyng*.
680 *And*. A, C, Ha, L, R, SZ: *For*. V: *For always to us*. C: *to us alway*. L: *to vs alwey*.
681 *bere*. V: *Bore*.
682 *it*. Ha, C, L, V, SZ: *to*. R: omitted.
683 *wondir keene*. A, Ha: *sharp and keen*. L: *wondir sheene*.
684 *Somwhile*. L: *som tyme*.
men may nat. L: *men nat may*.
hym. C: *hem*.
685 *at*. R: *that*.
morowhil. C: *morow*.
686 *empeere*. C: *emispere*.
689 *wynne*. A, Ha: *to wynne*.
by. C: *of*.
691 *a*. R: omitted.
692 *Al*. Ha: *And*.
694 *Evir entirmedlyd is*. C: *Entirmedlyd is euer*.
entirmedlyd. A, Ha: *entremelled*.
695 *soory*. L: *heuy*.
now$_4$. A: *and now*.
696 *aloffte*. A, Ha, V: *on lofte*.
697 *tonnes*. A, Ha: *stones*.
699 *That oon*. V: *the toon*.
is. A, Ha: omitted.
700 *ful*. A, Ha: *is ful*.
701 *of*. C: *on*.
703 *taste*. L, V: *cast*.
in. A, C, SZ: *the*.
or. A, Ha: *if*.
705 *nat*. C: omitted.
706 *For*. So M, SZ. A, C, Ha, L, R, V: *ffor*. MS: *ffo*.
that. V: *so*.
wil. A, Ha, omitted. V: *wel*.
first. R: *frust*.
707 *or*. L, V: *of*.
709 *of spak*. L: *spak of*.
spak. A, Ha: omitted. R: *spook*.
erwhyle. C: *here while*.
710 *bevere*. C: omitted.
so. C: omitted.
hed. C: *hert*.
to. A, Ha: omitted. C: *so*.
711 *ne*. R: omitted.
713 *he his beddyng whilom*. C, R: *he whilam hys beddyng*.
714 *now*. C: omitted.
nakyd. A: omitted.

715 *that*. R: omitted.
lay sleepyng. L, V: *sleepyng lay*
in. C: *on*.
717 *the*. A, Ha: omitted.
contek. C: *conflict*.
rise. A: *riche*. A later hand writes *rise* in right hand margin.
719 *boredoun*. A: *born downe*. Ha: *born adowne*.
720 *as*. A: omitted. Ha: *that*.
this. C, L, V: *this*.
721 *hym*. Ha: *hem*.
his way. A, C, Ha: *away*.
722 *rumour*. C: *the rumour*.
723 *renne*. A, Ha, L: *they renne*.
725 *hadde wrouht*. A, Ha: *wrought hath*.
this. V: *that*.
726 *han*. A, Ha: omitted.
727 *as*. A, Ha: omitted.
729 *for*. A, C, Ha, L, V, SZ, M: *soore*.
733 *or*. L: *of*.
734 *thouh*. C: *yf*.
and. C, L: *or*.
735 *with*. A, Ha: *man*.
736 *to ha*. R: *for to*.
737 *myht*. R: *my*. V: *fynde*.
739 *so*. A, Ha: omitted.
740 *hook*. L: *bothe hook*.
741 *las*. C: *place*.
742 *on*. R: *in*.
took. A, Ha: *toke on*.
this. A, Ha: *that*. C: *the*.
744 *nylt thu*. A: *wiltow nat*. Ha: *nyltow*.
747 *now*. V: *thou*.
feere. So A, C, Ha, L, R, SZ, M, V. MS: *fire*. I emend on the basis of sense as well as other MSS and previous editors. In some counties, including Suffolk, *feer(e)* is a variant spelling of *fire* (McIntosh, *Linguistic Atlas*, 4:170). The H scribe may have written *fire* because of his own spelling predilection or because of contamination from *desire* in line 746 above.
748 *crieth*. A, Ha: omitted.
751 *in*. R: *on*.
on. R: omitted.
752 *as*. R: *and*.
they hym founde. C: *he was found*.
753 *justice*. A, Ha: *iuge*.
754 *To seen a fyn he hopith of his sorwe*. V: omitted.
he. L: omitted.
755 *owne*. C: *onne*.
756 *the*. A, Ha: omitted.
757 *deth*. V: *the deth*.
758 *forby*. A, Ha: *to forby*.
759 *The*. A, Ha: omitted.
cheer. A, Ha: *face*.
761 *And*. A, C, Ha, L, R, V, SZ: omitted.
hym. V: *haue*.
leyseer to hym. A: *to hym leysour*.
762 *For*. A, Ha: *And*.
764 *seith*. V: *sith*.
nat yow. C, L, R: *yow nat*.
766 *this*. A, Ha: omitted.
767 *have*. L omitted.
wrouht. A, C, Ha: *done*.
769 *to*. C: *I*.
770 *his*. A, Ha, V: *hym*.
dedly. C: *dethes*.
771 *His herte*. C: *He*.
772 *for*$_2$. A, Ha: omitted.
774 *sure*. A: *sore*.
775 *al*. V: omitted.
her. Ha: *the*.
meekly he. A: *mekely they*. Ha, R, SZ: *mekely he*.
779 *many hym*. A: *manyon*.
781 *Which*. L, V: *that*.
glyde. C: *dyd glyd*.
783 *that*$_2$. A, C, Ha, L, R, V, SZ: *the*.
deede. Ha: *deth*.
784 *in*. A, Ha: *and in*.
785 *hard as*. A: *harder than*. V: *as hard as*.
786 *cruelté*. A, Ha: *cruel*.
to seen. So L, M, SZ, V. MS, C, R: *seen*. A, Ha: *tene*.
787 *ne were*. C: *ner*. L, R: *were*.
788 *The*. A, Ha: *that*. C: *of the*.
to. A, Ha: omitted.

789 *I*. V: *it*.
thus. A, Ha: *thus*.
susteen. V: *sustrene*.
790 *ungilté thus*. C: *thus vngilty*.
itake. A, Ha: *one I take*.
794 *that*. R: *thou*.
hyd. A, Ha: omitted.
796 *hih*. L: omitted.
797 *concelyd*. A, Ha: *couered*.
799 *weel*. A, Ha: *why*.
that. Ha: omitted.
800 *me*. R: omitted.
801 *in*. A, Ha: omitted.
esynesse. L: *he[?]synesse*. A very faint and indiscernible letter here.
802 *wrongfully is*. C: *is wrongfully*.
804 *gon*. A: omitted.
805 *the*. A, Ha: omitted.
aftir on me. A, Ha: *on me after*.
812 *me*. Ha: omitted.
817 *to*. A, Ha: *for to*.
fonge. C: *take*.
818 *and pleynly*. A, Ha: *plainly and*.
819 *And for my gilt receyven the redresse*. L: the scribe needlessly corrects the line by inserting *de* and *me* above the line after *receyven* and *the*, respectively.
for. A, Ha: *of*.
823 *ne*. C, L: omitted.
his. C, L, V: *in his*.
825 *let*. A: *lato*.
reserved. A, Ha: *obserued*.
827 *loos*. A, Ha: omitted.
he of gilt. A: *of gilt he*.
828 *the*. C: *thys*.
829 *verité*. C: *vertue*.
830 *falsnesse*. C: *falshede*. R: *falnesse*.
large. A, Ha: *larges*.
831 *to*. A, C, Ha: omitted.
wondren. C: *maruell*.
tho. A, Ha: *so*. V: *sore*.
832 *justices*. A, C, Ha: *iustice*. SZ: *justice*.
835 *they*. MS: *the*. A, C, Ha: *they*. L, R, V, M, SZ: *thei*.
836 *assent*. C: *thassent*.
hem. R: *hym*.
837 *the*. C: *ther*.
839 *for*. A, C, Ha: omitted.
840 *To*. A, Ha: *And*.
for. Ha: omitted.
842 *bothe*. R: omitted.
eek. Ha: omitted.
843 *And made mercy to goon aforn his myht*. R: omits line but copies it at end of stanza.
myht. L: *riht*.
844 *ful*. C: *both*. R: *for*.
resonable. A, Ha: *mesurable*. R: *eek resonable*.
846 *withyne*. C: *with*.
847 *so*. A, Ha: *for*.
trouthe. C: *sothe*.
shewe. R: *sewe*.
849 *frenship, joye*. V: *ioye frensshipe*.
850 *declaryd*. V: *doth clare*.
852 *that hard*. V: *hard that*.
853 *a*. A, Ha: omitted.
854 *so*. C: *of*.
855 *on*. R: *in*.
858 *wisshe*. So C, M, SZ. MS: *voisshe*. A, Ha: *wisshen*. L, R: *woish*. V: *wysse*.
863 *such*. R: *a soche*.
864 *the aeyer*. R: *Their*. V: *the heyre*.
the wedir. A, Ha: *whiche*.
865 *ne*$_2$. A, Ha, R: omitted.
867 *seel*. A, Ha: *ful seale*.
thenpreent. A, Ha: *the prynte*.
868 *armes*. A, Ha: *armour*.
armes hool. V: *hool armys for*
save. L: *have*.
869 *whan*. C: *whan that*.
hath thus. A, Ha: *thus hath*.
871 *hath*. MS: *hat*. A, C, Ha, L, R, V, M, SZ: *hath*.
hoom. A: *hym*. Ha: omitted.
873 *He*. A: *And*.
rayeth. L: *raicht*.
875 *ne*. A, Ha: omitted.
877 *halvendeel*. C: *half dele*.
878 *departyd be*. A, V: *be departed*.
880 *our*. V: *your*.
every. R: *at euery*.
882 *restooryd be ageyn*. C: *be storyd agayne*. Ha: *restored begayne*.

883 *avised*. A, Ha: omitted.
884 *contré*. L: *whedir contre*.
885 *your*. A, Ha: *my*.
dwelle. V: *to dwelle*.
886 *choys*. C: *ioyse*.
no more ye. R: *ye no more*.
887 *whersobe*. A, Ha: *whether so*. V: *whether so be*.
888 *trouthe*. C: *hert*.
hertys. C: *trouthys*.
889 *laste*. V: *lest*.
890 *witt*. C: *wehgte*.
896 *you*. C, Ha: omitted.
you moor. V: *more you*.
R ends here because the next leaf has been lost, as indicated by the catchwords *I sai you platly*.
897 *platly*. Ha: *plainly*.
so. Ha: omitted.
900 *tediousté*. L: *tediousness*.
902 *more*. A: omitted.
divyne. A, C, Ha, V: *to devyne*.
903 *gonne*. C: *began*.
904 *Thus of this tale to you I make an eende*. H: *lenvoye* appears in right-hand margin.
905 *On*. C: *of*.
906 *that*. A: omitted.
he. L: *god*.
907 *That*. A, Ha: *And*.
909 *This*. A, Ha: *This is*.
910 *seith*. A, Ha: *sey al*.
H: *Explicit quod lidgate* appears in right-hand margin.
Explicit A, Ha: *explicit ffabula duorum mercatorum De et super gestis romanorum*. C: *ffinit*. L: *Explicit de fideli amore duorum mecatorum*. V: *Explicit de ffideli amore duorum marcatorum*.

INTRODUCTION TO *GUY OF WARWYK*

Guy of Warwick was one of the most popular and best-known of English narratives, from its first appearance in literature as an Anglo Norman romance, *Gui de Warewic,* composed in the early thirteenth century to commemorate the marriage of an early Warwick earl,[1] through its many manifestations in romance and chronicle, in manuscript and printed books, down to the Romantic period.[2] As Alison Wiggins puts it, Guy is "England's other Arthur, his legend England's most successful medieval romance."[3] The full story encompasses the exploits and adventures of Guy, who, in his efforts to win the hand of the fair Felice, daughter of the Earl of Warwick, seeks and finds adventure both on the continent and in England. Shortly after marrying her and conceiving a son, Guy renounces his married and chivalric life and undertakes a pilgrimage to the Holy Land to atone for his deeds, encountering further adventures along the way; returning to England disguised as a pilgrim, Guy saves the country from Danish overlordship by defeating their champion, the dread giant Colbrond,[4] in single combat, after which he dies a saintly death, just before (or in some versions, just after) he is reunited with Felice.

---

[1] Henry, fifth earl of Warwick, to Margery d'Oilly. See Mason, "Legends of the Beauchamps' Ancestors," p. 31, who suggests a date of 1205; and Weiss, ed., *Boeve de Haumtone and Gui de Warewic,* pp. 12–13. *Gui de Warewic* is sometimes categorized as an "ancestral romance," a type of Anglo-Norman romance evincing an interest in nobility and ancestral heritage. Others in the group include *Waldef, Fouke de FitzWaryn,* and *Boeve de Hamptoun.* For a useful definition of this term, see Weiss, ed., *Boeve de Haumtone and Gui de Warewic,* pp. 1–2. See also Legge, *Anglo-Norman Literature,* pp. 139–75, especially 162–71 on *Gui de Warewic.* S. Crane [Danennbaum] redefines and recharacterizes the group, adding *Horn* and *Havelock.* See her "Anglo-Norman Romances of English Heroes" and *Insular Romance,* pp. 13–24.

[2] See R. Crane, who helpfully traces this popularity. The most significant and well-known Middle English versions of the tale are romances. The romance versions of *Gui* to which I refer in this Introduction are the following, with my abbreviations in parentheses: Anglo-Norman *Gui,* the original Anglo-Norman romance from the early thirteenth century, edited and translated by Weiss (*AN Gui*); the Middle English Stanzaic *Guy*, edited from the Auchinleck MS by Wiggins (*Stanzaic Guy*); the fourteenth-century Middle English romance version, edited by Zupitza (*Cauis*); and the fifteenth-century Middle English version, also edited by Zupitza (*Cambridge*).

[3] Wiggins, "Editorial Introduction," p. xv.

[4] Spellings for Colbrond and for Athelstan vary from version to version of the tale (e.g., *Colybrond, Collebrant, Ethelstan, Æthelstan*). For Lydgate, they are *Colybrond* and *Ethelstan.*

The legend of Guy reached the height of its popularity in the fourteenth and fifteenth centuries, circulating in a variety of romance versions.[5] Guy had also entered the chronicle tradition as a real historical figure inserted into the era of King Ethelstan's wars against the Danes by Pierre Langtoft, in whose *Chronicque d'Angleterre*[6] Guy battles Colbrond and defeats the Danes under Anlaf, who, having been defeated at Brunanburh by Ethelstan, has returned to besiege Winchester.[7] Langtoft's work was translated into English by the historian Robert Mannyng of Brunne, and thence into a variety of subsequent histories and chronicles.[8] Thus romance crossed into "history" and, as Velma Richmond explains, the "fusion of chronicle and romance became the mode for subsequent 'historical' treatments of Ethelstan's reign,"[9] with Guy of Warwick firmly embedded in history as the man who saved Ethelstan and all of England from the ravages of the terrible Danes.[10]

---

[5] The Middle English versions are those listed above in note 2. For a discussion of the English manuscripts and a comparison of the treatment of the Guy story in these, see Wiggins, "Manuscripts and Texts." For an overall discussion of the *Gui* narrative in the European tradition, see Weiss, "Home and Abroad" for a discussion of the Anglo-Norman *Gui* manuscripts, see Ailes, "*Gui de Warewic* in its Manuscript Context." For some useful overviews of the *Guy* narrative within the context of Middle English Romance, some useful beginning points are the following: Calin, *French Tradition and the Literature of Medieval England*; H. Cooper, *English Romance in Time*; Mehl, *Middle English Romances in the Thirteenth and Fourteenth Centuries*; S. Crane, *Insular Romance*; Loomis, *Mediæval Romance in England*; Legge, *Anglo-Norman Literature*; McDonald, ed., *Pulp Fictions of Medieval England*; Ramsey, *Chivalric Romances*; and Saunders, ed., *Companion to Romance*. The collection of essays entitled *Guy of Warwick: Icon and Ancestor,* edited by Wiggins and Field, is invaluable as a starting point for any investigation of the *Guy* legend, as is V. Richmond's *Legend of Guy of Warwick*, which provides a detailed discussion of the development of the legend and compares its many versions.

[6] Pierre's chronicle was translated by the fourteenth-century English chronicler Robert Mannyng of Brunne and incorporated into his own *Chronicle.* For Pierre Langtoft, see V. Richmond, *Legend of Guy of Warwick*, pp. 66–67 and Legge, *Anglo-Norman Literature*, pp . 168–69. For Langtoft's chronicle, see the 1866 edition by Thomas Wright, available online at: https://archive.org/stream/chronicleofpierr01pete#page/n9/mode/2up. For Brunne, see Robert Mannyng of Brunne's *The Chronicle*, ed. Idelle Sullens.

[7] It should be noted that the Danes actually never did besiege or attack Winchester in Ethelstan's time. However, the battle of Brunanburh did indeed take place. Langtoft's linking of this battle with Guy is perhaps what has given rise to the oft-repeated identification of the Guy-Colbrond battle with Brunanburh. See Legge, *Anglo-Norman Literature*, pp. 168–69; V. Richmond, *Legend of Guy of Warwick,* p. 68; and Rouse, *Idea of Anglo-Saxon England,* pp. 56ff. For a summary of the legend of Guy in the chronicle tradition, see V. Richmond, *Legend of Guy of Warwick,* pp. 65–76.

[8] I am aware that the terms *history* and *chronicle* are not synonymous, though I am using them somewhat interchangeably here for the purposes of this overview. For a clear and useful distinction between the two genres, see Gransden, "Chronicles," pp. 199–201. See also Dumville, "What Is a Chronicle?" and Given-Wilson, *Chronicles*. On the relationship between romance and history, see Field, "Romance as History, History as Romance."

[9] V. Richmond, *Legend of Guy of Warwick,* p. 68.

[10] The Danes and Norse attacked European coasts on and off from the late eighth to tenth centuries, in what is often referred to as the Viking invasions. By the tenth century, large groups of Danes and Norse occupied the British Isles. The Danelaw had been settled by the Danes as a result of the Treaty of Wedmore, the result of King Alfred the Great's victory over Guthrum, the Danish leader. In Scotland, a Danish/Norse king reigned, and an alliance of Scots, Danes, and Norse

Guy's battle with Colbrond is significant to cementing the medieval English understanding of its Anglo-Saxon past. Robert Rouse's valuable study of how Middle English romances presented this past illustrates the variety of ways medieval audiences understood and responded to the "fusion" of romance and history that Guy by the fifteenth century represented. Speaking of the Matter of England romances[11] specifically, Rouse writes that "as a form of popular history, many medieval romances can be seen to construct historical narratives that represent popular understandings of the past."[12] By the fourteenth century, in both chronicle and romance, Guy was figured as the savior of England, the embodiment of English heroism, while Colbrond became the very embodiment of evil, a "primal threat that underlies a possible Danish victory."[13] The Guy-Colbrond battle became the legend's central and most important episode, "a defining feature not only of Guy's career but of early English history."[14] As Jeffrey Cohen puts it, through this episode "England as a nation is being materialized through the body of Guy."[15]

Lydgate's poem focuses only on this last third of the tale: Guy's return to England as a pilgrim, his battle with Colbrond, and his death. It is thus considerably shorter than the longer romance versions with which the medieval audience would have been familiar, and it is also more self-consciously historical than the Middle English romance versions, emphasizing dates, locations, and names, underlining Guy's Warwick ancestral connections, and de-emphasizing both romance and hagiography. Yet it also mingles characteristics of the genres of history, romance, and saint's life, resisting easy categorization into one particular genre. The poem has met with little critical attention and even less approbation. Often considered a narrative and artistic failure, it has even been characterized as Lydgate's "worst poem."[16] Yet Lois Ebin suggests that, while the poem "is not of exceptional poetic merit, it nevertheless is . . . competent and strategically planned."[17] Lydgate's unique treatment of the *Guy* legend and the figure of Guy himself are attributable to his source, his patron, and his handling of structure, style, and theme.

---

repeatedly threatened Northern England. Alfred's descendants, including Ethelstan, repeatedly had to defend the northern borders of England against constant incursions from the north. Two good standard sources for information about this period are Stenton, *Anglo-Saxon England*, and Blair, *Introduction to Anglo-Saxon England*.

[11] Popular romance that focused on specifically English heroes, for example, *King Horn*, *Athelstan*, *Havelock the Dane*, *Beves of Hampton*, as well as *Guy of Warwick*. As articulated by twelfth-century French poet Jean Bodel, the three traditional "matters" of romance were those of France, Britain, and Rome, dealing with the exploits, respectively, of Charlemagne, Arthur, and Trojan heroes.

[12] Rouse, *Idea of Anglo-Saxon England*, p. 54.

[13] Rouse, *Idea of Anglo-Saxon England*, p. 63.

[14] Griffith, "Visual History," p. 118.

[15] Cohen, *Of Giants*, p. 95.

[16] Pearsall refers to the "tradition that regards [the poem] as Lydgate's worst" (*John Lydgate*, p. 167), and Schirmer wrote that it is often "held up as a prime example of Lydgate's style at its worst" (*John Lydgate: A Study*, p. 93). See, however, Nolan's "Lydgate's Worst Poem," which discusses Lydgate's "Tretise for Lauandres" (MacCracken, ed., *Minor Poems* 2:723).

[17] Ebin, *John Lydgate*, p. 80.

SUMMARY OF LYDGATE'S *GUY OF WARWICK*

Lydgate follows a chronicle version of the Guy legend for his own poem. His source is the eleventh chapter of a purported fourteenth-century Latin prose history of the West Saxons by Gerardus Cornubiensis, Gerard of Cornwall.[18] This history, if it existed,[19] has not survived except for this eleventh chapter, a brief and self-contained treatment of the Guy and Colbrond episode entitled *De bello inter Gwydonum de Warwick et Colbrondum* [*The Battle between Guy of Warwick and Colbrond*][20] which focuses on what would have been about the last third of the legend, Guy's return to England as a pilgrim, his battle with Colbrond, and his death.

Following Gerard, Lydgate's *Guy* focuses only on this final episode. It opens in the year 927, with a description of the fierce persecution of the Danes, who are besieging Winchester, King Ethelstan's capital. Ethelstan has been handed an ultimatum: he must either submit to the two cruel Danish princes, Anelaph and Gonelaph, or find a champion to fight for England in single combat against Colbrond. Ethelstan draws together his council to find a solution. They must find a champion, but none are to be found: their best hopes, Herald of Harderne and Guy of Warwick, are both out of the country, Herald searching for Guy's son, and Guy away on pilgrimage. In despair, Ethelstan takes to his room and prays for help before falling asleep, which arrives in the form of an angel who instructs him to arise at daybreak and find, at the north gate of the city, a pilgrim, from whom he will request and receive help. The focus now shifts to Guy, who, arriving in Portsmouth and hearing not only about the terrible Danish invasions but also about the absence of Herald and the death of his wife's father, makes his way to Winchester. After staying the night at a hospice just outside the north wall of the city, Guy enters the north gate, where Ethelstan, seeing the pilgrim he was to seek for and unaware of Guy's true identity, finds him and begs him for help. Guy demurs on the grounds that he is old and unaccustomed to armor, but at last agrees to help for the sake of the common profit. Arrangements for the battle are swiftly made: Guy and Colbrond come together on July 12 at Hyde Meadow, also known as Danemarche, just outside the city. Guy is victorious, confesses his identity to Ethelstan, refuses any reward, and makes his way to his own city of Warwick, where, continuing incognito, he spends three days among a group of beggars who are receiving alms from Felice. Removing to a hermitage near Warwick, he lives for two more years and, receiving

---

[18] Not to be confused with Giraldus Cambrensis (Gerard of Wales). For Gerard of Cornwall, see Rumble, "Gerard of Cornwall." See also V. Richmond, *Legend of Guy of Warwick*, p. 68. The account itself appears in two manuscripts, London, British Library MS Cotton Vespasian D ix, fols. 40–43, where it is entitled "Gwido de Warwicke et vxor eius Felicis" (See Ward, *Catalogue of Romances*, pp. 492–94), and Oxford, Magdalen College MS 147 (begins fol. 227a), where it is entitled "Narratio de Guidone Warwicensi auctore Gerardo Cornubiensi." See Gransden, *Historical Writing*, p. 493. Gerard's text is edited by E. Edwards, *Liber Monasterii de Hyda*, pp. 118–23; and Schleich, "Lydgates Quelle" (reproduced and translated in this volume; see Appendix 1); and printed by Hearne, *Chronicon*, pp. 825–30.

[19] Gerard is purported to have written this history, *De gestis regum West Saxonum*, and another, *De gestis Britonum*, but neither has been identified; they are known only by attribution in *Liber de Hyda* and in works by Thomas Rudborne, a mid-fifteenth-century monk and historian. For more on Rudborne and Gerard, see note 48 below.

[20] This is the title in the *Liber de Hyda*. See E. Edwards, *Liber Monasterii de Hyda*, p. 118.

notification of his death from an angel sent by God, sends his wedding ring and instructions to Felice for his burial; she arrives just after he dies, and efficiently makes burial arrangements for him and herself. She herself dies fifteen days later, but not before ensuring that their son, Reynborne, will inherit the earldom Guy held as her husband and that she, though she is a woman, can rightfully pass to their son. Lydgate ends the poem by referring to his source, Gerard Cornubiensis, and suggesting, in a typical modesty topos, that any blame for dullness ought to be placed on himself and not on Gerard.

PATRON, OCCASION AND DATE

Lydgate takes pains throughout the poem to show that he is following an authoritative source, characterizing his work as a "translacioun" (line 570) and frequently referring to the "the cronycleer," Gerard, whom he names at the end (lines 571–72). Particularly emphasized throughout the poem is the matter of ancestral inheritance: Guy's title, which he holds by virtue of being married to the daughter of the Earl of Warwick, will be readily passed to his son through Felice. This interest in inheritance, to which Lydgate gives more attention than Gerard, is connected to Lydgate's patron, Margaret de Talbot, eldest daughter of Richard Beauchamp, the thirteenth Earl of Warwick.

The Beauchamps, earls of Warwick since the thirteenth century, had long had an interest in connecting their family with Guy of Warwick, inserting the legendary figure into their own ancestry in order to bolster their prestige and power. The original Anglo-Norman romance, *Gui de Warwic,* had probably been composed to commemorate the wedding of the fifth Earl in 1205,[21] and, as Carol Fewster notes, "every earl of Warwick [since the late thirteenth century] leaves some evidence of a link created with the story."[22] David Griffith also observes that "all of the surviving images [in art and architecture] of Guy produced from c. 1360 have an explicit Beauchamp connection."[23] The Beauchamps named their heirs after Guy and his son Reynbourne;[24] they commissioned and collected books about him,[25] they accrued and bequeathed material objects associated with him, and a tower at

---

[21] See note 1 above.

[22] Fewster, *Traditionality and Genre*, p. 106.

[23] Griffith, "Visual History," p. 120.

[24] Earl William in the 1270s named his son Guy; Earl Thomas in the 1340s named his sons Guy, Thomas, and Reynbron. See Liu, "Richard Beauchamp," p. 272, and Fewster, *Traditionality and Genre*, p. 111.

[25] These texts include not only Lydgate's poem but also "the Irish Life *of Sir Guy,* composed before 1449, and the *Rommant de Guy de Warwick* of c. 1445, along with the undated 'second or fifteenth-century version' of *Guy of Warwick* (Cambridge University Library MS Fols. 2.38), which contains previously unnoticed internal evidence of a Beauchamp connection," (Driver, "Representing Women," p. 134). Griffith also notes Guy Beachaump's donation to Bordesley abbey of forty books, one of which was a "romaunce de Gwy" ("Visual History," p. 120). Griffith also notes that the "active promotion of Guy's cult by the fifteenth-century earls" (p. 124) also drove the creation of fifteenth-century histories of the Warwick earls, including the Beauchamp Pageant, the *Rous Roll*, and the Warwick Roll (Griffith, pp. 124–27). See also Fewster, *Traditionality and Genre*, pp. 120–24.

Warwick castle was named after him.[26] By the fifteenth century, the cliff near Warwick castle, formerly called Gybbeclyffe, had become identified as the hermitage to which Guy retired after his battle, and it was now known as "Guy's cliff";[27] Richard Beauchamp, Margaret's father, established a chapel and even constructed a statue of Guy (as a knight, not a pilgrim) there.[28] The Beauchamps' conscious "programme of architectural, artistic, literary, and ecclesiastical patronage [that] created the sense that the family enjoyed a direct lineage back to the historical founder of the dynasty"[29] has been well described by such scholars as Carol Fewster, Velma Richmond, Emma Mason, and Yin Liu, the last of whom gives a fascinating account of how Richard created and participated in a tournament at Guines designed to imitate the literary structure of chivalric romance. In this, as in much else, Richard, as Richmond points out, "cast[s] himself as a latter-day Guy."[30]

A powerful political family,[31] the Beauchamps were also consistent literary patrons of Lydgate. Richard had commissioned Lydgate's poem on "The Title and Pedigree of Henry VI" and his second wife, Isabella, had commissioned the "Fifteen Joys of our Lady." Richard is also associated in one manuscript with Lydgate's *Lives of St. Edmund and Fremund*.[32] Margaret's own interest in the story of Guy may have arisen from a desire to assert her ancestral claim as a Warwick daughter, through whom, like Felice, she could pass the earldom to her husband John Talbot.[33] These concerns are suggested by a rubric that prefaces the poem in two manuscripts:[34] "Her now begynnyth an abstracte owte the

---

[26] See Liu ("Richard Beauchamp," p. 271–72), Fewster (*Traditionality and Genre*, pp. 109–10; 112), Mason ("Legends of the Beauchamps' Ancestors," p. 33, 38n23), and Griffith ("Visual History," p. 121–23) for lists of such objects. The tower was built in the fourteenth century by the twelfth earl, Thomas (Griffith, "Visual History," p. 121).

[27] See Fewster, *Traditionality and Genre*, p. 113, and V. Richmond, *Legend of Guy of Warwick*, p. 473 n23, for interesting descriptions of how the name of the cliff evolved.

[28] On this statue, see Fewster, *Traditionality and Genre*, p. 113.

[29] Griffith, "Visual History," p. 120)

[30] V. Richmond, *Legend of Guy of Warwick*, p. 107.

[31] The Beauchamps had been at the center of English political and military power since at least the time of Edward I, when William Beauchamp became the ninth Earl of Warwick. On the Beauchamps in the fifteenth century, see such histories as Keen's *England in the Later Middle Ages*; Hicks, *English Political Culture in the Fifteenth Century*; Griffiths, *Reign of King Henry VI*; and Harriss, *Shaping the Nation.*

[32] Harley 7333. See Bale and Edwards, Lydgate's *Lives of SS Edmund and Fremund*, p. 14. For further discussion of this MS and the Beauchamp connection, see the discussion of manuscripts.

[33] As Driver points out, "the passing down of inheritance through the maternal line is not altogether unusual in the Middle Ages, nor is it the stuff of fiction" ("Representing Women," p. 143). The earldom of Warwick had, in fact, passed through the female line before: the seventh earl of Warwick, John de Plessis, attained the title from his wife Margery, 7th Countess of Warwick after the death of her brother Thomas, the sixth earl. The eighth earl, William Mauduit, succeeded to the title through his mother Alice de Newburgh, daughter of the fourth earl, Waleran, and heir and aunt to Margery. See Mason, "Legends of the Beauchamps' Ancestors," pp. 31–33; Mason, "Mauduit, William"; and Vincent, "Plessis, John."

[34] These are Harvard, MA, Houghton Library, MS Eng. 530 (HH) and London, British Library MS 7333 (Hr). The text which follows is from HH, fol. 4v.

cronycles in latyn made by Gyrade Cornubyence the worthy the cronyculer of Westsexse & translatid into Englishe be lydegate Daun Iohan at the request of Margret Countasse of Shrowesbury lady Talbot ffournyvale & lysle of the lyffe of that most worthy knyght Guy of Warrewyk of whos blode she is lenyally descended." The intent of this rubric is clearly to establish Margaret as a direct lineal descendent of Guy, an historical "fact," underlined by the implicit emphasis on Lydgate's reliability as translator and the historicity of his material, a Latin prose chronicle by a named author also known for his history of West Saxon kings.[35]

Margaret may have been particularly interested in the Guy story and its historicity because of her own family circumstances. She was the eldest daughter of Richard and his first wife, Elizabeth Berkely, and in about 1424 she married John Talbot,[36] who would have expected to become the next Earl of Warwick after Richard, inheriting the title through Margaret. The poem could have been written to commemorate Margaret's wedding or indeed that of her father, who remarried in 1423 after Elizabeth's death the previous year. Either occasion would have been appropriate for a poem that stressed Margaret's lineage and implicitly her claim as the eldest daughter to pass the title of Earl to her husband. Though these hopes would have been dashed when Richard had a male heir, Henry, born in 1425, and then a daughter, Anne, there was always the possibility that Margaret could assert a claim in the event that these children did not live. After Richard died in 1439, there was protracted legal wrangling between Richard's first and second families over the inheritance, the "Beauchamp Trust,"[37] and after both Henry and his daughter died, making his sister Anne in 1449 the full heir, the first family continued to press their claims. One imagines Margaret in particular, who was apparently a formidable woman,[38] pressing hard to wrest back the title, but apparently this was never seriously a possibility; Anne's husband, Richard Neville, became the next Earl of Warwick. However, as Martha Driver notes, John Talbot never gave up his hope of becoming Earl, directing in his will (1452) that he be buried in the new chapel of Warwick, "in case that eny time hereaftre y may actayne to the name and lordeship of Warewik as right wolle."[39]

---

[35] Carol Fewster also makes this point, going on to note that "Margaret Talbot's interest may have been the reason that Lydgate used a Latin historiographical and pietistic source . . . which stresses inheritance heavily" (*Traditionality and Genre*, p. 124; also see p. 115). Fewster's view is that the prefatory rubric makes a general rather than a specific point about heredity (pp. 117–18).

[36] On the date of Margaret's marriage to Talbot, see Frankis, "Taste and Patronage," p. 89. Pollard, "Talbot, John," gives the date of the marriage as "c. 1424".

[37] See Hicks, "Beauchamp Trust," especially pp. 137–39 and 141–42. See also Fewster, *Traditionality and Genre*, pp. 117–18, for a useful summary.

[38] Margaret and John were also involved in legal battles involving the settlement of Margaret's mother's, Elizabeth Berkeley's, estate; in this connection, Griffiths notes that Margaret was "particularly tenacious and indomitable — witness the chilling inscription on her tomb, 'Her reson was *Til deth departe*.'" (Griffiths, *Reign of King Henry VI*, p. 572). Griffiths cites Gibbs, et al., *The Complete Peerage*, for the inscription. See Griffiths, p. 600n61.

[39] Driver, "Representing Women," p. 151. Driver cites Conlon, ed., *Le Rommant de Guy de Warwik et de Herolt D'Ardenne* (p. 22n24), for the words from the will.

These events speak to Margaret's interest in the Warwick inheritance and may bear on the date of the prefatory rubric's composition, if not the poem's.[40] The rubric had to have been composed after 1442, when John Talbot was created Earl of Shrewsbury, and indeed it was this that led Robinson and Richmond to date the actual poem to the 1440's.[41] However, as A. S. G. Edwards points out, the rubric need not be contemporary with the poem's composition, and most scholars suggest the 1420s as the more likely decade.[42] This is probably the period during which two more *Lives* of Guy, both connected with John Talbot, were written. The French Prose *Guy* is extant in two manuscripts, one of which is a luxury manuscript presented by Talbot to Margaret of Anjou on her marriage to Henry VI in 1445. As John Frankis has shown, this version was very likely written in England in the 1420s and commissioned either by Talbot himself or by Richard Beauchamp.[43] Frankis also notes an apparent influence of this life of Guy on Lydgate's version.[44] Another life of Guy, the *Irish Life of Sir Guy of Warwick*, is also connected with Talbot: in Middle Irish, it was, as Driver says, "very probably" composed "by a person in the circle of Margaret . . . and . . . John, who was (from 1414 to 1419, in 1425, and again from 1445 to 1447) Lieutenant or Justiciar of Ireland."[45] It seems hardly coincidence that "during these years *Guy of Warwick* was translated into Irish."[46] Driver goes on to note that in this Irish version, Guy's father-in-law the Earl of Warwick is called "Richard of Warwick," clearly a "nod to Richard Beauchamp."[47] All of this evidence points to the early 1420s as a date for Lydgate's poem.

---

[40] Fewster makes this interesting point: "The prologue may be a pointed reminder, with precise relevance to Margaret Talbot's own situation at a particularly troubled time in her fortunes" (*Traditionality and Genre*, pp. 116–17), and she goes on to note that the rubric "probably appeared at a time when [Margaret's] inheritance was in jeopardy" (p. 124).

[41] See Robinson, "On Two Manuscripts," p. 197, and V. Richmond, *Legend of Guy of Warwick*, p. 124.

[42] See A. S. G. Edwards, "The *Speculum Guy de Warwick*," p. 88n33. On the dating of the poem, most scholars agree on the 1420s. See Zupitza ("Lydgate's *Leben des Guy von Warwick*," p. 26), Schirmer (*John Lydgate: A Study*, p. 92), Pearsall (*John Lydgate*, p. 167), Frankis ("Taste and Patronage," p. 88) and Fewster (*Traditionality and Genre*, p. 116). There is some textual evidence that might lend support to a date in the 1440s, though it is speculative. In his bio-bibliography, Pearsall notes the strange absence in the poem of any references to Richard Beauchamp, Margaret's father: "it is odd that there is no mention of [him], customarily regarded as the paragon of chivalry, in the poem" (*Bio-Bibliography*, p. 32). But there are two references in the poem to Felice's recently deceased father in lines 181–86 and line 316. If the poem had been written in the 1440s, just after Richard died in 1439, these would be a way of honoring his memory. Also suggestive is the appearance in the Peterborough manuscript (P) of the name Richard in place of Rowand at line 316 (fol. 58v). Here the recently dead Earl is explicitly named Richard.

[43] See Frankis, "Taste and Patronage," especially pp. 87–89.

[44] Frankis suggests that the location of Guy's hermit chapel in Lydgate is influenced by the *Prose Guy*. See Frankis, "Taste and Patronage," p. 88.

[45] Driver, "Representing Women," pp. 137–38.

[46] Driver, "Representing Women," p. 138.

[47] Driver, "Representing Women," p. 138.

THE IMPORTANCE OF HISTORY

Gerard's chronicle version of *Guy* may have appealed to both Margaret and Lydgate because of its apparent historical authenticity. Both Gerard and Lydgate open with the language of the historian, placing the narrative precisely into context (lines 1–6). The poem is full of details that anchor the narrative in time and place, but perhaps most striking of all is the exact dating of the Guy-Colbrond battle to July 12 (line 371). Only Gerard and Lydgate name this date and only one other chronicler, Thomas Rudborne, who was probably following Gerard, notes the year as 927.[48]

This particular date is linked to a documented historical event pivotal to the reign of Ethelstan. On July 12, 927,[49] Ethelstan, having driven the Danes from Northumbria earlier that year, called together and gained the peace pledges of four powerful kings (Constantíne of Scotland, Owain of Strathclyde, Hywel of the Welsh, and Ealdred of English Northumbria) at the river Eamont. The Treaty of Eamont marked, says Sarah Foot "in formal ceremony the profound significance of Ethelstan's acquisition of direct rule over Northumbria and the change in his royal status from king of the West Saxons and Mercians

---

[48] Rudborne, an historian and mid-fifteenth century monk of St. Swithun's was the author of *Historia Major Wintoniensis*, an ecclesiastical history of Winchester. As part of his short chapter on the reign of Ethelstan in the *Historia*, Rudborne gives a brief account of the battle and pinpoints the year: "Actum est enim Duellum inter Gwydonem de Warewyk & Gigantem Colbrandum anno Dominicæ Incarnationis DCCCCXXVII & anno ejusdem Regis Athelstani tertio" (Rudborne, *Historia Major*, p. 212). For more on Rudborne, see Rumble, "Rudborne, Thomas." Rudborne also specifies the location of Hyde Mede, "olim Denemarch appellatus est, prope Monasterium de Hyda" (Rudborne, *Historia Major*, p. 212). This wording recalls both Gerard and Lydgate. However, while Rudborne cites Gerard as his source in several places in the *Historia Major*, he does not do so in this chapter on Ethelstan and the Guy-Colbrond battle. The nature of the relationship between Rudborne and Gerard is puzzling. Gransden suggests that Rudborne "probably derived his account of the combat . . . from [Gerard's account]" (*Historical Writing*, p. 493). She goes on, however, to suggest that Rudborne may have invented Gerard (*Historical Writing*, p. 494n1), a suggestion acknowledged but then refuted by Rumble, who notes that the "citation of Gerard's works by the [*Book of Hyde*] and also by Lydgate indicates both an earlier and a wider currency than just Rudborne for them, and allows the possibility that Gerard actually existed" ("Gerard of Cornwall"). Gransden also suggests that Rudborne may actually have written the *Book of Hyde* (*Historical Writing*, p. 395n30; "Antiquarian," pp. 302–03 and 303n19–20). Gransden does not deal with the particulars of Gerard's life of Guy in either work, though she mentions the Magdelen MS and notes that it is printed in Hearne (*Historical Writing*, p. 493).

[49] The appearance in Gerard and Lydgate of this specific date is not noted by V. Richmond, Rouse, or A. S. G. Edwards. Rouse mentions Gerard only once, citing Gransden on Rudborne's sources (*Historical Writing*, p. 395n30 and p. 492) and quoting Sharpe, who says only that "Gerard of Cornwall is known only from citations in the work of Thomas Rudborne and in another Winchester text attributed to him; his [i.e., Rudborne's] source [for the brief account of the Guy-Colbrond battle noted above in note 48] remains unidentified" (Sharpe, *Handlist of Latin Writers*, p. 138; quoted in Rouse, *Idea of Anglo-Saxon England*, p. 143n36). This remark suggests that Gerard's account of the Guy-Colbrond battle is not extant, which, of course it is, though it is true that Gerard's putative *De Gestis Regum West Saxonum* or *De Gestis Britonum* are not. See Rouse, *Idea of Anglo-Saxon England*, pp. 142–44.

to ruler over all the English peoples."[50] Thus Guy's triumph over Colbrond takes place on the same date as Ethelstan's triumph over Northumbria. The specification of the date adds to the historical sense Lydgate was striving for, and, interestingly, also implicitly refutes the chronicle tradition's association of the Guy-Colbrond battle with the Battle of Brunanburh in 937.[51]

Specific references to and locations in the city of Winchester also add to the sense of historical authenticity. Winchester had been associated with the Guy legend from its inception, no doubt because of its military and administrative significance during the Anglo-Saxon and post-Conquest periods, and its connections to the legend have been well noted by scholars.[52] Often cited, for example, is eighteenth-century literary historian Thomas Warton's anecdote that in 1338 a minstrel entertained the bishop of Winchester and the monks of the cathedral priory of St. Swithin with a *Song of Colbrond*,[53] and Warton also tells us of Colbrond's axe, kept "in the treasury of St. Swithin's priory until the dissolution" and of the painting of the battle in "the north transept of [Winchester] cathedral till within [Warton's] memory."[54]

Gerard adds to these general associations, however, with unique narrative and geographical detail which Lydgate either reproduced or adapted. For example, on his return to England, Gerard's Guy arrives in Portsmouth whence he makes his way to Winchester. Arriving late, he takes shelter in a hospital dedicated to the Sacred Cross located 250 paces from the north wall near a new monastery.[55] Lydgate adapts the references slightly but still maintains the sense of geographical and historical authenticity: Guy shelters in an "old hospytall . . . Two hundrid pas withoute the north wall / Where stondeth now a menstre ful roiall" (lines 322–25).[56] This minster is Hyde Abbey, located very

[50] *Æthelstan: The First King*, p. 20; see also pp. 18–20 and 160–63. See also Foot, "Æthelstan." See also Blair, *Introduction to Anglo-Saxon England*, p. 85.

[51] On the association of the Guy-Colbrond battle with the Battle of Brunanburh, see note 7 above. V. Richmond also suggests that Gerard dissociates the battle from that at Brunanburh but says he does so by locating it at Hyde Mede (*Legend of Guy of Warwick*, pp. 68–69). However, she ignores Gerard's precise dating, which is stronger evidence for the dissociation. See note 49 above.

[52] Winchester itself, as King Alfred's capital and a significant military/administrative center throughout the Anglo-Saxon and Post-Conquest periods, had been associated with the Guy legend since its inception. As Rouse points out, Winchester also has strong associations with other English romances, particularly the Arthurian romances, but also *Havelok the Dane* and *Sir Orfeo* (*Idea of Anglo-Saxon England*, p. 134). Rouse goes on to discuss the significance of Winchester and its landscape features as "urban signifiers" (*Idea of Anglo-Saxon England*, p. 136). See his chapter on Winchester, pp. 134–56.

[53] See Warton, *History of English Poetry*, 1:89 and 1:93. See also Ward, *Catalogue of Romances*, p. 480, and Rouse, *Idea of Anglo-Saxon England*, pp. 140–41, Bradbury, *Writing Aloud*, pp. 1–2, and V. Richmond, *Legend of Guy of Warwick*, p. 76.

[54] See Warton, *History of English Poetry*, 1:89n*r*. See Rouse for other connections between the legend of Guy and the city of Winchester (*Idea of Anglo-Saxon England*, pp. 138–40).

[55] For Gerald's phrasing, see Appendix, p. 150. On the name of this hospital, see Explanatory Note to line 322.

[56] On Gerard's "new monastery" and the "menstre ful roiall," see Explanatory Note to lines 324–25.

near the battle site pinpointed by both Gerard and Lydgate as Hyde Mede, later known as Danemarche ("The place callyd of antyquyte / In Inglyssh tonge named Hyde Meede / Or ellis Denmark," lines 378–80).[57] The name Hyde Mede is explained by the presence of the abbey; that of Danemarche, though it may have come to be associated with the Danes, actually had been in use for centuries.[58] Winchester Cathedral, too, is a significant location. It is highlighted both as the place to which the crowd processes after the battle and to which Guy brings Colbrond's axe. Gerard says, and Lydgate implies, that the axe is still there: "Wich instrument thorugh al this regyoun / Is yit callid the ex of Colybrond" (lines 437–38).[59]

LYDGATE'S GUY

Lydgate not only reproduces many of Gerard's historiographic details but also follows Gerard's narrative structure, which differs significantly from that of the romance versions. These open with Guy's return to England and only later shift to Ethelstan. In Gerard and Lydgate, the situation is reversed. The poem opens with Ethelstan and the Danish invasions. Guy makes his appearance about halfway through when he arrives at Portsmouth. His return to England is directly linked to Ethelstan's prayer for deliverance; thus the delayed entrance both illustrates God's merciful hand and emphasizes Guy's significant place in an historical

---

[57] This name apparently persisted for many years. Warton asserts that "Guy fought and conquered Colbrond . . . just without the northern walls of the city of Winchester, in a meadow to this day called Danemarch." See *History of English Poetry*, 1:89nr. See also note 58 below. The location is associated with Hyde Abbey, just outside the north wall of town, where, not coincidentally, Guy spends the night when he arrives in Winchester.

[58] Gerard and Rudborne are the only historians to provide these names for the battle site, perhaps providing evidence for Gransden's speculation that Rudborne may have invented Gerard (see note 48 above). In this detail as well as in pinpointing the year as 927, Rudborne's account matches Gerard's. However, there are many differences between the two accounts, not least of which is length. The name Danemarch may have been in use since as early as the 11th century. See Ward, *Catalogue of Romances*, p. 480, and the note on that page. Rouse's contention, in an otherwise very useful discussion of the connections between Winchester and the battle, that Rudborne was the first to make a connection between "Guy's gigantomachia and [the name] Denemarche" (*Idea of Anglo-Saxon England*, p. 143), cannot be completely trusted, as he does not take Gerard into account in his discussion (see note 49 above). For Rouse's discussion of the battle and the name, see pp. 142–43.

[59] According to Warton, the axe remained in St. Swithun's priory in the cathedral until the dissolution of the monasteries. See *History of English Poetry*, 1:89nr. An account of Guy-associated Winchester artifacts very similar to Warton's is to be found in *The History and Antiquities of Winchester* (1773), whose anonymous author adduces as evidence for Guy's existence and the Guy-Colbrond battle the name of "the place where the battle was fought, which has ever since been called Danemark, . . . the battle axe of Colbrand, which was preserved in the cathedral till the reformation[,] a painting of the combat even now . . . visible on the wall in the north transept of the same church, and a representation of a great and little man in combat, . . . till within a few years past . . . visible on a stone in the city-wall, opposite the place of engagement, which has ever since been called Colbrand's chair" (*History and Antiquities of Winchester* 2:19). Rudborne also tells us that Colbrond's axe is kept in the cathedral in St. Swithin's priory (Rudborne, *Historia Major*, p. 212). See also Rouse, who notes the competing Beauchamp tradition that Guy's armor, including his axe, was part of the collection of Beauchamp family heirlooms. Rouse has some interesting speculations about possible rivalry between Warwick and Winchester; see *Idea of Anglo-Saxon England*, pp. 144–46.

and patriotic narrative. But Lydgate also alters Gerard's account in some significant ways. He expands Gerard's relatively short prose account to 592 lines of eight-line ballad stanzas,[60] adding description, moralizing exempla, and didactic observation particularly in the first part of the poem, creating a moral as well as historical dimension to the English-Danish conflict. Lydgate also adds emphasis to the ancestral theme, gives Guy and Felice a kind of practicality present neither in Gerard nor the romances, de-emphasizes both romance and hagiography, and enlivens the narrative with direct speech. Throughout, Lydgate underlines Guy's historical authenticity as English hero and true Warwick ancestor.

After its chronicle-like opening, the poem's opening stanzas are filled with action, creating a vivid account of the terrifying ferocity of the Danes. Building on Gerard, Lydgate portrays the Danes as the embodiment of evil as they sweep down on Winchester with fire and blood.[61] A kinesthetic sense is palpable in the swift, savage action which spares no one, not even "women greet with chylde" (line 16). Lydgate vividly and effectively contrasts the red Danish fury with the pale helplessness of the English. While Danish fires burn fiercely on the hills, the people below are "[f]or verray dreed of colour ded and pale / Whan the stremys ran doun of red blood / Lyk a gret ryver" (lines 30–32). These opening stanzas are also effective in establishing the moral framework. The great sin of the Danes is pride, the subject of the next few stanzas, which replace the arresting imagery and movement of the poem's opening with a series of didactic observations and exempla showing that, while God punishes the proud and tyrannical, he is merciful to the virtuous. While this material may seem merely digressive, its purpose is to frame the crisis in ethical terms: God will be "mercyable" (line 87) to those who deserve it. Ethelstan will gain God's favour and intervention because of his virtue and nobility: "The hand of God stood always in his myght / To chaunge his trouble into prosperyté" (lines 79–80).

Ethelstan and his council must decide whether to submit to the Danes or find a champion to engage the giant Colbrond[62] in single combat. Only now does Guy's name appear in the poem, in the first of what will be three passages on the Warwick ancestry. In each instance, Lydgate greatly expands Gerard's brief exposition, making the Warwick line of succession a major theme in the poem.[63] The passages occur at significant narrative moments: here near the beginning, with the council's wish that even one great English champion — Rowand, Herald, or Guy — were available to fight Colbrond (lines 165–85);

---

[60] The ballade stanza (rhyming *ababbcbc*) was much used by the French poets such as Mauchaut but not adopted with much enthusiasm by English poets such as Chaucer and Lydgate. Chaucer uses it in The Monk's Tale (hence this form is sometimes called Monk's Tale stanza) and in "An ABC," but he preferred rhyme royal, a seven-line stanza rhyming *ababbcc*, or couplets. We cannot with consistency link stanza form to genre in Lydgate, who uses the ballade stanza for short lyrics as well as some longer works in addition to the *Guy*, such as the *Lives of SS Edmund and Fremund* and *Legend of St. Austin at Compton*; couplets for the *Siege of Thebes* and *Troy Book*; and rhyme royale for the *Fall of Princes*, *Life of Our Lady*, and the *Fabula*.

[61] Despite his overall judgment of the poem as narratively clumsy, Pearsall seems to approve of this opening section as "the only part of the poem that shows any power" (*John Lydgate*, p. 167).

[62] For the figure of the giant in folktale, legend, and romance, see Cohen, *Of Giants*, especially pp. 87–90 and 95.

[63] While other versions of the legend also mention the passing of the title through Felice to Guy, Lydgate's insistent emphasis is significant. As Driver notes, Lydgate in particular is "most emphatic" about this inheritance ("Representing Women," p. 142).

next, when Guy arrives in England (lines 284–316); and third, when Guy dies (lines 553–68). Each set of stanzas emphasizes Felice's lineage and virtue and blurs the line between the fictional and the real, intertwining praise for the Warwick line with praise for Guy, shaping him as an authentic Warwick ancestor.

The first of these passages fills in the "back story" of Guy and Felice—his abandonment of her, their unborn son, and the chivalric life in order to live like a pilgrim. The initial focus is on Raynborne, Felice and Guy's son, who will inherit the Warwick title through Felice, the legitimate heir now that her father Rowand is dead (line 177). Felice, Rowand, and Guy are all presented as exemplars: Felice is the highest example of "trouthe and womanhede" (line 180),[64] Rowand, of "noblesse and manheede" (line 181), and Guy, of chivalry and virtue. Guy's roles of knight and pilgrim are carefully balanced here. He is the best knight of his time, the "lode sterre" of manhood (line 168), but he is also so virtuous, perfect, in fact (line 194), that he has forsaken the world for the love of Christ (line 192). This innate virtue has led him to reject "wordly pompe" (line 198) and to become "Goddis knyght" (line 195). Guy embodies the physical and spiritual qualities that will enable him to fight Colbrond and save England. Set within this passage on the Warwick succession, the description of Guy's multiple virtues intermingles praise for him and for the Warwicks.

The second extended Warwick reference is strategically embedded in the account of Guy's arrival in England, a pivotal moment in the narrative. The eponymous hero has finally arrived on England's shores and entered into the poem. The moment is heightened by its positioning — Guy arrives implicitly as God's agent, an answer to Ethelstan's desperate prayer for help — and by a recapitulation of the Warwick material. Emphasized again are Felice's virtue and Raynborne's legitimate inheritance through her of the earldom, made illustrious by her dead father. Again, Guy is presented as both knight and pilgrim, with initial descriptors stressing his martial role. The "noble famous knyght" (line 293) steps ashore, sent by God "taccomplisshe in knyghthood fynally / The laste empryse of his hih renoun" (lines 299–300). He is the "kyngys champioun" (line 301) in pilgrim garb, and in these capacities he will come through Winchester's north gate where Ethelstan waits. It is worth noting that, though Ethelstan sees only a lowly pilgrim, it is in the language of knighthood that he appeals for help, begging him "to underfonge this knyhtly hih empryse" (line 347), and to be his "champion" (line 351).

The final set of passages emphasizing the Warwick inheritance is positioned very near the poem's end. Here, Lydgate seizes a final opportunity to praise Felice, stress the ancestral theme, and articulate Guy's worthiness as ancestor: "the stok descendyng of antyquyté / To Guy [Raynbourne's] fader be tytle of mariage, / After whos deth, of lawe and equyté" (lines 561–63) Raynbourne will inherit the title. Guy is the inevitable and natural beneficiary of Felice's inheritance, which will come to fruition in their son. Again, Guy's physical and heroic qualities are balanced with his spiritual and pilgrim attributes. Guy's "parfight lyf" (line 580) of "vertuous governaunce, . . . wylful povert, hard goyng, and penaunce" (lines 580–81), is also characterized by his "marcyal name" (line 578), "knyghtly excellence" (line 575) and "noblesse" (line 577). When Guy sends for Felice just before he dies, he does so as a "notable, famous, worthy knyght" (line 529). Lydgate's final reference to him is as "sir Guy" (line 586). Felice has been praised likewise in the highest terms. As the inheritor of the

---

[64] For a useful analysis of the women in *Guy* stories and of the figure of Felice in particular, see Driver, "Representing Women."

Warwick title, she is of impeccable virtue, the very example of noble womanhood. At the end of the poem, three stanzas are devoted to describing her excellence, her practicality, and her obedience in following Guy's instructions about preparing his tomb (lines 521–44).

In all three of these extended passages on the Warwick inheritance, Guy's virtue is shown to reside in his multiple roles as knight, pilgrim, agent of God, and authentic ancestor. Lydgate keeps these in careful balance throughout the poem[65] by de-emphasizing hagiography and romance. Lydgate consistently keeps the poem from edging into romance, and this is echoed by a parallel movement away from hagiography. In Middle English and French romance versions of the tale, Guy prays before going into battle with Colbrond; he is armed with glittering and bejeweled armor; the battle is rendered in exciting blow-by-blow detail, and there is much jubilation and singing of the "Te Deum" on Guy's victory. Guy reveals his identity to Ethelstan, retires to a hermitage, and dies a saintly death just as Felice arrives for an emotional reunion with her dying (or newly dead) husband. However, these romance and hagiographical motifs are muted or absent in Lydgate's poem. Preparations for the battle, rendered in practical and legalistic language, sharply contrast with the praying or arming of the romances:

> Tyme set of Jule upon the twelfth day, *on 12 July*
> Place assigned, and meetyng of thes tweyne;
> The accord rehersed, the statute, and the peyne, *penalty*
> Doubylnesse and fraude set asyde
> As the partyes were boundyn in serteyn,
> For short conclusioun therby to abyde. (lines 371–76)

Nor is the battle itself given much attention.[66] Most striking, however, is Lydgate's treatment of Guy's death. In many versions of the tale, Guy's dead body emits the sweet odor of sanctity, a sign of God's favor reserved only for saints or the very saint-like. Angels carry Guy's soul to heaven, and sometimes miracles attend his death: his body is too heavy even for a hundred men to move it, the sick are sometimes healed. Here, however, Guy's death is quiet and humble. When he receives an angelic message that he is to die, he sends for Felice, who, when she arrives, finds him lying "dedly and pale of face" (line 528). Conspicuous by its absence is any sweet odor emanating from his body. Nor do any miracles attend his death. There is no trouble moving his body; no sick are healed. Felice follows Guy's burial instructions and prepares for her own death. That Lydgate does not accord Guy a saintly death is a significant deviation not only from the romance tradition but also from Gerard and his source. It speaks to the balance Lydgate achieves in Guy's portrayal. It is neither Guy's saintliness or his romantic heroism celebrated in his death but, rather, his

---

[65] A. S. G. Edwards also remarks on the relationship between Guy's "knightly and devotional dimensions" but suggests that "it is these spiritual dimensions that shape Guy's conduct which are given greater prominence in the narrative" ("The *Speculum Guy de Warwick*," p. 89).

[66] On the portrayal of the battle, Derek Pearsall remarks somewhat unkindly that "the narrative slithers forward without perceptible motion, so that one is not even aware . . . that the battle of Guy and Colbrand . . . has begun" (*John Lydgate*, p. 168). A. S. G. Edwards points out that the lack of focus on the battle creates "much greater emphasis . . . on the process by which Guy's role as champion is established and the aftermath of his victory, his identification of himself to the king, and his return to Warwick" ("The *Speculum Guy de Warwick*," p. 89).

humanity. Lydgate, that is, consistently works to depict Guy as neither saint nor romance hero but an historically authentic figure, a man of extraordinary virtue and bravery and a legitimate Warwick ancestor.

Direct speech helps to characterize Guy in this way. In Lydgate's source, direct speech occurs only twice, the angel answering Ethelstan's prayer and Guy revealing his true identity. Lydgate, however, increases this number: Ethelstan's heartfelt prayer is voiced,[67] the angel speaks to him twice, and Guy himself speaks four times, agreeing to fight Colbrond (lines 357–60), responding to Ethelstan's desire to learn his identity (lines 449–64), revealing that identity (lines 470–72), and vowing never again to remove his pilgrim garb (lines 487–88). These direct speeches not only vivify the narrative but they also function significantly to humanize Guy. In his very first words, spoken in response to Ethelstan's appeal for help, Guy articulates a concern for the common good. He replies, that is, as neither saint nor knight: "For comoun profit good wil shal nat fayll, / My lyf juparte to set thys lond in ese" (lines 359–60). Unlike the responses of the romance Guys, there are no references to God, to patriotism, or to chivalry in this reply.[68] The reference to "comoun profit" does not appear in other versions of the Guy story, nor is it in Gerard. This is Lydgate's innovation, and, in the manner of John Gower, its use takes Guy out of the realm of romance and hagiography and into the English world of citizenship and the common good.[69] As Anthony Black points out, the term referred not only to goods themselves which collectively "would benefit all indiscriminately, such as internal and external peace, and the prosperity of the realm" but also "the promotion of common interests, the integrity of one's territory and the preservation of common assets. There was much emphasis on the subordination of the individual to communal need."[70] The common profit included a

---

[67] Ethelstan's prayer is reported indirectly in Gerard, the *AN Gui,* and in the Middle English romance versions. Of Ethelstan's prayer A. S. G. Edwards cogently notes that direct speech "emphasize[s] the power of prayer and divine agency in directing the course of earthly affairs and resisting the forces of evil the Danes embody" ("The *Speculum Guy de Warwick,*" p. 89). Edwards does not address the other instances of direct speech in the poem.

[68] Guy agrees to fight Colbrond for various reasons in other versions: out of pity for Ethelstan and "with God's grace" (Weiss, ed., *AN Gui,* lines (10999–11008); for God and to "make Inglond fre" (Wiggins, ed., *Stanzaic Guy,* line 2969); for "goddys loue in trynyte / And for yow all beseche me" (*Cambridge,* lines 10123–24); and out of pity: "Now ye all for help crye / I shall for yow do thys bateyle: With help of god wyll I not fayle" (*Caius,* lines 10511–13). It is worth noting here the substantive textual variant to line 359 in HH and Hr that equally emphasizes this idea: "To the comoune goode my servyce shall not fayle" (see Textual Note to line 359).

[69] For a detailed discussion of this concept of common profit as Lydgate intends it, see Peck, *Kingship and Common Profit,* p. xxi: "The key to Gower's encyclopedic moral philosophy is 'comun profit,' by which he means the mutual enhancement, each by each, of all parts of a community for the general welfare of that community taken as a whole. It applies to the community of faculties within an individual man as well as the state of England with its individuals and its three estates. Each part has its natural rights. If one part deprives another, not only does the deprived part suffer from the onslaught but the oppressor is diminished too, for he loses the benefit of his larger self which he has affronted. To diminish another is to diminish oneself. Conversely, if one is capable of taking joy in another's success, and promotes that success for 'l'onour et le commun proufit' (*Mirour,* [line] 12905), he will himself grow and find a joy as great as his own successes hold."

[70] Black, "Individual and Society," p. 596.

dimension of *caritas* (Christian love and friendship) but it was grounded at its core in the community, the *civitas*.[71] That Lydgate gives this phrase to Guy suggests a different sort of heroism than that found in other iterations of the character. Though Guy is certainly a pilgrim, an agent of God, and a heroic champion, he is also very much a decent Englishman.

Guy's three other direct speeches reinforce his humanity and humility, their tone consistent with Lydgate's reshaping of the legend away from romance and hagiography. Guy replies to Ethelstan's question about his identity with a set of practical instructions about where they must meet, outside the city, "Noon but we tweyne beyng in presence / With trouthe assured that ye shal be secré" (lines 459–60), and he even adds a rather informal "ye gete no more of me" (line 461).[72] The terms with which he reveals his name to Ethelstan are dutifully meek and respectful, and his final words carry the force of some emotion and immediacy, reinforcing his innate humility. With"pitous wepyng" (line 485) Guy re-dons his pilgrim garb and declares "Duryng my lyf, it may noon other bee, / Schall I never doon off this garnement" (lines 487–88).

In his poem, Lydgate transforms the legend of Guy, shaping his source material and the tradition to his purposes. Skillfully exploiting the possibilities in Gerard's condensed narrative to enhance the moral, historical, and ancestral dimensions of the Guy legend, Lydgate links the figure of Guy intimately not only to the Warwick line but also to English history. Without downplaying Guy's virtue, spirituality, or humility, Lydgate strengthens his humanity, practicality, and authenticity. Herein lies Lydgate's unique contribution to the Guy legend.

MANUSCRIPTS

Lydgate's *Guy* is indexed in IMEV 875. Like the *Fabula*, the poem is extant in seven fifteenth-century manuscripts, a number which suggests the poem was reasonably popular and well-known. All of the manuscripts except for P participate in a large group of manuscripts that share a number of Lydgate texts in common.[73] The texts of *Guy* fall into two groups, Group A and Group B, as distinguished by Robinson.[74]

Group A

The texts of *Guy* in Houghton Library, MS Eng. 530 and British Library, MS Harley 7333 are closely similar, both also have a truncated envoy, omit three stanzas (lines 265–88), contain an alternate version of lines 230–40, and are headed by a rubric attributing the patronage of the poem to Margaret Beauchamp. Both manuscripts were at one time thought to have

---

[71] Black, "Individual and Society," p. 597.

[72] This phrase is probably not, however, an attempt on Lydgate's part to characterize Guy; it is a conventional "filler" line.

[73] First identified by Hammond ("Two British Museum Manuscripts"), this group of manuscripts demonstrates a variety of inter-relationships involving content, scribe/s, and provenance. For more information on these manuscripts, please see the Introduction to *Fabula* in this volume, under "Manuscripts" and "Note on the Text" pp. 25–28.

[74] See Robinson, "On Two Manuscripts," especially pp. 177–97.

been copied in whole or in part by John Shirley,[75] but scholars now agree that both are derived from a lost Shirley exemplar.[76] Both manuscripts also exhibit a strong Beauchamp connection in addition to the rubric: Houghton Library, MS Eng 530 ends with a prose *Brut*, which breaks off during the reign of Henry VI, accompanied by an annotation that in this year (1439) Richard Beauchamp "the gode erle of Warwyke" died. As Margaret Connolly points out, this information is pertinent to the date of the manuscript, since the "new chapell" where Richard's body is said to lie was not completed until 1464.[77] British Library, MS Harley 7333 also contains a reference to Beauchamp in a headnote to the text of Lydgate's *Lives of SS Edmund and Fremund* (written in honor of Henry VI's Christmas 1433 visit to Bury St. Edmunds), and Richard is also named as having commissioned Lydgate's "Title and Pedigree of Henry VI," a poem that appears uniquely in this manuscript.[78] Both HH and Hr have been well-described.[79]

Cambridge, MA, Harvard University, Houghton Library, MS Eng. 530 (HH): quarto, 211 leaves, on paper, dating from between 1440 and 1464, containing six items of historical and didactic material, including *Guy* which appears on fols. 4v–12v.[80]

---

[75] Robinson felt that four of the six items in HH were copied by Shirley, based on his analysis of hand as well as a letter from Henry Bradshaw to the then owner of the MS that accompanies the manuscript ("On Two Manuscripts," pp. 177–79). As Mooney notes, this ascription was repeated for a number of years until it was corrected in 1950 by A. I. Doyle ("Professional Scribes," pp. 131–32). The ascription may still be found from time to time; see, for example, V. Richmond (*Legend of Guy of Warwick*, p. 124) and Fewster (*Traditionality and Genre*, pp. 115–16).

[76] The correction was made by Doyle. See Mooney "Professional Scribes," p. 132 and Voigts, "Handlist of Middle English in Harvard Manuscripts," p.17. On both manuscripts' relation to Shirley, see also Connolly, *John Shirley*, pp. 173–75, and Mooney, "John Shirley's Heirs," especially pp. 190–95.

[77] Connolly, *John Shirley*, p. 173.

[78] The relevant portion of the headnote to the *Lives* is as follows: "now late translated oute of latyne into Englisshe by daun Iohn Lydgate religeous of the same place at [th]e comandement of kyng henre the vi. solempnising [th]ere his ffeste of Cristemasse [th]e yeere of his tendre age of the speciall instaunce of Richard beauchamp Eorlle of warwike." The complete note can be found in Bale and Edwards, *Lydgate's Lives of Ss Edmund & Fremund*, p. 14, from whom I take this text, and Mooney, "John Shirley's Heirs," p. 193n25. The rubric is puzzling in that the poem was commissioned by Abbot William Curteys, not Beauchamp, as the headnote seems to imply. See also Connolly, *John Shirley*, pp. 175 and 187n19, and Mooney's work.

[79] For HH, see especially Robinson, "On Two Manuscripts"; Voigts, "Handlist of Middle English in Harvard Manuscripts"; Conolly, *John Shirley*, pp. 172–73; and Mooney, "John Shirley's Heirs," pp. 194–95. For Hr, see Manly and Rickert, *Text of the Canterbury Tales*, 1:207–18; Bale and Edwards, *Lydgate's Lives of SS Edmund & Fremund*, pp. 13–14; Connolly, *John Shirley*, pp. 173–75; and Mooney, "John Shirley's Heirs," pp. 190–95. A printing error on p. 195 of this article suggests that Hr's text of Lydgate's *Guy* is acephalus, but it is not.

[80] The items in the manuscript are, in order, *Compleynt of Christ, Guy, Three Kings of Coleyne, Governaunce of Princes, Serpent of Division*, and the prose *Brut*. Robinson felt all except for *Governaunce* and *Serpent* were in Shirley's hand ("On Two Manuscripts," p. 180). Robinson's description and edition of the *Guy* text is still valuable, though it must be supplemented by those of later scholars. See Voigts, "Handlist of Middle English in Harvard Manuscripts." See also Mooney, "John Shirley's Heirs," pp. 194–95, and Connolly, *John Shirley*, pp. 172–73.

London, British Library, MS Harley 7333 (Hr): a large manuscript, over 200 pages, dating from between 1450 and 1460.[81] It consists of seven parts, or booklets, written by multiple scribes,[82] containing works by Chaucer (including *The Canterbury Tales*) and others; and seven works by Lydgate, including *Guy* and the *Lives of SS Edmund and Fremund*. John M. Manly and Edith Rickert's suggestion that the manuscript was associated with the religious house of St. Mary de Pratis in Leicester has been accepted by most scholars.[83] *Guy* appears on 33r–35v, preceded by the same rubric that appears in HH.

Group B

These five manuscripts all contain complete texts of *Guy*; that is to say that they contain a full eight-line envoy and three stanzas missing in Group A; they also share the same version of lines 230–240. None of them include the rubric present in the two Group A texts. The "sister manuscripts," British Library, MS Lansdowne 699 and University Library, MS Vossius Germ. Gall Q.9 are closely related.

London, British Library, MS Lansdowne 699 (L): 176 leaves, on paper, quarto, mid to late fifteenth century.[84] The contents include Chaucer's "Fortune," "Truth,"[85] and seventeen Lydgate items, including the *Fabula,* all of which, other than the *Lives of SS Albon and Amphibal,* are also found in University Library, MS Vossius Germ. Gall Q.9. *Guy* appears on fols. 18v–27v with the rubric *Incipit Guydo de Warwik.*[86]

Leiden, University Library, MS Vossius Germ. Gall. Q.9 (V): quarto, 135 leaves, late fifteenth century.[87] *Guy* appears on fols. 17r–29v. The poem is entitled (in a different hand) *Danico invasio regnante Ethelstano un cum historia Guidonis de Warwik.*[88] V is closely related to L, not only in the number and order of Lydgate items (both manuscripts have the first eighteen items in common, ten of which appear in the same order) but also in its texts of both the *Fabula* and *Guy.*[89]

---

[81] See Seymour, "Lives of SS Edmund and Fremund," pp. 19–20.

[82] For a description, see Manly and Rickert, *Text of the Canterbury Tales*, 1:207–18 and Bale and Edwards, *Lydgate's Lives of SS Edmund & Fremund*, pp. 13–14. See also Mooney, "John Shirley's Heirs," pp. 190–95, and Connolly, *John Shirley*, pp. 173–75.

[83] *Text of the Canterbury Tales*, p. 214. See, for example, Bale and Edwards, *Lydgate's Lives of SS Edmund & Fremund*, p. 14.

[84] See also the description of L on p. 26 of this volume.

[85] Counted as one item by both Robinson and the cataloguer of Lansdowne manuscripts. Including the two short Chaucer poems and the fragmentary *Life of St. Giles* with which the manuscript begins, there are nineteen items.

[86] For descriptions of this manuscript, see Reinecke, ed., *Saint Albon and Saint Amphibalus*, pp. xi–xii; Van Dorsten, "Leyden 'Lydgate Manuscript,'" p. 320; and Hammond, *Chaucer: A Bibliographical Manual,* pp. 331–32.

[87] See also the description of V on p. 26 of this volume.

[88] For a description, see Van Dorsten, "Leyden 'Lydgate Manuscript.'"

[89] The texts are not identical, but very similar, as the Textual Notes in this volume illustrate.

Cambridge, Cambridge University Library, MS Trinity R.3.21 (T): a large composite anthology, once owned by John Stow; made up of several booklets copied by three scribes, containing mainly religious and didactic works, several in duplicate, and a number of works by Lydgate. It shares its main scribes with Trinity MS R.3.19, and another scribe with two of the *Fabula* manuscripts, Harley 2251 and Add. 34360. *Guy* is found on fols. 305r–314r and is entitled *A Tale of Guy & Colbrond.*[90]

Peterborough, Peterborough Central Library (P): a small book, on paper, late fifteenth century, contains only seven items, of which only the final two, Lydgate's *Verses on the Kings of England* (IMEV 882; fols. 49r–52v) and the *Guy* (fols. 54–63) are in English. The other five items, in Latin, consist of hagiographical and liturgical material focused mainly on St. Edward.[91] The scribe identifies himself as Thomas Sandon on fol. 48r; he certainly wrote the Latin items and probably the Lydgate ones as well. The final stanza of Lydgate's *Verses on the Kings* provides an approximate date: it refers to Henry VI's burial in 1471 at Chertsey Abbey and is thus before 1484 when Henry's bones were moved to Windsor.[92]

Oxford, Bodleian Library, MS Laud Misc. 683 (Ld): a large Lydgate anthology, on vellum, with 151 leaves; its first section, fols. 1–107, originally a separate manuscript, contains religious and didactic works by Lydgate, including his *Testament. Guy of Warwick* appears on fols. 65–78. Anthony Bale and A. S. G. Edwards suggest that its contents "point to a Suffolk provenance."[93] Several works show a connection to or interest in Lydgate's own monastery, Bury St. Edmunds. The many prayers to saints include prayers to St. Robert, a local saint, and to St. Edmund. The manuscript also contains part of *Miracles of St. Edmund* — it is the only manuscript to contain this work without the accompanying *Lives of SS Edmund and Fremund*[94] — and Lydgate's *Life of St. Giles,* written for Abbot Curteys of Bury St. Edmunds. These contents seem to point clearly to a Suffolk provenance and local interest in the devotional; several other works, including the *Guy* (fols. 65–77v) as well as the prayers to St. Thomas and St. George illustrate a "general English devotional patriotism."[95] There is a blanket attribution to Lydgate on f. 105r: "Al the langage that heerre be forn ys wretyn was maad and compiled by damp Johannis Lydgate monk of Seynt Edmundys Bury on whos sowle now [Jesu] have mercy." This note must have been written after 1449, the year Lydgate died. Nevertheless, this is not far off the date of 1444 suggested by Bale and Edwards.[96]

---

[90] For a comprehensive description of this manuscript, see Mooney, "Scribes and Booklets."

[91] These are Aelred's *Life of St. Edward,* Aelred's homily for the translation of Edward's relics on his feast day (October 13, 1163), an account of the translation, and two sequentiae (liturgical hymns), one for St. Edward and one for St. Leonard. Brief manuscript descriptions are provided by Ker, *Medieval Manuscripts*, pp. 170–71 and Jackson, "In translacione sancti Edwardi," pp. 47–49.

[92] Ker dates the manuscript to between 1471 and 1483. See Ker, *Medieval Manuscripts*, p. 171.

[93] Bale and Edwards, *Lydgate's Lives of Ss Edmund & Fremund*, p. 17.

[94] Bale and Edwards, *Lydgate's Lives of Ss Edmund & Fremund*, p. 17.

[95] See Bale, *The Jew in the Medieval Book*, p. 115; and Bale, "House Devil," p. 190.

[96] Bale and Edwards, *Lydgate's Lives of SS Edmund & Fremund*, p. 17.

The text for the present edition is provided by Laud Misc. 683.[97] It has a very probable Suffolk provenance and clear connections to Lydgate's own monastery: Bale writes that Ld "comprises a regional eulogy to Suffolk and East Anglia,"[98] A. S. G. Edwards notes that it is one of a group of manuscripts "that seem to have been professionally produced from exemplars that may derive ultimately from . . . Bury St. Edmunds."[99] Its first section, fols. 1–105r, originally a separate manuscript, is clearly meant to be a Lydgate anthology, with a blanket scribal ascription of all of the texts to Lydgate. MacCracken and Zupitza also based their editions on Laud, but neither had access to all of the manuscripts.

A NOTE ABOUT MANUSCRIPTS AND CONTEXTS

The manuscript contexts within which Lydgate's *Guy* appears suggest a strong interest in the exemplary and in the historical. In this respect, it is consistent with the manuscript contexts within which the Anglo-Norman *Gui* appears as well; as both Judith Weiss and Marianne Ailes point out, the material with which *Gui* appears often bespeaks an overt interest in the historical, suggesting, as Weiss remarks, that "its readers may have regarded it as history."[100] This also appears to be the case with Lydgate's *Guy of Warwick*, which consistently appears with material pertaining to the history of England and/or with English monarchs. Five of the manuscripts include Lydgate's *Verses on the Kings of England*,[101] two, HH and Hr, contain the *Brut*, L and V contain the "histories" of Arthur and Constantine from Lydgate's *Fall of Princes*, and P centers on the exemplary and historical with its focus on Edward as king and saint. Overall, the contents of the manuscripts containing Guy can be described as collections of mainly short, didactic works that show a marked interest in the historical and the exemplary. Taking note of this fact, and singling out, in addition to the historical material, such works as *Life of St. Giles* (L, V, and Ld) and *Legend of St. Austen at Compton* (L and V), to which I would add *Life of St. George* (T), A. S. G. Edwards remarks that "these [manuscripts] provide the most obvious parallels to the historical and hagiographical

---

[97] Although one might expect that HH or Hr, with their close affiliations to the Beauchamp family, might have been chosen, their texts of Guy are not only incomplete (see pp. 100–01 above) but also generally inferior to those of the Group B manuscripts, particularly Ld. A glance at the textual notes will make this clear. The Zupitza and MacCracken editions are also based on Ld.

[98] Bale, *The Jew in the Medieval Book*, p. 115; Bale, "House Devil," p. 190. In *The Jew in the Medieval Book*, Bale asserts that "Laud Misc. 683 is one of several similar vernacular MSs produced at Bury in the fifteenth century," p. 216n49. Here he cites Seymour, "Some Lydgate Manuscripts," who, though he does not explicitly say that Laud Misc. 683 was produced at Bury, suggests that it is a distinct possibility. See Seymour, pp. 10 and 12.

[99] A. S. G. Edwards, "The *Speculum Guy de Warwick*," p. 90. See also p. 90n43, where Edwards cites his article "Fifteenth-Century Middle English Verse," pp. 104–05, in which he writes that Laud Misc. 683 is one of a group of manuscripts that seem to be connected to Bury St. Edmunds, p. 104.

[100] Weiss, "Home and Abroad," p. 2n3; Ailes, "*Gui de Warewic* in its Manuscript Context," pp. 21–22.

[101] The "Verses" appear in Hr, L, V, T, and P. On the appearance of the Verses in a variety of manuscripts and manuscript contexts, and on the many versions of these, see Mooney, "Lydgate's Kings."

elements in *Guy of Warwick*."[102] Laud Misc. 683 paradoxically both deviates from and reinforces this pattern. It does not contain the *Verses* or the *Brut*, but it does show a marked connection with material concerning St. Edmund. This material has clear connections with the same historical period that *Guy* purportedly belongs to. In fact, the descriptions of Danish ferocity and slaughter in *Lives of SS Edmund and Fremund* show clear similarities with the same sorts of descriptions in *Guy*.[103] Thus the contents of Ld also evince an interest in the exemplary and the historical.

NOTE ON THE TEXT

As outlined in the General Introduction, I have followed METS principles in preparing this edition of *Guy*. Scribal abbreviations are silently expanded; I have taken the macron to indicate *m/n*. Other strokes and flourishes I have considered otiose. I have also silently joined or separated words where not to do so would be confusing; for example, *hym silff* becomes *hymsilf* (line 318), while *Infeere* becomes *in feere* (line 456). I have tried to punctuate with a light hand while at the same time using punctuation as an aid to reading Lydgate's loose, paratactic sentences. Often these lack a finite verb or a clear grammatical subject; in these cases, punctuation can do only so much. The textual notes record any emendations I have made as well as substantive variants from the six other manuscripts that record significant differences in meaning. I have not included variations in spelling, or grammatical or other morphological variants (for example, *wer/werne*, *drawith/draw*, *been/ben/byn*), though on occasion I have included an interesting or unusual example. Where, however, the forms are significantly different (e.g., *eke/also*), I have included the variant. And if it is uncertain as to whether a variant records a different word or simply a different spelling, for example *dool/dulle*, I include this as well. Where more than one witness records the same variant, I include only one form, usually from the manuscript sigla that comes first alphabetically. I do not make a special point of indicating where my text differs from MacCracken's or Zupitza's, nor do I draw attention to where there may be errors or omissions in one or the other of their collations. I have not usually noted whether variants are scribal corrections, that is, added or inserted above the line or after a cancellation, and I have included marginalia only when it is of particular interest.

---

[102] A. S. G. Edwards, "*Speculum Guy de Warwick*," p. 90.

[103] See Explanatory Note to line 6.

GUY OF WARWYK

Here gynneth the lyff off Guy of Warwyk

1

Fro Cristis birthe complet nyne hundrid yeer
Twenty and sevene by computacioun, *In the year 927*
Kyng Ethelstan, as seith the cronycleer,
Reynyng that tyme in Brutys Albyoun, *England*
Duryng also the persecucyoun
Of them of Denmark, wich with myhty hond
Rod, brente, and slouh — made noon excepcioun *Rode, burnt, and slew*
By cruel force thorughout al this lond,

2

Spared nouther hih nor louh degré, *neither*
Chirchis, collegis, but that they bete hem doun,
Myhty castellis and every greet cyté
In ther furie, by fals oppressioun,
On to the boundys of Wynchestre toun;
With suerd and feer they madyn al wast and wylde, *fire*
And in ther mortall persecucyoun
Spared nat women greet with chylde.

3

In this brennyng, furious crueltė,
Two Denmark pryncis, pompous and elat, *proud and haughty*
Lyk woode lyouns void of all pité, *lions crazed with anger*
Did no favour to louh nor hih estaat.
Allas! this lond stood so dysconsolaat,
Froward Fortune hath at hem so dysdeyned, *Perverse; turned scornfully against them*
Mars and Mercurie wer with hem at debaat,
That bothe the kyng and pryncis wer distreyned *compelled*

4

By froward force to take hem to the flyght, *warlike; put them*
Thes Danyssh pryncis ageyn hem wer so wood. *them; furious*
On hih hilles ther fyres gaf suych lyght, *gave*
Fortune of werre in suych disjoynt tho stood, *in such a plight then stood*

The peple robbed and spoiled of ther good, *property*
For verray dreed of colour ded and pale,
Whan the stremys ran doun of red blood,
Lyk a gret ryver fro mounteyne to the vale.

5

Paraventure for sum old trespace, *Perchance; wrongdoing*
As is remembrid of antyquyté,
Of o persone hap, fortune, and grace *From one; chance*
Myhte be withdrawe, in cronycles ye may see:
Reed how the myhty famous Josue *Joshua*
Was put abak thre dayes in batayll,
The thefte of Nachor made Israell to fle
Out of the feld, and in ther conquest faile.

6

Thus by the pryde and veyn ambycioun
And cruel furie of thes pryncis tweyne
This rewm almost brouht to destruccyoun, *realm*
The swerd of Bellona gan at hem so disdeyne, *held them in such contempt*
Lordis wer pensif, the porail gan compleyne. *anxious; poor wretched people*
Oon of thes tirauntys callid Anelaphus,
And as myn auctour remembreth in serteyn,
The tother was named Genaphelus.

7

This myschef, wers than strok of pestilence, *calamity*
God with his punsshyng is founde mercyable:
Suerd of a tyraunt punssheth with vyolence,
With furious hand mortall and vengable.
Wher folk repente, the Lord is ay tretable *conducive to understanding*
That sit above, wich halt all in His hond,
But thes tirauntys, to scheden blood most able,
With suerd and flawme troubled al this lond.

8

God for synne, by record of scripture,
Hath chastysed many a greet cyté
And suffred hem gret myschef to endure; *allowed*
Record Jerusalem, record on Nynyvee; *For example*
Paris in Fraunce hath had his part, pardé, *indeed*
For leccherie and veyn ambucyoun;
Palpable examples at eye men may see *clearly*
Of Rome, Cartage, and of Troie toun.

9

This mater ofte hath been exemplefyed:
For lak of wisdam and of good consayll,
That peplys hertys wer nat full applyed
To sue vertu for ther owne avayll. *pursue; welfare*
Wynd of glad fortune bleuh nat in ther saill,
For ther dismeritées, God punshed hem of right:
Outrage and vices hath vengaunce at his tayll. *Wrongdoing*
Thouh kyng Ethelstan was a manly knyght,

10

Cruell Danys Inglyssh blood to scheede,
Ther swerd was wheet and ther fyres lyght. *honed*
Yit in cronycle, at leyser who lyst reede, *wish*
Kyng Ethelstan was a full noble knyght,
Though for a tyme eclypsed was his lyght;
Of his noblesse and royall magesté,
The hand of God stood always in his myght
To chaunge his trouble into prosperyté.

11

The sonne is hatter after sharpe schours, *hotter*
The glade morwe folweth the dirke nyght,
After wynter cometh May with fresshe flours,
And after mystys Phebus schyneth bright;
After trouble hertys be maad lyght,
And to conclude, lyk as I began,
God lyst to caste his mercyable syght *wished; merciful*
Upon his knyght, the forseid Ethelstan.

12

In this mater forther to procede:
Constreynt of werre and gret adversyté
Made hym to drawe, in cronycle as I reede, *[Ethelstan]*
With alle his lordis of hih and louhe degré
To have a counsayll at Wynchestre, the cyté,
Som remedye in all haste to provyde
Ageyn the malys and furious cruelté
Wrouht by the Danys in ther marcyal pride. *martial (warlike)*

13

Of al the lond gadryd were the statys,
Remedye to schapen in this mateere;
Pryncys, barouns, bysshopis, and prelatys
In that cyté assembled wern in feere. *together*
Hap and Fortune shewyd hem hevy cheere, *Chance; looked doleful*
Ther hope turned to dysesperaunce, *despair*

Knyghthood of armes had lost the maneere,
So destitute they were of spere and launce.

14

In that party was no remedye, *group*
Redres to fynde, nor consolacyoun. *Redress*
Mars set abak all ther chevalrye, *put aside*
Thus stood the lond in desolacyoun.
Strong wer the Danys, proud by ambucioun; *arrogance (overweening ambition)*
Kyng Ethelstan, by constreynt and distresse,
Held with his lordis a counsayll in that toun
To fynde a mene his myschef to redresse, *means (way)*

15

By grace of God how this myht ben amendyd,
Recure to fynde of ther adversyté. *Remedy*
Breefly to telle, they were thus condescendyd *agreed*
Benbassatrie, or mene of som tretee, *By negotiation*
Streyghtly driven of necessyté,
The kyng of Denmark with homage for to queme, *placate*
Or under tribute to have this liberté
As a soget rejoysshe his dyademe;[1]

16

Or ellis, pleynly of partyes covenaunt, *both parties having agreed*
Kyng Ethelstan for hym to fynde a knyght
With Colybrond of Denmark, the geaunt,
Day assigned to entre with hym in fyght,
For to darreyne atween hem to the right, *to decide by combat*
Who shal rejoisshe, with strong and myhty hond, *rule*
To holde a septre by manhood and by myght, *scepter*
And have poscessioun in quyete of this lond. *in peace*

17

The kyng, the lordis, beyng there present,
Withoute respight or loud dylacyoun *delay*
To yeve answere of ther fynall entent *give*
How they list quyten hem: for short conclusioun, *wished to acquit themselves*
Outher to make a resygnacyoun
Of septre and crowne, outher to fynde a knyht,[2]
As I seyde erst, to be ther champioun *previously*
Geyn Colybrond to entryn into fight. *Against*

[1] Lines 119–20: *Or to pay tribute to the king of Denmark, / As a subject giving over his sovereignty*

[2] Lines 133–34: *Either to surrender / scepter and crown, or to find a knight*

18

The Denmark dukis, of malys importable, *intolerable malice*
Wood and wylful in ther marcyal rage,
In outher wise lyst nat be tretable,
Requyred in haste benbassat or massage *by negotiation or message*
To have answere or pleggis for hostage, *pledges*
Of this convencioun relacioun to sende *agreement; report*
How they caste hem to puttyn in morgage *decided; trial by combat*
The lyf of tweyne to make a fynal ende. *two*

19

This apoyntement so streitly was forth lad, *strictly*
Of furious haste they wolde have no delay,
Kyng Ethelstan so hard was bestad, *beset*
And alle his pryncis put in gret affray; *consternation*
Afore Wynchestre the proude dukis lay,
The kyng withinne astoned in his mende, *stunned (bewildered)*
And weel the more because he knew no way
In his dyfence a championn to fynde.

20

Knew no bet mene as in this mateer *better way*
Redres to fynde to resoun accordyng
Than by assent to taken hym to prayeer, *himself*
He and his lordis to wakyng and fastyng,
Pore and riche, withoute more tarying, *without delay*
Alle attonys, as they wern of degré, *all together; according to rank*
With salte teris resembled in ther wepyng
By penaunce doyng to folk of Nynyvee. *performance of penance*

21

From hih estatys doun to the porayll, *wretched*
Of alle degrees founde was no wyght *no one*
To underfonge th'emprise of this batayll *undertake; task*
Ageyn the geaunt of Denmark for to fight.
Herald of Harderne, the noble famous knyht,
Callid in his tyme, of prowesse nyh and ferre, *near and far*
Fader in armes in every manhis sight, *man's*
Next Guy of Warwyk of manhood lode sterre. *Next to; guiding star*

22

This seide Herald beyng tho absent, *then*
Out of this rewm to seke the sone of Guy
Callid Raynbourne in contrees adjacent
And alle the provyncis that stoode faste by, *nearby*
Wich in yong age was stole traytourly
By straunge marchauntis, ongoodly lad a way. *wickedly*

Felyce, his moder, wepyng tendirly
For his absence, compleynyng nyht and day,

23

Born by dyscent to ben hir fadris hayr, *heir*
Hir yonge sone, Raynborne, to succede.
In hir tyme was holde noon so fayr,
Callid the example of trouthe and womanhede.
Rowand, hir fader, for noblesse and manheede,
Erl of Warwyk, named oon the beste knyht *one [of]*
That was tho dayes, in story as I reede; *[in] those*
But he, allas, flouryng in hys myght,

24

Paide his dette of deth onto nature;
By Parcas sustren was spoune his lyves threede.
And, as the story remembreth by scripture,
Whan that Felyce conseyved hadde in deede
By seyde Guy, sone after, as I reede,
He lyk a pilgrym, endewed with all vertu, *imbued*
The nexte morwe chaunged hath his weede *garments*
And spedde hym forth for love of Crist Jhesu;

25

Forsook the world, onknowe to every wight,
Of hih perfeccyoun to leven in penaunce, *to live*
Left wyf and kyn and bekam Goddis knyght, *became God's*
Whom for to serve was set all his plesaunce.
Content with lytel, Crist was his suffysaunce:
In wordly pompe he lyst not to sojourne.
Callyng ageyn onto remembraunce
Kyng Ethelstan, my penne I wyll retourne

26

As I began, in ordre to proceede,
Of his compleynt to make mencyoun.
Not clad in purpil, but chaunged hath his weede,
Blak for mornyng and desolacyoun,
Because there was in all his regyoun
Founde no persone his quarell to dyfende;
To God above seyde this orysoun *prayer*
Bespreynt with teris, His grace doun to sende: *Sprinkled*

27

"O Lord," quod he, "of moost magnyfycence,
Cast doun Thyn erys unto my prayeere. *ears*
Remembre nat upon my greet offence,

But fro my synnes turne away Thy cheere; *face*
Disespeired, stondyng in doubyll were *indecision*
To lese my kyngdam, septre, and regalye
But medyacioun of Thy moder deere *Unless*
Be gracious mene to save my partye.

28

My feith, myn hope, my trust, myn affyaunce, *solemn promise*
All hoolly restith in Thy proteccyoun; *wholly*
My sheeld, my sheltroun, my suerd, and eek my launce *protective phalanx*
Be blont and feble, my power is bore doun;
But grace with mercy list be my championn *Unless*
Thorgh Thy support, my foon shal me encombre." *foes*
While Ethelstan seyde this orysoun,
Or he was war, he fyll into a slombre. *Before he knew it*

29

For wach and trouble lay in an agonye, *Because of sleeplessness and anxiety [he]*
Devoutly knelyng by his beddys syde,
The Lord above, wich can no man denye
That asketh grace with meeknesse void of pride,[1]
For His servaunt lyst gracyously provyde,
Which of His goodnesse sente an aungel doun, *Who*
Bad hym nat dreede, but set al feer a syde,
Wich of His mercy had herd his orysoun.

30

Toward the kyng cast his look benygne,
Bad hym truste al hoolly in his grace,
By a tookene and an entyeer signe *token; excellently perfect*
Which shal be shewed to hym in riht short space;
Of sleep adawed, the kyng left up his face, *From; awakened; lifted*
Marked every thyng and prudently took heede, *Noted*
To whom the angel his hevynesse tenchase *to chase away*
These wordis hadde, in story as I reede:

31

"From thee voide al dyspeir and dreede! *yourself cast off*
Whan Aurora shewith hir pale light
Tomorwen, erly arys and take good heede, *arise early*
For Crist Jhesu, of His gracyous myght,
To thy requeste hath cast doun His sight;
Trust upon Hym, and in thy trust be stable;

[1] Lines 227–28: *who can deny no one / Who asks for grace with meekness and humility*

He shall conserve of equyté and ryght
Thy roiall tytle, for He ys mercyable.

32

At Phebus upriste, set no lenger date: *do not delay*
Whan silver deuh doth on the flours fleete, *dew; fall gently*
Make thy passage toward the north gate,
Or that the sonne with his fervent heete *Before*
Hath on the levys dryed up the weete. *leaves; moisture*
Abide there meekly and God shal to thee sende
Fyrst among pore, a pilgrym thou shalt meete;
Entrete hym goodly thy quarell to dyfende.

33

Clad as a pilgrym in a brood sclaveyn, *cloak*
Old and forgrowe amongys the porayll, *covered with long hair (bearded)*
Marke hym weell, and be riht weell serteyn *Note*
At thy requeste that he schall nat fayll
To accomplysshe manly thy batayll;
Trust on hym weell, and for thy purpartye, *rightful inheritance*
With Goddis myht that he schall prevayll,
In this mater thyn axing nat denye."

34

The woordis seid as ys rehersed heere
Onto the kyng by revelacyoun,
The angell dyd onwarly dysapeere, *suddenly*
And Ethelstan of greet devossioun
Gaf thank to God of this avysioun;
Neuly rejoisshed out of all hevynesse, *made glad*
With two bisshopis, as maad ys mencyoun,
And erlis tweyne forth he gan hym dresse; *earls; he set forth*

35

Thankyng the lord of His benygne graunt
As he was bounde, of humble affeccyoun,
With his bisshopis and erlys exspectaunt, *expectant (hopeful)*
At thilke party northward of the toun, *that section*
Lyk as the aungell, for short conclusioun,
Had told the hour onto the kyng but late, *just lately*
Whan poore folk for sustentacyoun *food*
Hadde in costom to entren at the gate.

36

As the cronycle breefly doth compile,
Unto purpos maketh rehersayll
Of John Baptyst afore in the vygyle, *earlier [in the story]; night*

How Guy of Warwik maad his arryvaylle
At Portysmouth, myn auctour wil nat fayle;
In his writyng assignyng hour and tyme,
By grace of God, wich may most avaylle,
Tellith how Guy evene at the hour of pryme, *exactly at sunrise*

37

Whan briht Phebus, with his gold tressed bemys,
On hillis hih gan shewe his hevenly lyght
Erly on morwe, and with his hoote stremys
Dried up the deuh as perlis silver bright, *dew*
Whan seide Guy, the noble famous knyght,
Repeired was from his long pylgrymage, *Returned*
Fro Portysmouth took his weye right,
To Wynchestre holdyng his vyage. *proceeding on his way*

38

By grace of God I deeme trowly, *believe*
Guy was hom sent into thys regyoun
Here taccomplisshe in knyghthood fynally *to accomplish*
The laste empryse of his hih renoun, *great undertaking*
He for to be the kyngys championn,
Onknowe of alle; but whan he cam to lond,
To hym was maad pleyn relacyoun
Of his requestis, how it did stond; *what the situation was*

39

They told hym firste in ordre ceryously, *in succession*
Harald Harderne, that was so good a knyht,
Was goon to seke the sone of Guy, *seek*
Gretly desired of every maner wight, *everybody*
Wich by discent was born of verray riht
By tytle of Felyce, famous in womanhede,
At his repair, with grace of Cristis myght, *On his [i.e., Guy's son's] return*
Erl of Warwyk justly to succede.

40

They told hym also of the grete stryf
Tween them of Denmark and Ethelstan the kyng,
And how that Rowand, fader to hys wyf,
Old erl of Warwik, ful notable of levyng, *eminent during his lifetime*
Was ded also; and Guy herd everythyng,
Of hih prudence kept hymsilf clos, *did not reveal himself*
Lyk a pilgrym his leve there takyng,
Goth to Wynchestre anoon as he aroos. *as soon as*

41

Guy took his loggyng whan it drouh to nyht *lodging; night drew [on]*
With pore men at an old hospytall, *almshouse*
Wery of travayl, onknowe to every wight,
Two hundrid pas withoute the north wall
Where stondeth now a menstre ful roiall. *(see note)*
The next morwe, anoon as Guy awook,
God was his guyde, in especyall,
Mong pore men the riht weie he took

42

To the north gate, as grace did hym guye, *guide*
By resemblaunce, so entryng into toun,
As David whilom cam ageyn Golye
To helpen Saul,[1] by grace of God sent doun;
So for refuge and for savacyoun,
Bothe of the kyng and of al this lond,
Guy was provided to be ther champioun
Ageyn the pompe of proude Colybrond. *Against*

43

By his habite and his pylgrym weede, *garments*
Thilke tyme clad in a round sclaveyn, *That; cloak*
Of whos array whan the kyng took heede,
Sauh Goddis promys was nat maad in veyn,
Took up his herte and knew riht weel serteyn
God faileth never His frend on see nor lond.
With wepyng teris, his chekis spreynt lik reyn, *sprinkled*
For verray gladnesse he took Guy by the hond,

44

Besekyng hym in moost louly wyse, *Beseeching; way*
With sobbyng cheer that routhe was to see, *pitiful*
To underfonge this knyhtly hih empryse *undertake; noble task*
For Goddys sake and mercyfull pyté,
To do socour in this necessyté,
In his dyfence that he wyll nat fayll
Geyn Colybrond his champioun for to be, *Against*
For his party darreyne the batayll. *part to undertake*

45

Guy, wonder sad of look and of vysage, *very; expression*
Feynt and wery and dulled of travayll, *Faint*

[1] Lines 330–32: *He entered the town / resembling David, [who] long ago came against Goliath / to help [King] Saul*. See note.

Made his excuse that he was falle in age,
And out of ews more to be clad in mayll. *no longer accustomed*
"My wil," quod he, "Yif it myhte avayll
The cruell ire of Danys to appeese,
For comoun profit good wil shal nat fayll, *(see note)*
My lyf juparte to set thys lond in ese." *jeopardize my life*

46

The kyng, the lordys made greet instaunce *entreated*
To this pylgrym with language and prayers;
Guy, for to doon unto the kyng plesaunce
For Jhesus sake and for his moder deere,
Ys condescendyd, lyk as ye schall heere, *agreed, as you shall hear*
With Goddys grace, after the covenaunt, *agreement*
As the convencyoun justly doth requere, *treaty*
At place assigned to mete the geaunt.

47

Of this empryse was maad no long delay
This convencyoun pleynly to darreyne,
Tyme set of Jule upon the twelfth day, *on 12 July*
Place assigned, and meetyng of thes tweyne;
The accord rehersed, the statute and the peyne, *penalty*
Doubylnesse and fraude set asyde,
As the partyes were boundyn in serteyn,
For short conclusioun therby to abyde.

48

Withoute the gate, remembred as I reede, *Outside of*
The place callyd of antyquyte
In Inglyssh tonge named Hyde Meede
Or ellis Denmark,[1] nat fer from the cyté,
Meetyng togedre there men myghte see
Terryble strokys lyk the dent of thonder,
Sparklys out of ther harneys flee, *armor flew*
That to beholde it was a verray wonder.

49

The old pylgrym quyt hym lyk a knyght, *acquitted himself*
Spared nat the geaunt to assaylle;
On his left shulder smet at hym with suych myht, *smote*
Undir the bordour of his aventayll *chain mail*
A streem of blood gan by his sydes rayll; *gush*
The geaunt wood, this hydous Colybrond, *infuriated*

[1] Lines 378–80: *In antiquity, the place called / in English Hyde Meede / or Den Marche*

Thoughte it sholde gretly hym avayll *help*
That Guyes suerd was broke out of his hond.

50

Whan Danys sauh Guy had lost his suerd,
They cauhte a maner consolacyoun; *received a kind [of]*
Guy, lyk a knyght in herte nat aferd,
Requered manly of the champioun,
Sith he of wepnys hadde so gret foysoun, *abundance*
To graunte hym oon that hour in his difence; *one*
But Colybrond of indyngnacyoun
To his requeste gaf noon audyence,

51

For he was set on malys and on wrak *evil*
To execute his purpos set on pryde,
And while that he and Guy togedre spak,
All attonys Guy sterte out asyde, *at once (suddenly)*
Cauhte a pollex, lyst no lenger byde, *poleax; wishing to delay no longer*
Smette the geaunt evene in the firste wounde, *Smote; right*
Made his strok so myghtyly to glyde,
That his left arme and shuldir fyll to grounde;

52

With wich strok, the geaunt Colybrond
Al his armure and boody was maad reed,
Stoupyng asyde, gan reche forth his hond *reach*
To take a suerd, wherof Guy took heed.
God and grace that day gaf hym suych speed
To put his name ever after in memorie,
Fleih with his ax, smet off the sturdy heed *Flew*
Of the geaunt and hadde of hym vyctorye.

53

This thyng accomplisshed by grace of Goddis hond
And by the prowesse of Guy this noble knyght,
They of Denmark, as the statute bond,
Han crossed sail and take ther weye right
Toward ther cuntré, nouther glad nor light, *country; neither*
Ther surquedye and ther pompe oppressed. *pride*
Kyng Ethelstan, by grace of Goddys myht,
Hadde of Denmark the pompe ful repressed.

54

Ther froward pompe with meknesse was repressed *wicked*
By Guy of Warwyk, as maad is mencioun,
The kyng, the clergye, devoutly have hem dressed, *prepared themselves*

Pryncys, barouns, and burgeis of the toun, *burgesses (citizens)*
With al the comounte; for short conclusioun, *community*
Hih and lowe, to speke in generall,
Hym to conveie with proscessioun
Onto ther chirche callyd Cathedrall. *(see note)*

55

This seide Guy, ther knelyng on his kne,
With gret meknesse made his oblacioun *presented as an offering*
Of thilke ex, with wich aforn that he *ax*
Hadde of Danys slayn the champioun,
Wich instrument thorugh al this regyoun
Is yit callid the ex of Colybrond, *still*
Kept among men of relygyoun
In the vestiarie, as ye schall understond. *vestry*

56

Whan al was doon, ther is no more to seyn,
Guy in al haste caste off hys armure,
Lyk a pilgrym put on his sclaveyn. *pilgrim's cloak*
The kyng ful goodly after dyd his cure, *tried very hard*
That he myhte the grace so recure *obtain*
Of this pilgrym to tellyn and nat spare,
In secre wyse to tellyn his aventure, *tell of his experience*
What was his name pleynly to declare.

57

"Certys," quod Guy, "Ye must have me excused,
Touchyng your ascyng and your petycioun. *About; question*
Beth nat besy and lat no more be mused *concerned; wondering*
In your desire for noon occasioun;[1] *for no reason*
To myn excuse I have ful greet resoun,
For I shal never dyscure this mateer *reveal*
But under bond of a condycyoun, *Unless*
Assuraunce maad tween yow and me in feere: *between; together*

58

Alle your pryncys avoided by absence, *sent away*
Sool be oursilf, out of this cyté, *Alone by ourselves*
Noon but we tweyne beyng in presence,
With trouthe assured that ye shal be secré *discreet*
Duryng my lyf — ye gete no more of me.
To no persone, I aske no more avayll

[1] Lines 451–52: *Don't be troubled or worried / for any reason in your desire [to know who I am]*

Of feith and oth, to hih nor louh degré, *[Than your] faith*
That ye shall never dyscure my counsayll." *reveal (discover)*

59

This thyng confermed by promys ful roiall,
Passed the subbarbys and boundys of the toun, *suburbs*
At a cros that stood feer from the wall,
Ful devoutly the pilgrym knelith doun
To sette asyde all suspecyoun.
"My lord," quod he, "Of feith withouten blame, *truly [and] with respect*
Your lyge man of humble affeccyoun, *liege*
Guy of Warwyk trewly is my name."

60

The kyng, astoned, gan chaunge cher and face,
And in maner gan wepyn for gladnesse; *in a way (i.e., almost weeping)*
And al attonys he gan hym to enbrace
In bothe his armes, of royall gentylnesse,
With ofte kyssyng of feithfull kyndenesse,
With grete proffres on the tother syde, *offers; other*
Of gold, of tresour, and of gret rychesse
Withinne his paleys, yif he wolde abyde.

61

Alle thes profres meekly he forsook,
And to the kynges royall mageste
Hym recomaundyng, anoon his weie he took.
At his departyng, this avouh maad he *vow*
With pitous wepyng, knelyng on his kne
Unto the kyng in full humble entent:
"Duryng my lyf, it may noon other bee,
Schall I never doon off this garnement." *remove*

62

At ther departyng was but smal langage; *little conversation*
Sweem of ther speche made interupcyoun. *Sorrow over*
The kyng goth hom; Guy took his vyage *journey*
Toward Warwyk, his castell, and his toun,
No man of hym havyng suspecyoun,
Where day be day Felyce, his trewe wyf,
Fedde poore folk of greet devocyoun
To praie for hir and for hir lordys lyf,

63

Thrittene in noumbre, myn auctour writeth so.
Guy at his comyng forgrowe in his vysage, *heavily bearded*
Thre daies space he was oon of tho *those*

That took almesse with humble and louh corage; *alms; meek disposition*
Thankyng the contesse, in haste took his viage.
Nat fer fro Warwyk, the cronycle doth expresse,
Of aventure kam to an hermytage,
Where he fond one dwellyng in wyldirnesse. *a man*

64

To hym he drouh, besechyng hym of grace *approached*
For a tyme to holde there sojour; *to stay there temporarily*
The same hermyte, withinne a lytel space, *a short time*
By deth is passed, the fyn of his labour. *end*
After whos day Guy was his successour,
Space of two yeer, by grace of Cryst Jhesu, *For two years*
Dauntyng his flessh by penaunce and rigour, *Mortifying*
Ay more and more encresyng in vertu. *Always*

65

God made hym knowe the day he sholde deie
Thorugh His moost gracyous vysytacyoun
Be an angel, hys spirit to conveye *By*
After his bodyly resolucyoun, *dissolution (death)*
For his merites, to the hevenly mansioun;
After he sente in haste his weddyng ryng
Unto his wyf, of trewe affeccyoun,
Praied hir come to been at his deying, *death*

66

And that she sholde doon hir besy cure, *do her best*
By a maner wyfly dyllygence, *In the best possible way*
In haste ordeyne for his sepulture, *make arrangements for; burial*
With no gret cost nor with no gret dyspence;
Gan haste hir faste tyl she kam in presence
Where as he lay, dedly and pale of face;
Bespreynt with teris, knelyng with reverence,
The dede body swownyng she did enbrace. *swooning*

67

And as this notable, famous, worthy knyght
Sente hir to seyne eek be his massangeer, *Sent to tell her also by his messenger*
In that place to burye hym anoon right *immediately*
Where as he lay aforn a small auhteer; *altar*
And that she sholde doon trewly hir deveer *do her best*
For hirsilf dyspoce and provyde, *arrange*
The fifteenth day folwyng the same yeer,
To be buryed faste be his syde.

68

Hys hooly wyf of al this thyng took heed,
Lyk as Guy bad, lyst no lenger tarye — *had bidden; wished not to delay*
To quyte hirsilf of trouthe and womanheed; — *acquit*
She was ful loth from his desire to varye, — *reluctant*
Sente in al haste for the ordynarye — *ecclesiastical authority*
Whiche ocupied in that dyocyse; — *diocese*
She was nat founde in o poynt contrarye — *one*
Al thyng taccomplisshe, as ye han herd devyse.

69

And this mater breefly to conclude:
At his exequyes, old and yong of age — *funeral*
Of dyverse statys there cam gret multytude
With gret devoycyoun to that hermytage,
And, lyk a prynce with al the surplusage, — *trappings*
They took hym up and leyd hym in his grave,
Ordeyned of God, aforn of hih corage
Ageyn the Danys thys regyoun to save;

70

Whos sowle I hope restith now in glorye,
With hooly spiritis above the firmament.
Felyce, his wyf, ay callyng to memorie — *always*
The day approchyng of hir enterment,
Aforn ordeyned in hir testament — *will (final wish)*
Hir sone Reynborne be tytle of hir possede, — *by virtue of her title*
Heyr trewly born by lyneal dyscent, — *Heir*
In the erldam of Warwyk to succede,

71

The stok descendyng of antyquyté
To Guy his fader be tytle of mariage,
After whos deth, of lawe and equyté,
Reynborne to entre into his herytage.
After al this, his mooder, of good age,
Hath yolde hir dette by deth unto nature. — *yielded*
Beside hir lord in the hermytage,
With a good ende was maad hir sepulture.

72

For more auctorité as of this mateer,
Whos translacioun is suych in sentence — *wisdom*
Out of the Latyn maad by the cronycleer
Callyd of old Gerard Cornubyence,
Wich wrot the dedis with gret dilligence
Of them that wern in Westsex crowned kynges,

Gretly comendyng for knyghtly excellence
Guy of Warwyk in his famous writynges,

73

Of whos noblesse ful gret heed he took,
His marcyal name puttyng in remembraunce
The eleventh chapitle of his hystorial book — *chapter*
The parfight lyf, the vertuous governaunce, — *perfect (i.e., unblemished, faultless)*
His wylful povert, hard goyng, and penaunce,
Brought onto me a chapitle to translate.
Yif ought be wrong in metre or in substaunce,
Putteth the wyte for dulnesse on Lydgate. — *blame (responsibility)*

74

Meekly compiled under correccyoun,
Lyf of sir Guy by dyllygent labour,
Sette aside pryde and presumpcioun
Because he hadde of cadence no colour; — *[formal training in] metrics or rhetoric*
In Tullius gardyn he gadrid never flour — *Cicero's garden*
Nor of Omerus he kam never in the meede. — *Homer*
Praying echon of support and favour,
Nat to dysdeyne the clauses whan they reede.

Explicit

Explanatory Notes to *Guy of Warwyk*

Abbreviations: ***AN Gui***: Weiss, ed., *Boeve de Haumtone and Gui de Warewic: Two Anglo-Norman Romances*; ***CA***: Gower, *Confessio Amantis*; ***Caius***: Zupitza, ed., *The Romance of Guy of Warwick, Edited from the Auchinleck Manuscript* (EETS, 1883); ***Cambridge***: Zupitza, ed., *The Romance of Guy of Warwick: The Second or 15th-century Version* (EETS, 1875); ***CT***: Chaucer, *The Canterbury Tales*; ***Fabula***: Lydgate, *Fabula Duroum Mercatorum*; ***FP***: Lydgate, *Fall of Princes*; **Gerard**: Gerard of Cornwall, *Battle Between Guy of Warwick and Colbrond*; ***Guy***: Lydgate, *Guy of Warwick*; **HH**: Cambridge, MA, Harvard University, Houghton Library, MS Eng. 530; **Hr**: London, British Library, MS Harley 7333; **ME**: Middle English; **OE**: Old English; ***OED***: *Oxford English Dictionary*; ***Stanzaic Guy***: Wiggins, ed., *Stanzaic Guy of Warwick*; **TB**: Lydgate, *Troy Book*; **Whiting**: Whiting, *Proverbs, Sentences, and Proverbial Phrases*.

1–2 *Fro Cristis birthe . . . by computacioun.* Lydgate follows his source, Gerard, in providing the specific year, 927, for the action of the poem.

3 *as seith the cronycleer.* "As the chronicler says." The first of many direct references throughout the poem to Lydgate's source.

6 *Of them of Denmark.* The Danes. Compare the similar descriptions of Danish ruthlessness in Lydgate's *Lives of SS Edmund and Fremund* (ed. Bale and Edwards), especially Book 2 (*Edmund*), lines 1340–51 and 1366–85; Book 3 (*Fremund*), lines 2501–06, 2920–26, and 2934–40. The Danes, also known as Norsemen or Vikings, are consistently portrayed in historical and literary sources as incarnations of evil heathens, completely outside Christianity and civilization. The Anglo-Saxon Chronicle repeatedly describes their destruction of churches and monasteries, their use of fire, sword, and terror, and their pitiless slaughter of innocents. Lydgate particularly emphasizes and condemns their excessive pride, or hubris.

13 *Wynchestre.* Ethelstan's capital city. Winchester has a long association with the Guy legend because of its significance to the kings of Wessex and their ongoing battles against the Danes and Norse, who invaded not only from northern Europe but also Northumbria. Winchester was the capital of Wessex and *de facto* capital of England until the Norman conquest. The city is actively used by Lydgate and his source Gerard as an historical backdrop for the poem; see the Introduction for additional information and for the significance of geographical references and locations in and near Winchester.

18–20 *Denmark pryncis, pompous and elat . . . Did no favour to louh nor hih estaat.* The Danish princes are Anelaphus and Gonelaphus. See note to lines 46–48, below.

pompous and elat. A recurrent phrase describing a dangerously proud person who abuses his power or position. Examples can be found in both Lydgate and Chaucer; see, for example, Lydgate's *TB*, "þenvious fals contagiousté / Of þe serpent, pompos and elat" (5.37); and Chaucer's Monk's Tale, "This kyng of kynges proud was and elaat" (*CT* VII[B^2] 3357). Excessive pride is always condemned and is usually punished. Phillipa Hardman sees lines 18–20 as the main clause of one long, loosely constructed opening sentence ("Lydgate's Uneasy Syntax," p. 29), whereas I suggest that the opening sentence ends at line 16, with the Danes ("them of Denmark," line 6) as the implicit grammatical subject of the sentence. Long, paratactic constructions which often seem to lack a main verb or grammatical subject are typical of Lydgate's practice in this poem. For a useful reassessment of Lydgate's syntax and the difficulties in applying to it modern punctuation, see Hardman, "Lydgate's Uneasy Syntax," especially pp. 29–30 on *Guy*.

22 *Froward Fortune hath at hem so dysdeyned.* Lady Fortune, whose turning wheel can suddenly turn happiness into misery — or vice versa — is a familiar personage in medieval literature. While she is often figured as blind and disinterested, the random turns of her wheel affecting rich and poor, high and low alike, she can also be presented as a persecuting figure who actively seeks the destruction of someone's happiness. At this point, Fortune seems to have turned against the English, as they are forced to flee the cruel onslaught of the Danes. The phrasing here, "hath at hem so dysdeyned" seems to be a particularly Lydgatian collocution: see also *Guy*, line 44, and *FP*: "[T]hei gan ful pitousli compleyne, / That Fortune gan at hem so disdeyne" (lines 6836–37). A search using the MED quotations field for the phrase "at disdeyn" turns up several more examples, all of them from Lydgate (*MED* proximity search, *at* and *disdeyne*).

23 *Mars and Mercurie.* Mars is the Roman god of war, Mercury the messenger god. Mercury also represents eloquence. See Lydgate's *Siege of Thebes*, where Mercury endows Amphion with the "craft of rethorik" (line 219), *FP*, where Mercury is described as "cheeff lord and patroun / Off eloquence and off fair spekyng" (2.4544–45), and *Pageant of Knowledge*, where Mercury is both the "God of eloquence, and merchandyse" (line 102).

with hem at debaat. The phrase is somewhat ambiguous: if "hem" is taken as reflexive, then Mars and Mercury are quarreling with each other. If "hem" refers to the English, then both Mars and Mercury are assailing the English in the form of the Danish assaults and demands.

37 *Josue.* Successor to Moses, Joshua led the Israelites across the Jordan river to the promised land of Canaan, defeating a number of cities, notably Jericho, whose walls fell to the trumpets and shouts of the Israelites. See Joshua 6:3–20.

39 *Nachor.* The reference here must be to Achan, also known as Achar or Akar, who, disobeying God's injunction (Joshua 6:18–19), pillaged and kept some of the riches of Jericho for himself, thereby causing the Israelites to lose their next battle at the city of Ai. Achar is punished by stoning, after which the Israelites go on to victory. See also Joshua 7 and 1 Chronicles 2:7. There is a biblical Nachor,

but he is mentioned in Genesis only as brother to Abraham (see Genesis 11:22–29; Genesis 22:20–23) and father to Laban (see, for example, Genesis 11:22–29, Genesis 22:20–23). Further, that Lydgate must be referring to Achar, not Nachor, is made clear in the reference to stoning from the variant lines from Hr and HH: "Theffte of Nathor caused the aduersitee: / Till he was stonnyed they myght not prevayle" (lines 39–40). Note the *t* in *Nathor*, suggesting that the Hr and HH copyists may have misread the *c* for *t*, a not uncommon occurrence, or that they were working from a faulty exemplar.

44 *Bellona*. Roman goddess of war. The name stems from Latin *bella*, meaning war.

46–48 *Anelaphus . . . Genaphelus*. In many Middle English versions of the Guy legend, there is only one main enemy, the Danish king An(e)laf. Here, Lydgate follows Gerard who in turn follows the tradition of the *AN Gui*, in which there are two Danish opponents, the kings Anelaf and Gunelaf. Ward suggests that the name An(e)laf is a variation of the name of the real-life Danish King Olaf Guthfrickson, he who submitted to Ethelstan in 927 (see introduction to poem), and that Gunelaf derives from a kind of twinning of the name (Ward, *Catalogue of Romances*, p. 473). An(e)laf is the name of the Danish enemy in the OE *Battle of Brunanburh*. See Ward, *Catalogue of Romances*, pp. 471–72, 481, and 486, for further discussion of these names.

57–58 *God for synne, by record of scripture / Hath chastysed . . .* Lydgate develops the commonplace (begun in stanza 7 and continuing into stanza 9) that God will punish the wicked but will also have mercy on the repentant, listing as exempla cities that suffered for their wickedness, with the implicit suggestion that the English, because they are deserving, will receive God's help. Lists of *exempla* that prove or illustrate a principle or point are a typical medieval rhetorical device and one of which Lydgate was particularly fond.

60 *Nynyvee*. Nineveh. Jonah was sent by God to the wicked city of Nineveh to call on its people to repent or suffer destruction; when they did repent, God spared them. See Jonah 3:5–10.

61 *Paris in Fraunce*. Hr and HH: *Parys nerr hoome*. Perhaps a reference to the French civil war, a struggle for power between the Armagnacs and the Burgundians in the first decades of the fifteenth century against the larger backdrop of the Hundred Years' War between England and France. Henry V negotiated with both sides and concluded a peace with the Burgundians in 1420 with the Treaty of Troyes and his marriage to Catherine of Valois. However, Henry V's early death in 1422 and the accession of his infant son Henry VI to the thrones of France and England paved the way for more fighting both between the two factions and between England and France until the end of the war in 1453.

64 *Rome, Cartage, and of Troie*. Classical cities that suffered destruction at the hands of, variously, Gauls, Goths, and Vandals (who raided Rome), Romans (who raided Carthage), and Greeks (who raided Troy).

69 *Wynd of glad fortune bleuh not in ther saill*. The metaphor of Fortune as a capricious wind is not unusual in ME literature; as Stevens points out, "The

figure of Fortune as steerswoman or propelling force . . . finds wide expression in the Middle Ages" (Stevens, "Winds of Fortune," p. 305n5). Stevens also points to Gower's use of the figure in *Confessio Amantis* 5.7557, as well as Lydgate in *TB* 1.3392–93 and 5.630–35. See Lydgate, *TB*, "The wynde was good; the goddys fauourable / Fortune her frende, þouh sche be variable" (1.1235–36), and Chaucer, *Boece*, "The amyable Fortune maystow seen alwey wyndy and flowynge, and evere mysknowynge of hirself" (2.pr8.24).

71 *Outrage and vices hath vengaunce at his tayll.* "Sin and vice will bring vengeance as a consequence." Note the singular form of the verb and pronoun despite the plural subject.

81–85 *The sonne is hatter after sharpe schours . . . After trouble hertys be maad lyght.* This is the common trope of defining something by referring to its opposite. On Lydgate's use of this device, see the *Fabula*'s Explanatory Note to lines 113–18.

84 *Phebus*. Phebus Apollo, the sun.

117 *necessyté.* Philosphically, something that has to happen. See *Fabula,* explanatory note to line 100, for the relationship between Fortune and *necessité*.

118–22 *The kyng of Denmark . . . to fynde a knyght.* In Lydgate's source, Gerard, Ethelstan has three choices: he can give up his crown entirely; he can keep his crown but pay tribute to the Danes, essentially giving up all of his power; or he can find a champion. Lydgate seems to be preserving the idea of three choices, but the first two really are the same: the English can placate the Danes with homage or they can pay tribute to them, which seems to amount to the same thing; or they can find a champion.

123 *Colybrond.* Colbrond, Guy's giant opponent. The name *Colbrond* itself is etymologically related to images of fire and darkness: ME *col* (coal; see *MED col* (n. 2)) + *brand* (burning or fire; a torch. See *MED brand* (n.), sense 1a). In some versions of the tale, Colbrond is an African giant, in some a Saracen; in some he is specifically described as black. In all versions, however, he is fearsome and apparently invincible. In addition to the implicit David and Goliath trope (see note to lines 331–32 below), it should be noted that gigantomachia (combat with a giant) is a familiar motif in folktale and romance. King Arthur battles the giant of Mont St. Michel, for example, and Amadis of Gaul defeats the monstrous Endriago. Guy of Warwick himself, in the longer versions of the tale, has fought the giant Amoraunt in an earlier episode. On giants in romance, see Cohen, *Of Giants*, especially pp. 87–91, which focuses on the Guy legend in particular. See also Rouse, "Guy of Warwick as Medieval Culture-Hero," especially pp. 104–08.

159–60 *resembled in ther wepyng / By penaunce doyng to folk of Nynyvee.* In their penance, Ethelstan and his lords resemble the people of Nineveh, who repented of their wickedness. For Nineveh, see note to line 60 above.

Penaunce doyng. Literally, a doing of penance. The gerund is effective and striking.

165 *Herald of Harderne.* Also known as Herhaud or Heralt. Guy's mentor and companion; also tutor to Raynbourn, Guy's son. Here Lydgate takes the

opportunity to relate the background story not present in his version of the tale: the heroic Herald, who might have been able to take on Colbrond, is out of the country searching for Raynbourne, who has been kidnapped. See also note to line 171 below.

167 *manhis*. Man's. As late as Shakespeare's time, the possessive case was often thought mistakenly to be derived from the noun plus possessive pronoun ("man his"). For example, see Shakespeare, *Twelfth Night,* where Antonio says to Sebastian: "Once in a sea-fight 'gainst the count his galleys / I did some service" (3.3.26–27). The mistake derives from the OE and early ME inflections for the possessive singular: *mannes*, which, pronounced aloud, could sound like "man his."

168 *Guy of Warwyk of manhood lode sterre*. This is the first mention of Guy in the poem. That he is described as a lodestar suggests both the literal and figurative meanings of the term: literally, a lodestar shows the way for navigational purposes. Figuratively, a lodestar is a principle or person on whom one's hopes are fixed. See *OED lodestar*. Guy is thus both literally and figuratively one who can show the way.

171 *Raynbourne*. Guy's son with Felice, stolen by merchants. Herald is out of the country, searching for him.

181 *Rowand*. Felice's father, the Earl of Warwick. Through Felice, Guy inherits the title of Earl of Warwick. The inheritance through the maternal line is emphasized throughout the poem, dovetailing with the real-life situation of the Beauchamp-Warwick succession. See the Introduction to *Guy*, pp. 89–92.

186 *Parcas sustren*. The Parcae, or the three fates. In Roman mythology, the Parcae (Gk *Moirae*) spin, measure, and cut the thread of a person's life.

Sustren. An old plural form (compare *children*, *oxen*). Rowand's life has been cut short by the Fates.

190–91 *He lyk a pilgrym, endewed with all vertu, / The nexte morwe chaunged hath his weede*. A reminder of an earlier episode of the Guy legend: after having been married for just two weeks to Felice, for whom he had achieved many spectacular feats of arms, Guy suddenly repented of his warlike deeds, and, renouncing the world of chivalry and knighthood, donned the guise of a pilgrim and left England and Felice, newly pregnant, on a pilgrimage of atonement. Guy's change in clothes is a disguise, but it also signifies his inner change and change in outward goals. For more on this metaphor, see the *Fabula*'s explanatory note to line 545.

203 *chaunged hath his weede*. Ethelstan's clothing mirrors his state of mind and desperate situation. He is no longer clad in purple, a color signifying his royalty, but black, signifying his mourning and "desolacyoun" (line 204).

209 *"O Lord . . ."* Unlike the fourteenth or fifteenth century Middle English versions of *Guy*, the *Stanzaic Guy*, and the *AN Gui*, Ethelstan's prayer is rendered here in direct speech. Also in direct speech is the angel's reply to Ethelstan at lines 241–64, emphasizing, as A. S. G. Edwards points out, "the power of prayer and divine agency in directing the course of earthly affairs and resisting the forces

of evil the Danes embody" ("The *Speculum Guy de Warwick*," p. 89). For more on direct speech in the narrative, see the Introduction to *Guy*, pp. 99–100.

213 *doubyll were*. The *MED* glosses this phrase as "a state of doubt or indecision between two alternatives" (*wer(e* (n. 5), sense 1a). Usually the context states the two alternatives; see, for example, Lydgate's *TB* 4.2354–61, "Achille . . . brent in a double fyre / Of loue and Ire . . . And þus he stood in a double wer"; *FP* lines 4954–56: "Thus in a weer longe [time] she dede endure . . . Whethir she shal be tendre or cruel"; and *Temple of Glas* (ed. Mitchell), lines 651–52, "As man dispeired in a double werre [where]: Born up with Hope and than anon Daunger." Here, however, Ethelstan's angst seems not to derive from indecision about which alternative to choose — it is clear that the English would choose to fight Colbrand had they a champion like Herald or Guy — but, rather, from a deep worry about just what he is going to do given that they do not have a champion. "Double were" here, then, might more accurately be glossed as "deep and terrible worry," sense 1c rather than 1a.

230–40 *Which of His goodnesse sente an aungel doun . . . . in story as I reede*. Hr and HH have a substantively different reading. See Textual Notes to these lines.

241 *From thee voide*. . . Angel messengers, a sign of God's interest and favor, are found frequently in Biblical story and medieval hagiography. That God is intervening directly to guide Ethelstan to the place where he will meet Guy underlines what has been clear from the beginning, that God is indeed on the side of the English.

250 *fleete*. This unusual word means "to fall gently" (see *MED fleten* (v. 1), sense 3c). Interestingly, HH has "swete" here. Though this may seem a more apt word, "fleete" appears in all six of the other manuscripts as well as fulfills the grammatical construction expected by "doth" earlier in the line.

265–88 Omitted in HH and Hr. While Ward asserts that these three stanzas are "quite superfluous" (*Catalogue of Romances*, rpt., p. 495) in all five of the other MSS, it is more likely that they were simply omitted in error, as Robinson suggests: "It is easier . . . to assume that three stanzas were omitted in copying (they make, for example, an even page of the Leyden MS [V]) than to suppose that any one added to Lydgate's work" ("On Two Manuscripts," p. 195).

281–83 *As the cronycle breefly doth compile . . . Of John Baptyst afore in the vygyle*. A reference to Gerard, the chronicler, who had explained earlier that on the eve of St. John the Baptist's Day, Ethelstan had prayed for aid and that on the same day, early in the morning, Guy had landed in Portsmouth and traveled almost immediately to Winchester. St. John the Baptist's Day is 24 June. "Afore" is difficult grammatically to construe. Here, it seems to mean "earlier" (in the narrative). See *MED, affore* (adv.), sense b. Lydgate is orienting us in time: Guy arrives in Portsmouth in the early morning and leaves for Winchester almost immediately, arriving there in the evening. On the morning of St. John the Baptist's Day, he and Ethelstan meet at the north gate. The association between Guy and St. John's Day is also seen in the *AN Gui*, the fifteenth-century version, and the *Stanzaic Guy*. In the AN *Gui* and the fifteenth century version, Guy arrives in

Winchester on St. John the Baptist's day and on that same evening, Ethelstan prays for assistance and is answered by the angel (AN *Gui*, lines 10855, 10925; fifteenth-century version, lines 9997, 10065). The two meet at the north gate on the following morning, the day after St. John the Baptist's Day. St. John the Baptist's Day is also significant in Guy's combat with Armourant in both the AN and *Stanzaic Guy*; in the AN version, the combat takes place the day after June 24 (line 8571, Weiss, p. 191), in the Stanzaic, on the day before (lines 1291–92).

As Weiss points out, St. John the Baptist's day was when the summer solstice, midsummer's day, would have been celebrated all over Europe (AN *Gui*, p. 191). St. John the Baptist was a very popular medieval saint, but it is difficult to know why he is particularly associated with Guy. The association is unlikely to be connected with John's beheading and the head's being served on a platter at the instigation of Salome, daughter of Herod Antipas (See Matthew 14:1–12). It may rather have to do with John's having lived as a hermit, as Guy does at the end of his story, or with John's association with hope and deliverance: he foretold the coming of Jesus and is often seen as Jesus' precursor; he is also known for baptizing Jesus. For more information about John the Baptist, see the *Oxford Dictionary of Saints*.

288 *evene at the hour of pryme*. *Prime* is the first hour of the day after sunrise, about 6 am. This is when Guy departs from Portsmouth, where he has just arrived from the continent. Guy thus begins this final leg of his journey home just as the day dawns on the morning of June 23, the day before St. John the Baptist's Day. Traveling all day, Guy spends the night in Winchester and enters the city on the morning of St. John's Day, a day of celebration and hope. See note to lines 281–83 above.

295 *his weye right*. See note to line 328 below.

322 *hospytall*. A charitable institution for the needy. See *OED*, *hospital*, which traces the interesting history of this word and its relatives *hostel*, *hotel*, and *hospitable*. Guy is taking his lodging where it is certain no one will recognize or find him; this choice also reflects his humility. The hospice is located on the site where Hyde Abbey would have been located in 1110. See also note to line 324, below. Gerard, Lydgate's source, names this hospital specifically as the Hospital of the Sacred Cross, and it is tempting to see a reference here to the Hospital of St. Cross, an almshouse founded between 1132 and 1136 and which still exists as a continuing almshouse. See the hospital's website, "The Hospital of St. Cross" (hospitalofstcross.co.uk) and Jenkins, *England's Thousand Best Churches*, p. 256. If this were Gerard's intent, he was mistaken in its location, however, as it is south rather than north of Winchester. Perhaps this is why Lydgate did not reproduce the specific name.

324–25 *Two hundrid pas withoute the north wall / Where stondeth now a menstre ful roiall*. The "menstre," or minster, is Hyde Abbey, formerly known as the New Minster, which had been located within the city of Winchester next to the Old Minster, on the site of what is now Winchester Cathedral. When the Old Minster was demolished after the Norman conquest and a new cathedral built (Winchester

Cathedral), the New Minster was moved to the suburb of Hyde. The minster is "ful roiall" because it contained the bones of King Alfred, his wife, and his son, moved there when it was consecrated in 1110. Hyde Abbey was a Benedictine monastery until it was destroyed in the Reformation. For a history of the Abbey, see Doubleday and Page, "The New Minister." See also E. Edwards' introduction to *Liber de Monasterii de Hyda*, especially pp. xxiii–xxiv, xxvii–xxviii, and xliv–xlvi, and *The History and Antiquities of Winchester*, pp. 11–14.

328 *the riht weie*. Guy is guided by God to the north gate. The phrase the "right way" is also in Lydgate's source: "recto tramite." As Eric Auerbach points out, the "right way" is not merely directional but has an "ethical signification" (*Mimesis*, pp. 128–29) — it is the correct way. See also Cooper, *English Romance in Time*, p. 101.

331–32 *David . . . Saul*. David was the shepherd boy who defeated the giant Goliath with a stone and a slingshot. The well-known Biblical story tells of the plight of King Saul who faces a large force of Philistines and their giant champion Goliath, who, like Colbrand, challenges the Israelites to single combat. The boy David alone steps forward to take up the challenge and kills Goliath with the single shot of a stone from his slingshot. David becomes king of Israel after Saul. See 1 Samuel 17:37–51. The comparison of Guy to David is apt: both heroes step forward to the aid of their king, who faces an invading army; in both cases, the army is led by an apparently invincible and fearsome giant who issues a challenge; in both God ensures the outcome by sending a champion to defeat the giant singlehandedly and save an entire people. Note the mini epic-simile: "As David whilom cam ageyn Golye / to helpen Saul. . . So . . . Guy was provided to be ther champioun / Ageyn the pompe of proude Colybrond" (lines 331–36; emphasis mine).

342 *God faileth never His frend on see nor lond*. God never fails his friend on sea or land. Proverbial. See Whiting G211.

356 *out of ews more to be clad in mayll*. Guy protests that he is not accustomed to being in armor anymore.

359 *comoun profit*. For the common good; to the benefit of everyone. Lydgate's Guy is unique in agreeing to fight Colbrand for the common good. See Introduction to *Guy*, p. 99n68. There are numerous occurrences of the phrase in ME literature, particularly in Gower. In another well-known example, the dreamer/narrator in Chaucer's *Parliament of Foules* is told "What man . . . That lovede commune profyt . . . He shulde into a blysful place wende"; and Lydgate also uses the phrase in several places to underline the concept that one person can serve the common good (*Pilgrimage of the Life of Man*, line 3933); "[th]e Grekis . . . acordid . . . [th]at Achilles and . . . Pirrodus / For comoun profit . . . Schal take on hem [th]e charge of [th]is message" (*TB* 2.5397). For a brief history of the idea of the common good in medieval thought, see Black, "Individual and society," especially pp. 595–97. See also Kellie Robertson, who sums up the idea succinctly: "The Middle English variants of 'common profit' (including *comoun profyt* and *commune profit*) were the usual translation of *bonum commune*, itself an extension of the

classical concept of *res publica* that viewed the public good as a function of an individual's responsibility to society" ("Common Language," p. 212).

360 *My lyf juparte*. To jeopardize my life. Scribal readings of *juparte* vary (see Textual Note), but there are many examples of Lydgate using *iuparte* to mean "jeopardize." See, for example, Lydgate's *Siege of Thebes* (lines 1381, 1826); *Troy Book* (1.994, 1.2464; 2.224; 3.188); and *Fall of Princes* (1.878, 2.931, 2.3260). A *Literature Online* search of the scribal variations (*em/im parte/n*) yields only one example each of *inpartye*, *inpartyd*, and *enpartythe*, none of which fit the meaning here (*Literature Online*, http://www.literature.proquest.com).

371 The date, July 12, 927, is significant. On July 12, 927, an important agreement was reached at Eamont between King Ethelstan and his Northumbrian enemies, including Scots and Danes, by which they submitted to his rule. See note to lines 1–2 above and the Introduction to *Guy*, especially pp. 93–94.

379–80 *Hyde Meede / Or ellis Denmark*. Hyde Meadow, near the site of the monastery. That is, the battle takes place at a location that will later come to be called Hyde Meadow. It was known as Danemarch at least until the late eighteenth century. For more on this name, see the Introduction to *Guy*, p. 95.

399–400 *Colybrond of indyngnacyoun / To his requeste gaf noon audyence*. That Colbrond will not give Guy a weapon to continue the fight illustrates his complete lack of moral or Christian standing; he does not behave in a chivalric way because he cannot. He is completely outside of civilization.

432 *Onto ther chirche callyd Cathedrall*. A detail not included in the fifteenth-century version or the AN *Gui*. Lydgate and Gerard are emphasizing that it is the cathedral in town, Winchester Cathedral, not Hyde Abbey, to which the party processes.

438 *the ex of Colybrond*. This axe was purported to have been kept in St. Swithun's priory, the cathedral Benedictine monastery, until the dissolution of the monasteries by Henry VIII. See also Introduction to *Guy*, p. 95n59.

442–43 *Guy in al haste caste off hys armure / Lyk a pilgrym put on his sclaveyn*. In his change from armor to pilgrim garb, Guy rejects chivalric life again, once more becoming a pilgrim. See also note to line 488 below.

457–61 *Alle your pryncys avoided by absence . . . Duryng my lyf*. An extended ablative construction, outlining the conditions under which Guy will explain to Ethelstan who he is. Guy insists that Ethelstan never divulge his true identity.

461 *ye gete no more of me*. A common filler phrase. See also, for example, *Fabula* lines 490 and 852.

467 *At a cros*. Crosses were sometimes placed at crossroads or along byways for travelers passing outside the sacred places designated within cities.

484 *avouh*. While the *MED* lists only verbal meanings for *avouh* (*avouen*) the word is clearly meant to function as a noun here. The noun form is usually *vou(e*, but the *MED* acknowledges that forms with *a* are ambiguous (*MED vou(e* (n. 1)).

488 *doon off.* Note again the metaphorical force of the clothing Guy wears. His assertion that he will never remove his hermit's garment underlines his refusal of gold and riches from the king and illustrates his determination not to return to the knight's life but, rather, to remain as a hermit for the rest of his days.

492 *Warwyk, his castell, and his toun.* A reminder of Guy's close ties to the locality of Warwick.

499–500 *Thre daies space he was oon of tho / That took almesse with humble and louh corage.* This episode, in which Guy receives alms at the hand of Felice, who does not recognize him, is often given more dramatic effect in other versions of the Guy legend. In the fifteenth century version, the disguised Guy reminds Felice of her husband, and she asks a squire to tend especially to him (*Cambridge*, lines 10505–15). She feels a kind of kinship with this pilgrim and comes close to recognizing him.

502–03 *Nat fer fro Warwyk . . . Of aventure kam to an hermytage.* Here, Lydgate differs from his source, Gerard, who describes the hermitage as quite a distance from Warwick. John Frankis suggests as a reason for this discrepancy the possible influence on Lydgate of the Prose Guy, a French prose redaction of the *AN Gui,* extant in two manuscripts, one in England and one in France though probably both of English origin, and probably commissioned either by John Talbot or Richard Beauchamp (Frankis, "Taste and Patronage," pp. 80–81 and 88–89), in which the hermitage is described as being close to Warwick (Frankis, "Taste and Patronage," p. 88). In the second, or fifteenth-century version (*Cambridge*), the hermitage is similarly described as close to Warwick. Frankis suggests that Lydgate and the author of the fifteenth-century version have been influenced here by the Beauchamps, whether Talbot or Richard (Frankis, "Taste and Patronage," p. 88).

573–74 *Wich wrot the dedis with gret dilligence / Of them that wern in Westsex crowned kynges.* For Gerard's purported history of the West Saxon kings, see the Introduction to *Guy* in this volume, p. 88n20.

585–92 *Meekly compiled . . . .* This final stanza is truncated in HH and Hr. See corresponding Textual Note.

589–90 *In Tullius gardyn he gadrid never flour / Nor of Omerus he kam never in the meede.*

Tullius. Cicero, an important Roman orator and rhetorician.

Omerus. Homer. This familiar modesty topos, in which the poet protests his lack of rhetorical talent, is used frequently by Lydgate and here particularly recalls Chaucer's Franklin, who prefaces his tale by saying that he has never learned anything about the colors of rhetoric: I sleep nevere on the Mount of Pernaso, / Ne lerned Marcus Tullius Scithero. / Colours ne knowe I none, withouten drede, / But swiche colours as growen in the mede" (*CT* V[F] 721–24). See also Gower's closing words of the *Confessio Amantis* (ed. Peck, 8.3115–119):

> For thilke scole of eloquence
> Belongith nought to my science,
> Uppon the forme of rethorique
> My wordis for to peinte and pike,
> As Tullius som tyme wrot.

TEXTUAL NOTES TO *GUY OF WARWYK*

ABBREVIATIONS: HH: Cambridge, MA, Harvard University, Houghton Library, MS Eng. 530; **Hr**: London, British Library, MS Harley 7333; **L**: London, British Library, MS Lansdowne 699; **MS**: Oxford, Bodleian Library, MS Laud Misc. 683 (base manuscript); **M**: MacCracken, ed., *Lydgate's Minor Poems*; **P**: Peterborough, Peterborough Central Library MS, s. n.; **T**: Cambridge University Library, MS Trinity R.3.21; **V**: Leiden, University Library, MS Vossius Germ. Gall. Q.9; **Z**: Zupitza, ed., "Lydgate's *Leben des Guy von Warwick*."

Incipit *Here gynneth the lyff off Guy of Warwyk*. HH, Hr: *Her now begynnyth an abstracte owte the cronycles in latyn made by Gyrade Cornubyence the worthy the cronyculer of Westsexe & translatid into Englishe be lydegate Daun Iohan at the request of Margret Countasse of Shrowesbury ladyTalbot ffournyvale & lysle of the lyffe of that moste worthy knyght Guy of Warrewyk of whos blode she is lenyally descendid*. L: *Incipit Guydo de Warwik*. V: *Danico invasio regnante Ethelstano un cum historia Guidonis de Warwik*. T: *A Tale of Guy & Colbrond*.

1 *complet*. T: omitted.

3 *the*. Hr: omitted.

5 *also*. HH, Hr: *þane harde*.

6 *them of Denmark*. HH, Hr: *þe daanes*.
wich with. HH: *that with her*. Hr: *who che with þeire*.

7 *brent*. T: *Bruto*.
and. P: omitted.
made. T: *and made*.

9 *Spared*. HH, Hr: *They sparyd*.

10 *Chirchis collegis*. T: *Churche ne college*.
that they. HH, Hr: omitted. V: *thy*.

11 *every*. HH, Hr: *many*.

12 *furie*. HH, Hr: *wodnesse*.

14 *wylde*. V: *wylle*.
feer. HH, Hr: *ffuyre*. P, T: *fyyre*. V, L: *fyr*.

15 *And in ther mortall persecucyoun*. HH, Hr: omitted. HH supplies in the right-hand margin the following: *without all mercy they frett and frown*.

16 *Spared*. HH, Hr: *ne spared*.
greet. HH, Hr: *goon grete*.
chylde. V: *clyde*.

17 *this*. P: *the*.

18 *Two*. So HH, Hr. MS: *To*. L, V: *Too*. P, T: *The*.
Denmark. HH, Hr: *daanisshe*.

19 *void*. HH, Hr: *& voyde*.

20 *Did no favour*. HH, Hr: *no ffauour shewe*. T: *Shewyd no fauour*.
nor. Hr: *nor to*.
estaat. P: *degre*.

21 *so*. HH: *than*. Hr: *þoo*.
dysconsolaat. T: *desolate*.

22 *hath at hem*. HH, Hr: *at hem hath*.
so dysdeyned. V: *disdeyne*.

23 *Mars and Mercurie wer with hem at debaat*. HH, Hr: *Mercury & Mars held with hem debate*.
debaat. T: *bate*.

24 *That bothe*. HH, Hr: *So was*.
pryncis. HH, Hr: *lordes*.
and. T: *and þe*.

distreyned. HH, Hr: *þane constreyned*. V, L, P, T: *constreyned*.

25 *By froward force*. HH, Hr: *By fforce ellas*.
the. T: omitted.
flyght. P: *fyȝt*.

26 *Thes*. HH, Hr: *þe*.

27 *On hih hilles*. HH, Hr: *On hillis hie*. T: *on theyre hygh hylles*.
fyres gaff suych. HH, Hr: *beekens were so*.
suych. P: *gret*.
lyght. Hr: *bright*.

29 *robbed and spoiled*. HH, Hr: *spoyled & robbed*.
robbed. T: *they robbyd*.

30 *verray*. HH, Hr: *mortall*.

31 *the*. P: omitted.
red. HH, Hr: omitted.

32 *a*. HH, Hr: *þe*.
gret. HH, Hr: omitted.
fro. T: *fro the*.
mounteyne. HH, Hr: *the hille*.

33 *for*. HH, Hr: *ffrome*.
trespace. HH: *antiquite*.

34 *of*. HH, Hr, T: *of olde*.
antyquyté. HH: *trespace*.

35 *hap, fortune, and grace*. HH: *in cronycles as ye may see*.

36 *in cronycles ye may see*. HH: *on happe ffortune & grace*.

39 *The thefte of Nachor made Israell to fle*. HH, Hr: *The* is omitted.
Nachor. HH, Hr: *Nathor*.
made Israell to fle. HH, Hr: *caused þe aduersytee*.

40 *Out of the feld, and in ther conquest faile*. HH, Hr: *till he was stoonyd they myght not prevayle*.
in. L, P, T: *of*.
faile. T: *to fayle*.

41 *the*. P: omitted.
ambycioun. T: *Abusion*.

42 *And*. HH, Hr: *þe*.
furie. T: *furyes*.

43 *This*. HH: *þe*.
destruccyoun. P: *confusion*.

44 *The swerd of Bellona*. HH, Hr: *Bellonas swerd*.
so. HH, Hr, V: omitted. T: *to*.

45 *wer*. HH, Hr: omitted.

46 *Oon of*. HH, Hr: *On*.

47 *And as*. HH, Hr: *As that*.

48 *tother was named*. V: *the thodir so mamed*.

50 *God*. T: *ffor god*.
with his punisshyng. HH, Hr: *to punysshe offt*.

51 *Suerd*. P, T: *The sword*.
a. L, V: omitted.
punssheth. HH, Hr: *sleþe ffolke*. P: *smyth*.

52 *With furious hand mortall and vengable*. HH, Hr: *þeyre ffuryous handes ben wode & vengeable*. T: *Thorough furyous Ire & mortall vengebyll*.

53 *Wher*. T: *There*.
the Lord. HH, Hr: *oure lorde*. T: *god*.
ay. T: *euer*.
tretable. HH, L: *mercyable*.

54 *wich halt all*. T: *with merci*.
wich. HH, Hr: *&*.

55 *But thes tirauntys, to scheden blood most able*. HH, Hr: *thise twoo to shedyn blode thyrauntes full able*.

56 *troubled*. HH, Hr: *they troubled*.

57 *for*. HH: *for the*.
by. HH, Hr: omitted.

58 *Hath chastysed*. HH, Hr: *Chastised hath*.
greet. HH, Hr: *ffayre*.

59 *hem*. HH: omitted.

60 *Record*. HH, L, T: *Recorde of*.
on. HH, L, P, T: *of*. Hr: omitted.

61 *Paris in Fraunce*. HH, Hr: *Parys nerr hoome*.
pardé. V: *payd*.

62 *veyn*. HH, Hr, L, P, T, V: *ffals*.
ambucyoun. T: *Abusion*.

63 *examples at eye*. V: *at eye examplis*.
at eye. HH, Hr: *her*. T: *as*.

65 *This mater ofte hath been*. T: *The mater hath oft be*.

66 *For lak*. HH, Hr: *Lackyng*.
of$_2$. HH: omitted.
wisdam. P: *witte*.
67 *peplys*. HH, Hr: *ffolkes*.
wer. HH, Hr: *ne wer*.
68 *To*. HH, Hr: *ffor to*.
69 *Wynd of glad fortune*. HH, Hr: *Of glad fortune the wynde*.
Wynd. T: *The wynde*.
in. HH, Hr: omitted.
70 *of*. HH, Hr: omitted.
72 *Thouh*. P: *And yit*.
Kyng Ethelstan. HH, HR: *Edelston king*.
73 *Cruell*. HH, Hr: *þese cruwell*. P: *Of cruell*.
Inglyssh. HH: *þis Englissh*. Hr: *þenglisshe*.
74 *swerd was*. HH, Hr: *swerdes wer*.
75 *Yit*. P: *And yit*.
in. L: omitted.
cronycle. Hr, L, P, T, V: *cronycles*. HH: *the cronnycles*.
at leyser. HH, Hr: omitted.
who. V: *who so*.
lyst. HH, Hr: *list bokes*.
77 *his*. V: *his his*.
78 *nobless and royall*. HH, Hr: *ryall and marcyall*.
noblesse. P, T: *nobilness*.
79 *God*. V: *good*.
always. T: *euer*.
in his myght. P: *with the ryght*.
82 *folweth*. HH, Hr: *is next*.
85 *After*. HH, Hr: *Next the*.
trouble. L, P, T, V: *gret trouble*.
87 *to*. Hr: omitted.
mercyable. HH: *counfortable*.
88 *Upon his knyght, the forseid Ethelstan*. HH, Hr: *to recounforte his knyght kynge Ethelstan*.
89 *In*. HH, Hr: *thus in*.
90 *adversyté*. P: *necessite*.
91 *cronycle*. L, P, T, V: *cronycles*.
92 *alle*. HH, Hr: omitted.
93 *have a*. HH, Hr: *holde*.
at. P: *in*.
the. HH, Hr, P: omitted.
94 *Som*. HH, Hr: *theyr*.
in all haste to provyde. HH, Hr: *in haste for to*. P: *to fynde and hastyly*.
95 *and*. Hr: *of*.
97 *the lond*. HH, Hr: *this reaume*.
98 *Remedy to schapen*. HH, Hr: *to ben avysed hole*.
100 *In that cyté*. HH, Hr: *At Wynchestre wer they*.
101 *Hap*. HH, Hr: *hope*.
102 *Ther hope*. HH, Hr: *ffor theyre trust*.
turned. HH: *ffell in*. Hr: *ffel vn*. T: *was turnyd*.
to. V: omitted.
104 *spere*. HH, Hr: *swerd*.
105 *that*. HH, Hr: *theyre*.
party. HH: *prayer*.
was. Hr: *þere was*.
108 *the*. HH: *in þis*.
109 *Strong wer the Danys*. HH: *The daneys stronge*. Hr: *þe danys so strong*.
proud. HH: omitted. T: *and proud*.
110 *Kyng*. HH: *þis*. Hr: *þus*.
by. V: *in*.
111 *that*. V: *the*.
112 *to*. V: omitted.
113 *By*. HH: *Be the*.
this. HH, Hr: *hit*.
115 *telle*. HH, Hr: *seyne*.
116 *Benbassatrie, or mene of som tretee*. Hr: omitted.
117 *Streythtly*. T: *Streyte*.
of. HH, Hr: *of pure*.
Hr adds in left margin between 117 and 118: [*?re*]*cord ryght as ye shall see*.
118 *The kyng of Denmark*. HH, Hr: *Alle þo danys*.
for. P: omitted.
119 *this*. T: *hys*.
121 *ellis pleynly*. HH, Hr: *to appoynte*.
partyes. HH, Hr, L, P, T, V: *parties bi*.
124 *Day*. L, T, V: *A day*. P: *At day*.
assigned. T: *sygned*.
in. L: *to*.

125 *to*. P: *ii* [i.e., *two*]. HH, Hr: *twoo*.
126 *with*. HH: *the*.
127 *a*. HH, Hr: omitted.
by$_2$. P: omitted.
128 *in quyete of*. HH, Hr: *hooly in*.
129 *beyng there*. Hr: *ther beyng*.
130 *loud*. HH, Hr, L, P, T, V: *long*.
131 *fynall*. HH, Hr: *ffull*.
132 *How they list quyten hem*. HH, Hr: *Tacquyte hem selfe*.
hem. L: omitted.
134 *and*. Hr: *of*.
outher. HH, Hr, P: *or elles*. T: *orelles*.
135 *ther*. HH, Hr: *his*. T: *the*.
137 *Denmark*. HH: *danyes*. Hr: *danyshe*.
138 *wylful*. HH, Hr: *contrarye*.
139 *lyst*. Hr: *ne lyst*.
be. HH, L, P, T, V: *to ben*.
141 *or*. HH, Hr: omitted.
for. HH, Hr: *or*.
142 *this*. V: *the*.
convencioun. L: *relacioun relacioun*.
relacioun. HH, Hr: *aunswer*.
to. HH, Hr: *for to*.
143 *How*. P: *If*.
caste hem. HH: *purpossen*. Hr: *purposid*.
144 *The*. HH, Hr: omitted.
145 *so*. HH: *ffull*.
146 *furious*. HH, Hr: *yrous*.
haste. T: *Ire*.
they. HH, Hr: *the danys*.
have. HH, Hr: omitted.
147 *so hard was*. HH: *was so harde*.
so. P: *ful*.
149 *the*. HH, Hr: *thise*.
150 *mende*. L, P, V: *mynde*.
151 *And weel*. HH, Hr: *ffulle moche*.
weel. L: *wele*. V: *wyll*. P, T: *well*.
152 *to*. T: *for to*.
153 *Knew no bet*. HH, Hr: *kouþe thenke no*. T: *And knew no mene*.
as in. L: *in al*.
mateer. T: *manere*.
154 *Redres*. HH, Hr: *remedy*.
to$_2$. HH, Hr: *be*.
155 *Than*. HH, Hr: *but*.
hym. T: *hem*.
156 *to*. HH, Hr, P: *in*.
157 *Pore*. HH, Hr: *þe poure*.
withoute more. HH, Hr: *to make no*.
158 *attonys*. HH, Hr: *echon*.
159 *salte*. HH, Hr: *bytter*.
resembled in. HH, Hr: *semed be*.
160 *By*. HH, Hr: omitted.
to. HH, Hr: *as*. P: *like*.
161 *hih*. L: *his*. HH, Hr, T: *the hye*.
162 *Of*. HH, Hr: *Soughte*.
founde was. HH: *but they ffynde*. Hr: *but they fonde*.
164 *Ageyn the geaunt of Denmark for to fight*. HH, Hr: line omitted.
for. P: omitted.
165 *Harderne*. T: *order*.
the. Hr, P: *that*. T: *and the*.
noble. HH, Hr: *goode*.
Hr adds a line between 165 and 166: *Koud not be found in nomans syght*.
167 *in*$_1$. HH, Hr: *of*.
in$_2$. HH: *to*.
168 *of manhood*. HH, Hr: *most knyghtly*.
lode sterre. P: *þe lodsterre*.
169 *This*. HH, Hr, L, P, T, V: *The*.
beyng tho. Hr: *thoo beyng þens*. T: *tho beyng*.
172 *alle*. T: *in all*.
173 *yong age*. HH, Hr: *his youthe*.
174 *By straunge*. HH, Hr: *And by*.
ongoodly. V: *vngodly*.
175 *tendirly*. HH, Hr: *ryght tendrely*.
176 *compleynyng*. HH: *wepyng*.
177 *hir*. HH, Hr, L, V: *his*.
178 *yonge*. HH, Hr: *dere*.
to. HH, Hr: *ffor to*.
179 *In*. HH, Hr: *In alle*.
180 *the*. HH, Hr, L: omitted.
and. L: *in*.
181 *Rowand*. HH, Hr: *Ronaulde*. P: *Rewynd*. T: *Rowland*.
182 *Erl*. HH, Hr: *þan eorlle*.
oon. HH, Hr: omitted. P: *on of*.
beste. T: *boldyst*.

183 *That was*. HH: *levyng*. Hr: *levyng in*.
184 *allas*. HH: *was so*. Hr: *ellas so*. P: *forsoth*.
185 *Paide*. V: *Pay*.
of. L, V: *bi*.
186 *was*. HH, Hr: *þat*.
his. HH, Hr: *þe*.
187 *And*. HH, Hr: omitted.
189 *seyde*. Hh, Hr: omitted. P, T: *the said*.
sone affter. HH, Hr: *hir sone Reynebroune*.
as. HH, Hr: *as þat*.
190 *He lyk a pilgrym*. HH, Hr: *The next morwe*.
He. L, P, T, V: omitted.
endewed. P: *endowed*.
all. HH, Hr: omitted.
191 *The nexte morwe*. HH, Hr: *Lyche a pilgrym*.
192 *hym*. T: *hymsylf*.
193 *to*. HH, V: *of*.
194 *hih*. HH, Hr: omitted. T: *hys*.
195 *and*$_2$. HH, Hr: omitted.
kyn. P: *child*.
bekam. HH, Hr: *became so*.
196 *for*. V: omitted.
was. P: *he*.
197 *Crist*. T: *for cryst*.
his. P: omitted.
198 *In*. T: *With*.
pompe. HH, Hr: *wellthe*. P: *pryde*.
he lyst not to. HH, Hr: *hym list no more*.
199 *onto*. HH, Hr: *nowe to*.
200 *Kyng*. HH, Hr: *To*.
wyll. V: *well*.
201 *As I began in order*. HH: *Ryght as I ffyrst gan*. Hr: *Right as I firste gave for*.
202 *make*. HH, Hr: *make clere*.
203 *but*. HH, Hr: omitted.
205 *Because there was*. HH, Hr: *þis was the cause*.
206 *Founde no persone*. HH, Hr: *was ffounde no man*.
207 *seyde*. HH, Hr, P: *he saide*.
208 *His grace doun*. HH: *some grace hym*. Hr: *some grace to him*.
to. P: *wold*.
210 *Cast doun*. HH, Hr: *Enclyne*.
211 *upon*. HH, Hr: *lord*.
212 *But fro*. HH, Hr: *ffrome alle*.
turne. HH, Hr: *þou tourne*.
thy. HH, Hr: *my*.
213 *Disespeired*. HH, Hr: *I dispeyred*.
stondyng. P: *I stonde*.
in. T: *thus in*.
214 *kyngdam*. HH, Hr: *reaume*.
216 *gracious mene*. HH, Hr: *benygne lord*.
partye. HH, Hr: *prayer*.
217 *My feith, myn hope*. T: *My hoope my feythe*.
219 *My sheeld, my sheltroun*. HH, Hr: *shelde & sheltroun*.
eek. T: omitted.
220 *Be*. HH, Hr: *Alle*.
power. HH, Hr: *ffortune*. V: *pore*.
221 *But grace with mercy list be my champioun*. HH, Hr: *Saue grace & mercy I haue no chaumpyon*.
be. T: *to be*.
222 *Thorgh Thy*. HH, Hr: *But thou*.
223 *this*. HH: *this his*. Hr: *þus his*.
224 *Or he was war*. HH, Hr: *hym alle vnwist*.
he fyll into. T: *was fall in*.
into a slombre. HH, Hr: *in slepe & slombyr*.
225 *trouble*. HH, Hr: *thoughte*.
lay. P: *he lay*.
226 *Devoutly knelyng*. HH, Hr: *knelyng devoutly*.
Devoutly. T: *Benygnely*.
by. HH, T: *besyde*.
228 *grace*. P: *mercy*.
with meekness void. HH, Hr: *& is devoyde*.
230–40 *Which of His goodnesse sente an aungel doun. . . .in story as I reede*. These ten lines are substantively different in HH and Hr. HH reads as follows:

Sent an aungell Ethelston to recounforte
Be twene midnyght & the morwe tyde
Spake to the kynge as I cane me reporte
I goddes aungell sent ffrome hevenly kynge
ffor to releesse thyn hevy perturbaunce
Whether thou slepe or that thou be wakyng
God hath resceyued thy prayer & penaunce
þyne pytous wepyng & alle thyne olde greuaunce
shall hastly chaunge to ioy & to plesaunce
Ne drede the not but haue thou in remembraunce
As I to the shall nowe here expresse

Hr exhibits four substantive variants from HH:

233 *cane me*. Hr: *schall you*.

238 *plesaunce*. Hr: *blyse*. There is clearly a correction written over an erasure. The erased word looks very much as if it could have been *plesaunce*.

239 *thou*. omitted.

240 *shall nowe here expresse*. Hr: *here right shall nowe expresse*. Robinson suggests that these lines may represent an alternate version of the poem because they seem closer to Gerard (p. 196). Whether or not this is so, these ten lines (with or without Hr's correction of the breach in ballad-stanza by the rhyme in HH's line 238) are arguably less effective than the version represented by L and the other "Group B" texts.

231 *dreede*. T: *feare*.
feer. T: *drede*.
a syde. V: *on side*.

232 *mercy*. P: *goodness*.

233 *cast*. P: *he cast*.

234 *Bad*. T: *And bade*.

235 *entyeer*. T: *vttyr*.

236 *in riht*. P: *in*. T: *withyn*.

240 *hadde*. T: *harde*.

241 *thee*. MS, L, P, V: *the*. T: *thee*.
voide. HH, Hr: *to avoyde*.

242 *Whan*. HH, Hr: *Whan þat*.
hir. P: *his*.

243 *Tomorwen, erly*. HH, Hr: *Eorly to morowe*.

244 *Crist Ihesu*. P: *Ihesu Crist*.

245 *sight*. T: *sute*.

246 *upon*. HH: *well in*. Hr: *well on*.
in. T: *yef*.
trust. HH, Hr: *hope*.

247 *shall*. HH, Hr: *will*.
and. HH: *& of*.

248 *for He ys*. HH, Hr: *he is so*.

249 *Phebus*. HH, Hr: *the sonne*.
set. HH, Hr: *ne sette*.

250 *flete*. HH: *swete*.

251 *toward*. HH, Hr: *vn to*.

252 *that*. P: *euer*.

253 *Hath on the levys*. HH, Hr: *on leve & herbe hath*.
weete. HH, Hr: *hete*.

254 *Abide there meekly*. HH, Hr: *Mekely þer byde*.
God. V: omitted.
to. P, T: omitted.
thee sende. P: *thi d[?] send*.

255 *Fyrst among*. HH, Hr: *Amonges the*.

256 *hym goodly*. HH, Hr: *þou hym*.
thy. T: *the*.

257 *Clad as a pilgrym*. HH, Hr: *symply arayed*.
in a brood. HH: *in a rowe*. Hr: *and cladde in rovghe*.

259 *Marke*. HH, Hr: *Thou merke*.
riht weell. HH, Hr: *thou full*. L: *riht trist*.
weell$_2$. P: omitted.

261 *To*. HH, Hr: *ffor to*.

262 *on*. P: *in*.
and. HH: omitted.

263 *Goddis myht that*. HH, Hr: *myght of god*.
schall. HH, Hr: *shalle the ther*.
L: ~~*Newly reioissed out of all hevynisse*~~.

265–88 *The woordis seid. . . hour of pryme*. These stanzas are omitted in HH and Hr.

265 *The*. P: *Thes*.

267 *dyd onwarly*. T: *vnwarely dyd*.

270 *Neuly*. T: *And newly*.
271 *two*. MS: *too*. P: *ii*. T: *two*. L, V: *too*. I have made this same emendation at lines 324 and 510.
as. V: omitted.
274 *humble*. P: *dew*.
276 *At*. T: *Alle*.
279 *Whan*. T: *When that the*.
280 *in*. T: *of*.
at. P: *in*. T: *into*.
at the. V: *atte*.
282 *Unto*. P: *vnto a*.
287 *By*. T: *By the*.
288 *how*. T: *how that*.
289 *briht Phebus*. HH, Hr: *Phebus bryght*.
gold tressed. HH, Hr: *golden*.
290 *hih*. T: omitted.
291 *on*. T: *in the*.
and. HH, Hr: omitted.
hoote. HH, Hr: *feruent*.
292 *perlis silver*. HH, Hr: *silver perlys*.
293 *Whan seide*. HH, Hr: *And that*.
seide. P, T: *the said*.
Guy the noble. P: *noble Guy*. HH: *Guy þat noble*.
294 *long*. HH, Hr: omitted.
295 *took*. HH, Hr, P, T: *he toke*.
296 *To*. HH, Hr: *Vnto*.
holdyng. HH: *strayte he held*. Hr: *streght heelde*.
297 *By*. HH, Hr: *By the*.
trowly. HH, Hr: *hit trwly*.
298 *thys*. HH, L, T: *his*.
301 *He*. HH: *here*.
for to be. Hr: *for toke*.
303 *hym*. T: *whom*.
304 *how*. HH, Hr: *how þat*.
305 *They told hym firste*. HH: *he tolde the kynge*. Hr: *he tolde þe knyht*.
306 *Harald*. HH, Hr, P: *harald of*.
307 *the sone*. HH, Hr: *Reynebroune þe*.
308 *maner*. T: *maner of*.
310 *tytle*. HH, Hr: *cleyme*.
famous. HH, Hr: *clene of*.
in. P: *of*.
311 *Cristis*. T: *goddes*.
his. P: omitted.
312 *Earl*. HH, Hr: *þeorldame*.
313 *They told hym also*. HH, Hr: *Men tolde eke Guy*.
grete. HH, Hr: *dredefull*. T: omitted.
314 *them of Denmark*. HH, Hr: *the danys*.
315 *that Rowand, fader*. HH: *Rohauld þat was ffader*. Hr: *Rohauld was ffadir*.
to hys wyff. HH, Hr: *to Guys wyffe*.
Rowand. P: *Richard*. T: *Rowlond*.
316 *Old*. HH: *þe olde*. Hr: *þe older*.
ful. HH, Hr, P: omitted.
318 *clos*. HH, Hr, T: *full close*.
319 *his leve there*. Hr: *ther his leve*.
320 *Goth*. T: *went*.
Goth to Wynchestre. HH, Hr: *to Wynchester gooyth*.
321 *Guy*. HH, Hr: *he*.
took. T: *to*.
loggyng. HH, Hr: *herboroughe*.
322 *at*. HH, Hr: *therat*. T: *in*.
old. Hr: omitted.
323 *Wery*. T: *Were*.
onknowe to every wight. HH, Hr: *whan hit droughe to night*.
to. P: *of*.
324 *without the north*. HH, Hr: *& ffyffty ffrom þe*.
325 *Wher*. L: *Ther*. T: *Where as*.
stondeth now. T: *now stondeth*.
now a menstre. Hr: *a mynster nowe*.
327 *was his guyde*. HH, Hr: *guyded hym ther*.
his. P: omitted.
328 *Mong pore men*. HH, Hr: *with oþer poure*.
330 *into toun*. P: *the town*. HH, Hr, T: *into the towne*.
331 *whilom*. T: *somtyme*.
333 *for*$_1$. T: *for the*.
335 *provided*. T: *prouyd*.
336 *pompe*. HH, Hr: *danys*.
of proude Colybrond. HH, Hr: *& ffuryous Colbronde*. L: *of fowle Colibrond*.
337 *By*. HH, Hr: *boþe be*.

338 *Thilke tyme*. HH, Hr: *þo*.
clad in a round. HH: *eclade with a rowe*. Hr: *ecladde al with a rowght*.
339 *Of*. T: *on*.
kyng. T: *kynde*.
340 *Sauh*. P: *he saw*.
promys. HH, Hr: *be hest*.
341 *Took*. HH, Hr, T: *he tooke*.
up his herte. HH: *good hede*. Hr: *good herte*.
his. P: omitted.
riht weel serteyn. HH, Hr: *well ffor certayne*.
342 *never*. HH, Hr: *not*.
on. HH, Hr, T: *in*.
lond. Hr, T: *in lond*.
343 *lik*. HH, Hr: *as*.
344 *For verray*. HH, Hr: *of hye*.
he. HH: omitted.
took. Hr: *to*.
345 *Besekyng*. HH, Hr: *Requeryng*.
in. HH, P, T: *in the*. Hr: omitted.
louly. P: *humble*.
346 *was*. P: *it was*.
347 *this knyhtly hih*. HH: *the dredfull*. Hr: *þis dredfull*.
349 *this*. HH, Hr: *þat*.
350 *In his dyffence that he*. T: *In thys that ye*.
wyll. L: *hym*.
351 *for*. HH, Hr, L, P, T: omitted.
352 *For*. T: *ffrom*.
darreyne. HH, Hr: *to derrain*.
the. HH, Hr, P: *this*. T: *hys*.
353 *of look and*. Hr: *and looke of*.
of$_2$. P, T: omitted.
354 *and*$_2$. HH, Hr: *ffull*.
of. HH, Hr: *of his*.
355 *was*. P: omitted.
356 *And*. HH, Hr: *longe*.
more to be clad in. HH, Hr: *to were plate or mayll*.
357 *he*. HH, Hr: *Guy*.
Yif. Hr: *if þat*.
it. V: *I*.
myhte avayll. HH: *may prevaylle*.
358 *to appeese*. HH, Hr: *ffor to peese*.
359 *For comoun profit good wil shal nat fayll*. HH, Hr: *To the comoune goode my servyce shall not fayle*.
360 *juparte*. MS: *in parte* (or *iu parte*). V: *Iuperte* (or *Inperte*). L: *Iuperte* (or *Inperte*). HH: *in Iuperde*. Hr: *in Iuberde*. P: *ieperdye*. T: *to in* (or *iu*)*patte*. M: *juparte*. Z: *inparte*. This emendation is based on several considerations, the first of which is the difficulty of determining whether MS, V, L, and T read *in* or *iu*. However, in Hr and HH, this is fairly clearly intended to be *iu*, given the preceding word *in*. T adds another layer of difficulty (although MacCracken reads *im parte*, I cannot concur). However, I do agree with MacCracken in making the final emendation to *juparte*. While Zupitza's *inparte* can make sense, it is much rarer (see *MED imparten/emparten*); further, the evidence of HH, Hr, and particularly P, as well as Lydgate's own usage, suggests that the best reading is *iuparte*, "jeopardize" (see *MED juparten*). See also the Explanatory Note.
to set thys lond. HH, Hr: *this lande to sette*. P: *and set*.
361 *kyng*. T: *kyng and*.
362 *To*. T: *Of*.
this. Hr: *his*.
363 *Guy, for to doon onto*. HH: *And he most mekely doo*. Hr: *And he moste mekelye to do*.
364–65 *For Jhesus sake . . . ye schall heere*. P: transposes.
365 *Ys*. HH: *ye*.
367 *requere*. HH, Hr: *appere*.
368 *At*. HH, Hr: omitted. T: *At a*.
assigned. T: *y sygnyd*.
mete. HH, Hr: *mete with*.
369 *long*. T: *lengor*.

370 *This*. HH, Hr: *þeise*. L, P, T: *The*.
convencyoun. HH, Hr: *covenauntes*. L: *condicion*. P: *bataill*.
371 *Tyme*. HH, Hr, T: *þe tyme*.
upon. HH, Hr: omitted.
372 *Place*. HH, Hr: *þe plase*.
and meetyng of thes. HH: *betweene hem*. Hr: *bytwene þeos ylke*.
374 *Doubylnesse*. HH, Hr: *Alle doublenesse*.
set. T: *to be set*.
375 *As*. HH, Hr: omitted. T: *Of*.
were. HH, Hr: omitted.
in serteyn. HH, Hr: *vnder a surtee pleyne*.
376 *For short*. HH, Hr: *in*.
therby to abyde. Hr, Hr: *ther to assent & byde*.
378 *of*. HH, Hr: *of olde*.
379 *Inglyssh*. HH, Hr: *oure*.
named. P: *called*.
Hyde. HH, Hr: *the Hyde*.
380 *Denmark*. HH, Hr: *Denmarche*.
nat fer from. HH, Hr: *vndir*.
the. HH, Hr, L, T: *that*.
381 *Meetyng togedre*. HH, Hr: *þey assembled*.
see. HH, Hr: *well see*.
382 *lyk*. Hr: *liche to*.
383 *Sparklys*. L: *sparkis*. HH, Hr, P: *Sparklis of ffuyre*.
harneys. T: *armes dyd*.
384 *a*. HH, Hr: omitted.
385 *old*. HH, Hr: *vnkouthe*.
386 *Spared*. HH, Hr: *he sparid*.
to. HH, Hr: *ffor to*.
387 *his*. HH, Hr: *whos*.
smet at hym. HH, Hr, P: *he smote*. L: *smet hym*. P: *he smote him*.
suych. Hr: *moche*.
myht. V: *a myht*.
388 *aventayll*. V: *aven entayle*.
389 *A*. HH, Hr: *þat*.
390 *wood*. V: omitted. T: *was woode*.
this hydous. HH, Hr: *þer with this seid*.
391 *Thoughte it sholde gretly hym avayll*. HH, Hr: *ffor to ben venged ne cast hym not to ffayle*. T: *That with all hys myght he gaue hym suche batayle*.
gretly hym. V: *hym gretly*.
392 *That Guyes suerd was broke*. HH, Hr: *brake Guys swerd on tweyne*.
393 *Whan*. HH, T: *Whane þe*.
sauh. HH, Hr, T: *saughe þat*.
394 *a maner*. HH, Hr: *þer by gret*. P: *in maner a*. T: *a maner of*.
395 *Guy, lyk a knyght in herte nat aferd*. HH, Hr: *þoughe he wer stonyed yit was he not afferd*.
396 *manly*. HH, Hr: *knyghtly*.
397 *he of wepnys hadde so gret*. HH, Hr: *þat he hade of weponys suche*.
398 *in*. V: *of*.
399 *Colybrond of*. HH, Hr: *of ffals ire &*.
400 *gaff*. HH, Hr: *he gave*.
401 *For*. HH, Hr: omitted.
set. HH, Hr: *hole sett*.
on wrak. T: *in wrethe*.
402 *To execute his purpos set on pryde*. HH, Hr: *ffor to be vengid of verray ffroward pryde*.
404 *All*. HH, Hr: *þane alle*.
out. P: *onto*.
asyde. L, V: *on side*. P: *a syde*. T: *on a syde*.
405 *Cauhte*. HH, Hr: *he caught*. T: *And caute*.
lyst. HH, Hr: *& list*.
byde. P: *abide*.
406 *Smette the geaunt evene in the firste wounde*. HH, Hr: *of knyghtly prowes þe Geaunt to confounde*.
the furste. P: *þat*.
wounde. P: *stound*.
407 *Made*. HH, Hr: *he made*. P: *And made*.
to. P: omitted.
408 *his*. P: *both his*.
409 *wich*. HH, Hr: *the whiche*.
410 *armure and boody*. HH, Hr: *harney & armure*. T: *body and armure*.
411 *gan reche forth*. HH, Hr: *he raught out*.
413 *and grace*. HH, Hr: *ffortuned hym*.
gaff hym. HH, Hr: *to haue*.

415 *Fleih with his ax*. HH, Hr: *with stroke of axe*.
Fleih. L: *ffleith*. T: *ffowte*.
the. V: omitted.
sturdy. HH, Hr: *geauntes*.
416 *Of the geaunt*. HH, Hr: *called Colbrond*.
hym. T: *hym the*.
417 *thyng accomplisshed*. HH, Hr: *bataille wonne*.
418 *prowesse*. HH, Hr: *manhode*.
Guy. HH, Hr: omitted.
this. L: *the*.
419 *statute*. HH, Hr: *covenauntes*.
bond. T: *was bonde*.
420 *take*. Hr: *to*.
ther. L: *the*.
421 *cuntre*. HH, Hr: *land*.
423 *by grace*. HH, Hr: *thus be*. T: *because*.
of Goddys. HH, Hr: *Crystes*.
424 *Hadde of Denmark the pompe ful repressed*. HH: *in wele recured as is to ffor exppressid*. Hr: *is wele recured as is to ffor exppressid*.
425 *Ther froward pompe with meknesse*. HH, Hr: *And eke the pryde of danys*.
was repressed. HH: *sore oppressed*. Hr: *so repressed*.
pompe. P: *pride*.
426 *is*. Hr: *his*.
427 *have*. HH: omitted.
428 *Pryncys*. HH: *prynces &*. T: *Bothe Pryncys*.
and. Hr: omitted.
429 *With al the comounte; for short conclusioun*. HH, Hr: *In oon assembled of pure devocyoun*.
430 *Hih*. HH, Hr, T: *Both hye*.
431 *Hym*. HH, Hr: *Guy*.
with. HH, Hr: *with þeyr*. T: *with a*.
432 *ther*. V, L: *the*.
chirche callyd. HH, Hr: *mynster & chyrche*.
433 *This*. T: *Thus*.
seide Guy. HH, Hr: *noble knyght*.
435 *thilke*. HH, Hr: *þat same*. P, T: *that*.
436 *Danys*. HH, Hr: *denmarke*.
the. HH, Hr: *þer her*.
437 *instrument*. HH, Hr: *wepon yit*.
al. T: omitted.
438 *Is yit callid*. HH: *yit is hit called*. Hr: *Yit is callid*. T: *ys callyd*.
of. HH, Hr: *of gret*.
439 *Kept*. HH, Hr: *And kept*.
440 *the*. HH, Hr: *theyr*.
as ye shall. HH: *I*. Hr: *yee schall*.
shall. L, P: *may*.
441 *is*. L, P: *was*.
442 *caste*. Hr: *he caste*.
443 *Lyk*. HH, Hr, T: *& lyche*.
put on his sclaveyn. HH: *clothed hym with*. Hr: *he clothid hym with*.
put. T: *cast*.
444 *The kyng*. HH, Hr: *Kinge Ethelston*.
ful goodly affter did his cure. HH, Hr: *did his besy cure*. P: *full goodly did his besy cure*. T: *aftyr full gladly dyd his cure*.
afftir. V: omitted.
446 *tellyn*. HH, Hr: *tell hym*.
spare. HH, P: *to spare*.
447 *to*. L, V: omitted. P: *of*.
tellyn. HH, Hr: *shewe*. P: omitted.
448 *What was his name pleynly*. HH, Hr: *his name to hym pleynely ffor*.
What. P: *And what*.
449 *Certes*. HH, Hr: *My lorde*. P: *Truly*.
Guy. HH, Hr: *he*.
450 *Touchyng*. P: *As touching*.
your$_1$. HH, Hr: *þis*.
and your. HH, Hr: *or*.
451 *Beth nat besy and*. HH, Hr: *ne be not besy ne*.
and. P: *nor*.
455 *of a*. HH, Hr: *this*. T: *&*.
456 *Assuraunce*. HH, Hr: *of assuraunce*.
maad tween. HH, Hr: *be you*. V: *be tweyn yo*. The rest of V's line missing because a corner of page is torn.
457 *avoided*. T: *devoydyd*.
458 *oursilff*. HH, Hr, P: *youre selfe*.

460 *that*. HH, Hr: omitted.
be. HH, Hr: *keep*.
secre. P: *pryvee*.
462 *I*. Hr: *I ne*.
463 *nor*. T: *&*.
465 *confermed*. HH, Hr: *ensured*.
ful. HH, Hr: *& wordes*.
466 *Passed*. HH, Hr, P: *they passed*.
subbarbys and boundys. HH, Hr, L, P, T: *boundes & subbarbis*. V: *bondis of subbarbis*.
467 *At*. HH, Hr: *out at*.
feer. T: *for*.
wall. P: *walls*.
468 *devoutly*. HH, Hr: *konyngly*.
469 *all*. HH, Hr: *alle menys*.
470 *Of feith*. P: *my lorde*.
471 *Your*. P: *Your own*.
472 *trewly*. HH: *sere truuly*. Hr: *sir*.
473 *gan chaunge*. HH: omitted. Hr: *chaunged*. P: *gan*.
and. P: *of*.
474 *gan wepyn for*. HH, Hr: *wepped ffor gret*.
475 *And*. HH, Hr: *þan*.
477 *With offte kyssyng*. HH, Hr: *with honde in honde*.
478 *With gret proffres*. HH, Hr: *Gret profyres made*.
479 *of*$_2$. HH, T: *&*. Hr: *and of*.
of$_3$. T: omitted.
of gret. HH: *muche*. Hr: *of muche*.
480 *yif*. Hr: *yf þat*.
481 *Alle*. HH, Hr: *but alle*.
meekly he. HH: *Guy clene*. Hr: *Guy þeire clene*.
483 *Hym*. HH, Hr: *with*.
484–90 *At his departyng . . . . speche made interupcyoun*. These lines are rearranged and recast in HH and Hr:

And pytous knelyng on his knee
At þat departing þis avowe made he
duryng Guys lyffe hit wille noon oþer be
He should neuer wer oþer garment
til Ihesu Cryste of mercy & pitee
here in this eorþe hathe ffor his soule sente.

Hr exhibits two substantive variants from HH:

484 *And petouse wepyng knelyng on his knee*.
486 Hr: ~~*Duryng Guyes lyf it wil noon oþer be.*~~

484 *maad he*. V: *he made*.
486 *in*. L, P: *with*.
full. P: *his*.
489 *but*. HH: omitted. L: *ful*.
490 *Sweem of ther speche*. HH, Hr: *þeyr hevynesse*.
Sweem. T: *S* is present, but the rest of the word is left blank. However, *Swem* is added in left margin.
491 *goth*. T: *went*.
took. Hr: *to*.
493 *man*. HH, Hr: *wyght*.
of hym havyng. T: *hauyng of hym*.
496 *for*$_2$. V: omitted.
hir$_2$. HH: *his*.
497 *writeth*. HH, Hr: *tellith*.
so. V: omitted.
498 *his*$_1$. Hr: omitted.
499 *Thre*. HH, Hr: *be thre*.
501 *in haste took*. HH, Hr: *made þan his*.
502 *Warwyk*. HH, Hr: *thens*.
503 *Of*. P: *By*.
505 *hym*. HH, Hr: *whome*.
506 *For*. HH, Hr, P: *As ffor*.
there. HH, Hr: *with hym*. P: *the*.
507 *same*. Hr: omitted.
a. Hr. omitted.
508 *the fyn*. HH: *& the ende*. Hr: *þe Ende*. P: *to the fyne*.
his. T: *thys*.
509 *whos day*. HH, Hr: *whome*.
day. T: *dethe*.
his. HH: *the*. Hr: *þer*.
successour. T: *socour*.
512 *Ay*. P: *Euer*.
513 *the*. P: *what*.
he. HH, Hr, L, P, T: *þat he*.
514 *moost*. HH, Hr: omitted.
515 *hys*. T: omitted.

517 *his*. HH: *whos*.
518 *Affter he sente in haste*. HH, Hr: *þan in alle hast he send*.
520 *come*. P: *to come*.
to been. HH, Hr, T: *& be*.
deyng. Hr: *[?e]onding*. The first letter is difficult to distinguish.
521 *And*. HH, Hr: omitted.
hir. HH, Hr: *ther hir*.
522 *By*. HH, Hr: *As by*.
a maner. P: *all maner of*. T: *maner of*.
wyfly. HH: *of wyffly*.
523 *ordeyne*. HH: *for to ordeyne*. Hr, T: *to ordeyne*. P: *tordeyn*.
524 *With no gret dyspence*. HH: *no gret reuerence*.
no$_2$. P: omitted.
525 *Gan haste hir faste tyl she kam in presence*. V: omits line.
Gan haste hir faste. HH, Hr: *she hastid hir*. P: *She hasted fast*. T: *And she gan hast fast*.
in. T: *to*.
526 *as he*. HH, Hr: *þat Guy*.
and. HH, Hr: omitted.
528 *swownyng*. T: *sowyng*.
swownyng she did. HH, Hr: *ffelyce did þer*.
529 *And as*. HH, Hr: omitted.
famous. HH, Hr: *& ffamous*.
worthy. L: *& worthi*. P: omitted.
530 *to seyne*. P: *word*.
eek. HH, Hr: omitted.
531 *that*. P: *that same*.
anoon. P: omitted.
532 *as*. HH, Hr, P: *þat*.
a. Hr: *in a*.
533 *And that she sholde*. HH, Hr: *And affter þis*.
534 *For*. HH, Hr: *þer ffor*.
hirsilf dyspoce. T: *her lyfe to dyspose*.
535 *The fifteenth day*. HH, Hr: *xv dayes*.
536 *To be buryed faste*. HH, Hr: *she to be buryed þer*.
his. HH, Hr: *Guyes*.
537 *this*. T: omitted.
thyng. HH, Hr: omitted.
heed. HH, Hr: *goode hede*.
538 *Guy*. HH, Hr: *he*.
lyst. HH, Hr: *& list*. P: *she list*.
539 *trouthe and*. HH, Hr: *wyffely*.
540 *She*. HH, Hr: *ffor she*.
ful. HH, Hr: omitted.
from. T: *of*.
541 *Sente*. P: *She sent*.
544 *Al*. HH, Hr: *Eche*.
thyng. L: *this*.
ye han herd. P: *she koud best*.
545 *And*. HH, Hr: *And alle*. P: *All*. T: *And in*.
this mater breefly. HH, Hr: *this coronycle ffor*.
546 *his*. HH: *whos*. Hr: *hos*.
old. HH: *bothe olde*.
547 *dyverse*. P: *grete*.
statys there. HH, Hr: *ffolke*.
549 *And lyk*. HH: *Eche a*. Hr: *lyche*.
551 *afforn of hih*. HH, Hr: *be marcyall*.
552 *the*. P: omitted.
to. T: *for to*.
553 *Whos*. P: *hos*.
I hope. HH, Hr: *I truste*. T: omitted.
555 *ay*. HH, Hr: omitted.
to. HH, Hr: *to hir*.
556 *The*. P: *That*.
approchyng. HH, Hr: *gan neyghe*.
557 *ordeyned in*. HH: *provyded of*. Hr: *provided in*.
hir. V: *ther*.
558 *Hir sone Reynborne be tytle of hir possede*. HH: *Reynebroune than Eyere ioustely to succede*. Hr: *Reynebroune than þeire ioustely to succede*.
possede. T: *to possede*.
559 *Heyr trewly born by lyneal dyscent*. HH, Hr: *be title of hir & lynyall discent*.
560 *In*. HH, Hr: omitted.
the. V: *ther*.
to succede. HH: *ioustely to possede*. Hr: *trewly to possede*. T: *to procede*.
561 *of antyquté*. HH, Hr: *downe be the pedugree*.

563 *deth*. V: *det*.
of. L, P, T: *bi*.
565 *Affter al this*. HH, Hr: *Claymyng his ryght*.
566 *unto*. P: *of*.
567 *the*. HH, Hr: *þat*.
568 *With a good ende*. HH, Hr: *whiche ended ffayr*.
was maad. HH: *& made was*.
569 *more auctorité as of*. HH, Hr: *ffor to auctoryse better*.
more. T: *none*.
of. T: *for*.
570 *is suych*. HH, Hr: *shewith þe*. V: *sewht in*. L, P: *seweth in*. T: *sheweth*.
571 *the*. HH, Hr, L: omitted. T: *a*.
the cronycleer. P: *cronicler*.
573 *Which wrot the dedis*. HH, Hr: *whiche whilome wrote*.
574 *Of them that wern*. HH, Hr: *dedes of hem*.
575 *for*. HH: *of*.
576 *his*. HH, Hr: *whos*.
578 *marcyal name*. HH, Hr: *knyghtly ffame*.
puttyng. HH, Hr: *to putten*.
581 *hard goyng*. HH, Hr: *hard lyggyng*. P: *his hard lyving*.
and. T: *in*.
582 *Brought onto me a chapitle to translate*. HH, Hr: *Alle sent to me in Englisshe to translate*.
me. T: *and*.
to. V: *for to*.
583 *metre*. P: *mater*.
in$_2$. HH, Hr, L: omitted.
584 *the*. HH, Hr: *alle the*.
for. HH: *of*.
dulness. P: *dowbilness*.
on. HH, P, V: *of*.
585 *Meekly compiled under correccyoun*. L: adds *Lenvoie* in left margin.
586 *Lyf*. P, T: *The lyf*.
585–92 *Meekly compiled under . . . . whan they reede*. This final stanza is shortened and recast as an Envoy in HH and Hr. The following text comes from Hr, as the final three words are unavailable in HH:

Lenvoye
Mekely translatid vnder correcciou[n]
Settyng a syde preyde and presompcioune
And praye echoon þ[at] shalle of hit take hede
ffavoure and supporte whan þei þe clause Rede

590 *Nor of*. T: *wherof*.
592 *the*. T: *these*.
whan they. T: *who ye*.
Explicit *Explicit*. L, V: *Explicit Guydo de Warwick*.

 APPENDIX: GVYDO DE WARWYKE[1]

Regnante in Anglia inclito rege Athelstano — anno dominiee incarnacionis, vero eiusdem regis regni tercio — in tantum Danorum crudelissime persecucionis inualuit rabies, quod terras conprouincialium tam crudeliter itinera legendo, depopulando inuasit, ut fere usque Wyntoniam non erat ciuitas, villa vel castrum, quod penitus non dirutum vel remaneret incombustum. Interea, acri ignessente furore, tanto elacionis stimulo insonuit barbarorum principum pompositas et ambicio, Anelaphi scilicet et Gonelaphi, quod regi Athelstano, tunc temporis cum suis prelatis et proceribus regni apud Wyntonyam ciuitatem super prouincie desolacione salubrius affectans festinati auxilii solamen, moram trahendi oportunam, nuncios dirigerent legacione sua triplici articulo roborata ita fungentes, scilicet aut rex Anglie regni sui diadema Danorum ducibus sine dilacione vna cum regno Anglie resignaret aut sub se regnaturus Athelstanus fidelitatem, homagium et tributum secundum voluntatem paganorum persolueret aut inter duos viros vtriusque partis ad inuicem valde pugnaces conserto prelio regis — regis videlicet vtriusque — et regni negocium expediretur, hoc superaddito ex parte Anelaphi, quod, si cedat victoria Athelstano, sine mora se cum suis compatriotis pro perpetuo regnum abiuratum, contrario permanente regni diadema abque contradiccionis innouacione sibi et suis, videlicet Dacis, concederetur.

Vltimo proposito rex Anglorum codescendens, apud Wyntoniam regni prelatos et ceteros magnates conuocat. Ipsis comparentibus sciscitatur ab eis, quis super se hoc prouincie lucrum, deuicto, barbarico gigante nomine Colbrando, adquireret premium pro reportato lucro recepturus. Set non inuento, dolore cordis Athelstanus concutitur pro maximo. Indicto igitur trium dierum ieiunio, cum precibus et lacrimis ad deum altissimum quam deuote profusis eius exorabant clemenciam, quatinus ipsis militem concedere dignaretur, qui pro illis iure et libertate regni inimicos inuictissime expugnaret. Timore enim nimio percutitur gens anglicana eo, quod non est, qui consoletur eam ex omnibus caris eius, Herando, milite inuictissimo, in transmarinis partibus agente perquirendo Reyburnum, filium Gwydonis, domini sui, comitis de Warwyk, qui furtim, cum adhuc infans esset, a mercatoribus ignote nacionis asportatus est; set et comes Rohandus, pater comitisse Gwydonis, vir inter mille bellicosus,

[1] Latin text edited by Schleich, "Lydgates Quelle," pp. 49–52.

GERALD OF CORNWALL'S *LIFE OF GUY OF WARWICK*[1]

When the famous king Athelstan reigned in England — in the [927th] year of Our Lord's incarnation, that is, the third year of his reign — the fury of the utterly cruel harrying of the Danes gained strength to such a pitch, since it so cruelly attacked the lands and the roads of the locals with pillaging and plundering, that almost right up to Winchester there was not a city, country house, or castle which was not thoroughly demolished or stood unburnt. In the meantime, with this fierce, burning frenzy, the pride and ambition of the barbarian princes Anelaph and Gonelaph resounded under such a goad of exaltation that they sent a delegation to King Athelstan, who was at that time with his prelates and nobles of the realm at the city of Winchester to seek speedy relief of the desolation of the province, delaying as necessary. The ambassadors delivered a message stiffened with a threefold ultimatum, namely, that either the king of England should transfer the crown of his kingdom to the leaders of the Danes without the least delay, along with the kingdom of England; or Athelstan should reign under them and render loyalty, homage, and tribute according to the will of the pagans; or a duel should be arranged between two mighty warriors, one from either side, in order to settle the business of the kingdom, that is, who would be king; and Anelaph added that, if the victory fell to Athelstan, he and his compatriots would quit the kingdom forever without delay; otherwise the crown of the kingdom would be granted in perpetuity to him and his, the Danes, without objection thereafter.

The king of the English agreed to the last proposal and summoned the prelates and other magnates of the kingdom to Winchester. When they were gathered, they were asked who of them would secure above and beyond his own interest, the good of the land by defeating a barbarian giant called Colbrand and receive a reward for restoring that wealth. But no one was found and Athelstan was struck to the heart with the utmost grief. So a three-day fast was proclaimed, and faithfully pouring forth prayers and tears to God Most High, they besought His mercy that He might deign to grant them a warrior, who for their sakes and the right and freedom of the kingdom might altogether invincibly drive out their enemies. For the English people were struck with terrible fear that there was no one who might relieve them of all their cares, since Herandus, a thoroughly invincible warrior, was busy in lands across the sea searching for Reyburn, the son of Guy, his lord, the count of Warwick, who while he was still an infant had been secretly carried off by merchants of an unknown nation; and Count Rohandus, the father of Guy's countess, a warrior amongst a thousand,

[1] Translation provided by Benjamin Garstad, Ph.D., Associate Professor of Classics, Department of Humanities, MacEwan University.

morte superueniente nature debitum soluit; Gwido vero in crastino sue desponsacionis, vir fortissimus ac in pugna robussimus, peregrini propositum suscepit et ignorabatur, quid de eo accideret.

Set altissimus, motus suorum fidelium lacrimis, nocte natiuitatis sancti Johannis baptiste, rege Athelstano apud castrum Wyntonie ante cubiculum prostrato, preces pro statu et patrie prosperitate deo recomendate et infra breue pre nimio vigiliarum tedio in soporem aliquantisper resoluto, misit dominus angelum suum, qui regem confortaret in agonia constitutum. Qui cum sic allocutus est: 'Athelstane rex, dormis an uigilas? Ecce, missus sum ad te angelus domini a domino Jesu Christo, ut dicerem tibi, ne timeres frustratus auxilio. Set cras mane surge et propera ad borialem portam ciuitatis et expecta ibi mendicancium pauperum aduentum, inter quos vnum peregrinum venientem reperies. Quem apprehensum reduc eum tecum et pugi onus super eum impone. Quod enim postulas, non negabit.' Hiis dictis angelus disparuit.

Rex, euigilans et deo pro sibi de supernis prestita reuelacione gracias agens, summo mane surgens, duos pontifices secum accipiens et duos comites, predictam adiit portam, expectans mendicancium aduentus horam, qua ciuitatem intrare solebant. Et ecce, nutu dei in vigilia natalis sancti Johannis baptiste, hora, qua sol oriendo primo radios mittit in terram, Gwydo, comes de Warwyk, miles strenuus et insignis, apud portysmowth Angliam, natale solum, reuisurus. Qui certificatus ab Angligenis de Herandi, militis nobilissimi, et filii sui, ut pretactum est, absencia et de morte comitis Rohandi, cuius filiam in coniugem acceperat, et de regis ac domini sui Athelstani et procerum regni angustia et mesticia, festinato cursu eadem die Wyntonie terminos petit. Perueniens nocte illa ad hospitale quoddam pauperum, quod tunc temporis ducentis quinquaginta passibus distabat versus borealem plagam a loco, in quo nunc nouum edificatum est monasterium, quod hospitale in honore sancte crucis erat fundatum, — ad quem locum ueniens, fatigatus ex itinere pernoctando, fatigata membra refocillando consolabatur.

Diem vero reportans, dum solis aureus reuoluitur axis, recto tramite ad sepe dictam ciuitatis cum suis sodalibus graditur portam, rege eius expectante aduentum, tamquam David, a patre luminum regi Sauli missus in golia philisteos deuicturus, et iste in Colbrando de Dacis triumphaturus. Quo viso, per peregrini habitum cognito, arripuit eum rex, introducens eum, et pre gaudio cum lacrimis Anglorum princeps imprecatur, vt sibi instante necessitate subueniat et cum inhumano illo Colbrando regni negocia pugnando pro victoria expedire. Qui, aliqualiter dissimulans, confitetur se etate debilem sudoreque peregrinacionis virtute vigoris soporata desiderare regis et procerum minime explere valentem.

Tandem, principum precibus et lacrimis victus, sperati auxilii promittit leuamen statutoque congressionis die — videlicet quarto idus iulii — conueniunt ambo, miles strenuus et inuisus ille Colobrandus, in loco quodam extra predictam portam, que modo anglice 'the hyde-mede' vocatur, qui vocabatur antiquitus et etiam a quibusdam adhuc appellatur 'Den-marche'. Qui dum mituos enses alter in alterum mitterent, prosiliebant ex ictibus ignes, ac si tonitrua coruscaciones procrearent, percussoque gigante super sinistrum

had died unexpectedly, paying his debt to nature; and indeed Guy, on the day after his marriage, a man superlatively brave and strong in battle, had taken up the pilgrim's vocation, not knowing what lay ahead.

But the Most High was moved by the prayers of his faithful, and on the eve of the nativity of St. John the Baptist, while King Athelstan was at the castle of Winchester, prostrate before his chamber, offering prayers to God for the safety of his homeland and then falling asleep for a time from sheer weariness at his vigil, the Lord sent His angel to encourage the king, who was fixed in agony. The angel spoke to him thus, "King Athelstan, do you sleep or keep vigil? Behold! I am an angel of the Lord sent to you by the Lord Jesus Christ that I might tell you not to be afraid or disappointed of hope. Rather, tomorrow morning get up and hurry to the north gate of the city and wait there for the arrival of some mendicant paupers, amongst whom you will find one who is a traveling pilgrim. Take him and bring him back with you and set the burden of the duel on him. For what you ask, he will not deny." With these words the angel disappeared.

The king, waking up and giving thanks to God for this revelation and taking two bishops and two counts with him, went to the gate mentioned earlier, awaiting the arrival of the beggars at the hour when they were accustomed to enter the city. And behold, by the will of God on the vigil of the birthday of St. John the Baptist, in the hour when the sun in its first rising sheds its rays on the earth, Guy, the Count of Warwick, a doughty and famous warrior, landed at Portsmouth, returning from his wanderings in distant parts across the sea once more to see England, his native land. He had been informed by his countrymen about the absence of Herandus, the most noble warrior, and of his own son, as was touched on previously, and about the death of Count Rohandus, whose daughter he had taken as wife, and about the predicament and sadness of his lord and king Athelstan and the nobles of the kingdom; and he set out by a speedy course for the bounds of Winchester on that very same day. He came that night to a certain hospice for beggars, which at that time stood against the north gate a hundred and fifty paces distant from the place in which a new monastery has now been built, founded as a hospice in honor of the Holy Cross. Coming to this place, and worn out by his journey through the night, he relieved his weary limbs by warming them.

While the golden axis of the sun was turned over, bringing back the day, he took the right way to the oft-mentioned gate of the city with his companions, where his king was awaiting his arrival. Just as David had been sent from the Father of lights by King Saul to defeat Goliath the Philistine, so Guy himself was intended to gain victory over Colbrand of the Danes. When he was seen and recognized by his pilgrim's garb, the king took hold of him and brought him inside, and with tears of joy the prince of the English besought him to undertake this pressing need and settle the business of the kingdom by fighting for victory with the beastly Colbrand. Guy demurred somewhat and insisted that, weak with age and the exertion of travel, he felt the want of his now-diminished strength and vigor and he would hardly discharge the office of king's and nobles' champion at all well.

At length, won over by the prayers and tears of these princes, he promised the assistance they wished for, and on the day decided for the duel, namely the fourth of the Ides of July [12 July], they both came together, the mighty warrior and the unbeaten Colbrand, in a certain place outside of the aforementioned gate, which is called in English the Hyde-Mede, a place which was anciently called and is also referred to by some up to the present as Denemarche. While they thrust their swords the one against the other in turn, and sparks leapt from their blows, as if those flashes might produce thunder, the giant was struck on the left

humerum erumpenteque sanguinis copia, ille, male meditacionis non ignarus, acri ignescens ira, in militem irruit confractoque militis mucrone ipsum reddit inermem: gaudium magnum Danis, timor nimius Anglis intonuit. Gwydo vero, dum aliquid genus armorum a Colbrando, cuius plurima erant, requireret, set voto suo non optento, dum diucius inter se sermocinarentur, ocius elabitur et celeriter de armis gigantis quandam sicam arripuit iterumque cum eo facta congressione cum proprio pagani instrumento sinistrum abscidit humerum. Quod prospiciens, inhumanus ille, nitens arripere gladium retro iacentem, post tergum cum manu dextera dum se inclinaret, Gwydo, leuata sica et fortiter ictum inferens, gigantem amputauit capud.

Quo facto, Danis repatriantibus nauibus inuectis, confusio nimia ipsis concipitur, dum ferox pugio trucidatur. Gwydo vero, sollempni processione a rege, clero et populo honorifice receptus, ad cathedralem ecclesiam Wyntonie deducitur, qui coram summo altari predictam sicam deo et ipsius ecclesie patrono optulit, quod instrumentum vsque hodie in vestiaro eiusdem ecclesie sub firma custodia reseruatur et vocatur Angligenis materna lingua 'Colbrondis axe' usque in presentem diem. Preterea depositis armis militaribus, peregrini habitu resumpto, Gwydoni insistit rex Athelstanus inquirendo, quid sit euis nomen et cuius condicionis vir esset. Ille uero regis peticioni minime fore satisfacturum respondit tali non obseruata condicione, quod extra ciuitatem, longe a Wyntonia, semotis regiis ministris, inter regem et comitem soliloquium admitteretur et nulli militis denudaretur consilium ex tune, quousque bini suum compleuerit cursum.

Promisso regio de hiis obseruandis sub iureiurando stabilito, procedunt ambo per viam, qua Gwydo ad ciuitatem tendebat, nemine subsequente, quousque, peruenientes ad quandam crucem, procul a ciuitate starent, vlterius non progredientes. Cum autem illie peruenissent, Gwydo, genua flectens humum: 'Domine', inquit, 'mi rex Athelstane, vester seruus in omnibus sum, fui et ero. Comes de Warewyk, Gwydo, nomen mihi imposuerunt me de salutiferi fontis suscipientes lauacro.' Quo audito rex ruit in eius amplexus gratanter eum osculando, multa sibi promittens donaria, si in eius conuersari vellet palacio. Qui, omnia relinquens et principi benignissimo suum recomendans secretum, dicit se habitem, quo tune iudutus erat, vit comite nunquam depositurum. Qui sibi inuicem cum lacrimis valefacientes, rex ad sua, Gwydo vero uersus Warewyk calles aggreditur.

Cum autem villam suam peruenisset, ignotus omnibus, tribus diebus vnus de tresdecim pauperibus, quos comitissa sua cotidie pro amborum corporis incolumitate animeque salute, ab vxore propria ignotus — scilicet resedendo — est depastus; post prandium sue perendinacionis graciarum acciones dilecte comitisse tamen vicem pro vice rependens, desertum peciit, longo itineris spacio pertransito inter opaca siluarum cuisdam heremite colloquio refoueri postulat solo.

Set, quo paulo ante mortis nexibus depresso, eius successorem Gwydo se ipsum constituit in multiplicium virtutem virens floribus. Duobus igitur inibi feliciter viuens annis, obitum suum biduo ante reuelacione presciens angelica, misit vnicum sibi seruientem ad vxorem suam cum anulo matrimonialis federis, sibi illud resignans, exortans eam, vt festinando se preparet ad eius perficere sepulturam, quem, cum venerit,

shoulder and a quantity of blood gushed forth, and he, not unacquainted with evil thinking, and burning with fierce anger, rushed against the warrrior, breaking the point of Guy's sword and rendering him weaponless. A great joy resounded amongst the Danes, and a greater fear amongst the English. When Guy asked for some kind of weapon from Colbrand, who had many, his plea was not granted, but when they had been conversing with each other for some time, Guy very quietly slipped away and quickly snatched a dagger from among the giant's weapons. When the duel resumed, Guy cut off the pagan's left arm at the shoulder with his own weapon. When that savage man saw this, he strove to seize the sword lying behind him, and while he bent backwards with his right hand, Guy raised the dagger and delivered a mighty blow that cut off the giant's head.

As soon as this happened, the Danes leapt aboard their homeward bound vessels. A great confusion had arisen amongst them while the fierce dagger worked its slaughter. Then Guy was received in solemn procession by the king, clergy, and people and led forth to the cathedral church of Winchester, where before the high altar he presented the aforementioned dagger to God and the patron of this same church, and this weapon is preserved under close guard up to the present day in the vestry of the same church and is called in the mother tongue of the English people "Colbrand's axe" to this very day. Meanwhile, once Guy had set aside his warlike weapons and resumed the garb of a pilgrim, King Athelstan pressed him, asking his name and of what position he might be. But he replied to the questioning of the king that he would very shortly give an answer, though not in such an open and public situation, but rather beyond the city, far from Winchester, distant from the royal ministers, where a private conversation between king and count would be possible. Guy would reveal his counsel to no one but the king when the two of them had finished their walk.

The royal promise to observe these conditions was granted and confirmed under oath, and they both went along the road by which Guy came to the city, and, arriving at a certain cross, they stood at a distance from the city and did not proceed any farther. When they arrived there, Guy knelt on the ground and said, "My lord king Athelstan, I am your servant in all things, have been and will be. The Count of Warwick, Guy, is the name they set upon me when they took me up from the cleansing water of the saving font." When he heard this, the king joyfully ran into his embrace, kissing him and promising him many gifts if he wished to return to the palace. But he, refusing all of them and commending his secret to the most kindly prince, said that he would never exchange his pilgrim's garment for that of a count. They bid each other farewell with tears, and the king went home and Guy went along the road to Warwick.

When, however, he arrived at his own manor he was not recognized by anyone, and for three days he ate as one of the thirteen paupers whom his countess [tended to] for the safety of their bodies and the salvation of their souls. He was unknown to his own wife, no doubt by keeping back; and, after dinner on the third day, he took his turn to give thanks to his beloved countess and sought a desert place, and after traveling a lengthy space of road amidst the shade of the woods he sought no more refreshment than the conversation of a certain hermit.

But, a little while before the hermit was weighed down with the bonds of death, he named Guy, fresh with the flowers of manifold virtues, as his successor. After Guy had been happily living there for two years, he foresaw his own death two days beforehand in an angelic vision; and he sent one of his attendants to his wife with his wedding ring, returning it to her and prevailing upon her to hurry and get ready to carry out his burial, since she would find him

ante altare in capella inueniet recubantem, debita in morte resolutum, additoque, quod peracto quindecim dierum curriculo post eius mortem nature debitum et ipsa erat persoluenda.

Hiis impletis, veniente vxore Gwydonis cum euisdem diocesis ordinario, cum clero et populo ad heremitagium viri sui, Gwydonis, et inuento corpore eius, sicut nunciatum fuerat, miro fragrante suauitatis odore et iacente totum in terra prostrato, eleuatum de terra principis more in eodem habitaculo, ut decuit, honorifice reconditum est. Circa cuius sepulcrum et ipsa, transactis XV diebus, vinculis carnis absoluta decentissime humata est, hereditatem paternam filio suo Reyburno relinquens, ut ipse memoriale parentum in pectoris sui armariolo quem tenerrime sigillando inprimeret, inde pro meritis celestia regna mercaturus.

Jstud extractum est ex scriptis Girardi Cornubiensis in libro de gestis regum Westsaxonum in capitulo XI et eciam habetur Wynton in tabula pendente iuxta maius altare ecclesie cathedralis sancti Stephani.

Explicit Gwydo de Warwyk et vxor eius Felicia.

lying before the altar in the chapel, having paid his debt in death, adding that fifteen days after Guy's death, she herself would pay her debt to nature.

When these things had been done, Guy's wife went with the ordinary of that diocese, with the clergy and the people, to the hermitage of her husband Guy, and when his body was found, just as it had been announced, it was fragrant with a marvelous smell of sweetness and lying stretched out full length on the ground. It was lifted up from the earth and in the manner of a prince was honorably buried in the same dwelling place, as was seemly. At this tomb she also, after fifteen days had passed, broke the chains of the body and was very properly interred, leaving her father's inheritance to her son Reyburn, that she might impress a memorial to his parents upon his breast with the most tender sealing, and so purchase heavenly kingdoms with her merits.

This extract is from the writings of Gerard of Cornwall, in the book about the deeds of the kings of Wessex, in the eleventh chapter, and it is also preserved on a tablet hanging by the high altar of the cathedral church of St. Stephan.

Thus ends "Guy of Warwick and his wife Felicia."

BIBLIOGRAPHY

Aertsen, Henk, and Alasdair A. MacDonald, eds. *Companion to Middle English Romance*. Amsterdam: VU University Press, 1990.

Ailes, Marianne. "*Gui de Warewic* in its Manuscript Context." In Wiggins and Field, *Guy of Warwick: Icon and Ancestor*. Pp. 12–43.

Alain De Lille. *De Planctu Naturae*. Trans. James J. Sheridan. Toronto: Pontifical Institute of Medieval Studies, 1980.

Alfonsi, Petrus. *The Disciplina Clericalis*. Ed. Eberhard Hermes. Trans. P. R. Quarrie. London: Routledge and Kegan Paul, 1977.

Andreas Capellanus. *The Art of Courtly Love*. Trans. J. J. Parry. New York: Columbia University Press, 1970.

Athelston. In *Four Romances of England*. Ed. Ronald B. Herzman, Graham Drake, and Eve Salisbury. Kalamazoo, MI: Medieval Institute Publications, 1999. Pp. 349–71.

Auerbach, Erich. *Mimesis: The Representation of Reality in Western Literature*. Trans. Willard R. Trask. Princeton, NJ: Princeton University Press, 1953.

Ayers, Robert. "Medieval History, Moral Purpose, and the Structure of Lydgate's Siege of Thebes." *PMLA* 73 (1958), 463–74.

The Babees Book: Aristotle's A B C, Urbanitatis, Stans Puer Ad Mensam, The Lytille Childrenes Lytil Boke, Etc. Ed. Frederick J. Furnivall. EETS o.s. 32. London: Trübner, 1868. Rpt. New York: Greenwood Press, 1969.

Bale, Anthony. "House Devil, Town Saint: Anti-Semitism and Hagiography in Medieval Suffolk." In *Chaucer and the Jews: Sources, Contexts, Meanings*. Ed. Sheila Delany. New York: Routledge, 2002. Pp. 185–210.

———. *The Jew in the Medieval Book: English Antisemitisms 1350–1500*. Cambridge: Cambridge University Press, 2006.

———. "A Norfolk Gentlewoman and Lydgatian Patronage: Lady Sibylle Boys and her Cultural Environment." *Medium Aevum* 78.2 (2009): 261–80.

Bale, Anthony, and A. S. G. Edwards. *John Lydgate's Lives of SS Edmund & Fremund and the Extra Miracles of St. Edmund. Edited from British Library MS Harley 2278 and Bodleian Library MS Ashmole 46*. Middle English Texts 41. Heidelberg: Universitätsverlag, 2009.

Banks, Mary Macleod, ed. *An English 15th Century Translation of the Alphabetum Narrationum of Etienne de Besancon*. EETS o.s. 126–127. London: Kegan Paul, Trench, Trübner, 1904–1905.

Barber, Richard, ed. *The Pastons: A Family in the Wars of the Roses*. Woodbridge: Boydell Press, 1993.

Barbour, John. *The Bruce*. Edinburgh: Canongate Books Limited, 1997.

Benson, Larry D., ed. *The Riverside Chaucer*. Third edition. Boston: Houghton Mifflin, 1987.

Bevis of Hampton. In *Four Romances of England*. Ed. Ronald B. Herzman, Graham Drake, and Eve Salisbury. Kalamazoo, MI: Medieval Institute Publications, 1999. Pp. 200–321.

Black, Anthony. "The Individual and Society." In *Cambridge History of Medieval Political Thought c. 350–1450*. Ed. J. H. Burns. Cambridge: Cambridge University Press, 1988. Pp. 588–606.

Blair, Peter Hunter. *Anglo-Saxon England*. London: Folio Society, 1997.

———. *Introduction to Anglo-Saxon England*. Third edition. Cambridge: Cambridge University Press, 2003. Rpt. Cambridge: Cambridge University Press, 2006.

Blamires, Alcuin, Karen Pratt, and C. W. Marx, eds., *Woman Defamed and Woman Defended: An Anthology of Medieval Texts*. Oxford: Clarendon Press, 1992.

Boethius. *Boethius: De Consolatione Philosophiae*. Ed. Mark Science. Trans. John Walton. EETS o.s. 170. London: Oxford University Press, 1927.

———. *Theological Tractates and The Consolation of Philosophy*. Trans. H. F. Stewart, E. K. Rand, and S. J. Tester. Loeb Classical Library 74. Cambridge, MA: Harvard University Press, 1973.

———. *The Consolation of Philosophy*. Ed. and trans. P. G. Walsh. Oxford: Oxford University Press, 1999.

Boffey, Julia. "Short Texts in Manuscript Anthologies: Minor Poems of John Lydgate in Two Fifteenth-Century Collections." In *The Whole Book: Cultural Perspectives on the Medieval Miscellany*. Ann Arbor: University of Michigan Press, 1996. Pp. 69–82.

Boffey, Julia, and John J. Thompson. "Anthologies and Miscellanies: Production and Choice of Texts." In *Book Production and Publishing in Britain 1375–1475*. Ed. Jeremy Griffiths and Derek Pearsall. Cambridge: Cambridge University Press, 1989. Pp. 279–315.

Bradbury, Nancy Mason. *Writing Aloud: Storytelling in Late Medieval England*. Urbana, IL: University of Illinois Press, 1998.

Breeze, Andrew. "Sir John Paston, Lydgate, and the *Libelle of Englyshe Polycye*." *Notes and Queries* 48 (September 2001), 230–31.

Brewer, Charlotte, and Barry Windeatt, eds. *Traditions and Innovations in the Study of Medieval English Literature: The Influence of Derek Brewer*. Cambridge: D. S. Brewer, 2013.

Brewer, Derek. *English Gothic Literature*. London and Basingstoke: The Macmillan Press Ltd., 1983.

———. *Studies in Medieval English Romance: Some New Approaches*. Cambridge: D. S. Brewer, 1988.

The British Library. *Catalogue of Illuminated Manuscripts*. Web. Accessed 8 November 2015. Online at http://www.bl.uk/catalogues/illuminatedmanuscripts/welcome.htm.

Burnley, J. D. *Chaucer's Language and the Philosophers' Tradition*. Cambridge: D. S. Brewer, 1979.

Calin, William. *The French Tradition and the Literature of Medieval England*. Toronto: University of Toronto Press, 1994.

Castor, Helen. *Blood and Roses: The Paston Family in the Fifteenth Century*. London: Faber and Faber, 2004.

Catalogue of the Harleian Manuscripts in the British Museum: With Indexes of Persons, Places, and Matters. Vol. 2. London: HMSO, 1808. Rpt. Hildesheim and New York: Georg Olms, 1973.

Chaucer, Geoffrey. *Works*. See Benson.

Childress, Diana T. "Between Romance and Legend: 'Secular Hagiography' in Middle English Literature." *Philological Quarterly* 57.3 (Summer 1978), 311–22.

Ciavolella, Massimo. "Medieval Medicine." *Florilegium* 1 (1979), 222–41.

Cicero. *Cicero: De Senectute, De Amicitia, De Divinatione*. Trans. William Armistead Falconer. Cambridge, MA: Harvard University Press, 1923.

Cohen, Jeffrey Jerome. *Of Giants: Sex, Monsters, and the Middle Ages*. Medieval Cultures 17. Minneapolis, MN: University of Minnesota Press, 1999.

Conlon, D. J., ed. *Le Rommant de Guy de Warwik et de Herolt D'Ardenne*. Chapel Hill, NC: University of North Carolina Press, 1971.

Connolly, Margaret. *John Shirley: Book Production and the Noble Household in Fifteenth Century England*. Aldershot: Ashgate, 1998.

Cooper, Helen. *The English Romance in Time: Transforming Motifs from Geoffrey of Monmouth to the Death of Shakespeare*. Oxford: Oxford University Press, 2004.

Cooper, Lisa H. "'His guttys wer out shake': Illness and Indigence in Lydgate's *Letter to Gloucester* and *Fabula duorum mercatorum*." *Studies in the Age of Chaucer* 30 (2008), 303–34.

Cooper, Lisa H., and Andrea Denny-Brown. *Lydgate Matters: Poetry and Material Culture in the Fifteenth Century*. New York: Palgrave Macmillan, 2008.

Coss, Peter. *The Origins of the English Gentry*. Cambridge: Cambridge University Press, 2003.

Crane, Ronald S. "The Vogue of *Guy of Warwick* from the Close of the Middle Ages to the Romantic Revival." *PMLA* 30 (1950), 125–94.

Crane, Susan. *Insular Romance: Politics, Faith, and Culture in Anglo-Norman and Middle English Literature*. Berkeley, CA: University of California Press, 1986.

Cropp, Glynnis M. "*Le Livre de Boece de Consolacion*: From Translation to Glossed Text." In *The Medieval Boethius: Studies in the Vernacular Translations of* De Consolatione Philosophiae. Ed. A. J. Minnis. Cambridge: D. S. Brewer, 1987. Pp. 63–88.

Curry, Walter Clyde. *Chaucer and the Mediaeval Sciences*. Oxford: Oxford University Press, 1926.

Curtius, Ernst Robert. *European Literature and the Latin Middle Ages*. Trans. Willard R. Trask. Bollingen Series 36. Princeton, NJ: Princeton University Press, 1983.

Dahlberg, Charles, ed. and trans. *The Romance of the Rose*. Third edition. Princeton: Princeton University Press, 1995.

Dalrymple, Roger. *Language and Piety in Middle English Romance*. Cambridge: D. S. Brewer, 2000.

Dannenbaum, Susan Crane. "Anglo-Norman Romances of English Heroes: 'Ancestral Romance'?" *Romance Philology* 35 (1982), 601–08.

———. "Guy of Warwick and the Question of Exemplary Romance." *Genre* 17.4 (Winter 1984), 351–74.

Dante Alighieri. *La Divina Commedia*. Ed. C. H. Grandgent. Boston: D.C. Heath Co., 1909–14. Revised by Charles S. Singleton. Cambridge, MA: Harvard University Press, 1972.

Davis, Norman, Richard Beadle, and Colin Richmond, eds. *Paston Letters and Papers of the Fifteenth Century*. 3 vols. EETS s.s. 20–23. Oxford: Clarendon Press, 1971–76. Rpt. Oxford: Oxford University Press, 2004–05.

Demaitre, Luke. "Bernard de Gordon." In *Medieval Science, Technology, and Medicine*. Ed. Thomas Glick, Steven J. Livesey, and Faith Wallis. New York: Routledge, 2005. Pp. 84–85.

Doubleday, H. Arthur, and William Page, eds. "The New Minster, or the Abbey of Hyde." *A History of the County of Hampshire*. Vol. 2 (1973), 116–22. *British History Online*. Accessed 15 November 2014. Online at http://www.british-history.ac.uk/vch/hants/vol2/pp116-122.

Driver, Martha. "'In her owne persone semly and bewteus': Representing Women in Stories of *Guy of Warwick*." In Wiggins and Field, *Guy of Warwick: Icon and Ancestor*. Pp. 133–53.

Dumville, David. "What is a Chronicle?" In *The Medieval Chronicle II: Proceedings of the 2nd International Conference on the Medieval Chronicle Driebergen/Utrecht 16–21 July 1999*. Ed. Erik Kooper. Amsterdam: Rodopi, 2002. Pp. 1–27.

Dupin, Henri. *La courtoisie au moyen age*. Paris: Editions A. Picard, 1906.

Dwyer, Richard. "Arthur's Stellification in the *Fall of Princes*." *Philological Quarterly* 57 (1978), 155–71.

Ebin, Lois. *John Lydgate*. Boston: Twayne, 1985.

———. *Illuminator, Vates, Makar: Visions of Poetry in the Fifteenth Century*. Lincoln: University of Nebraska Press, 1988.

Economou, George. *The Goddess Natura in Medieval Literature*. Notre Dame, IN: University of Notre Dame Press, 2002.

Edwards, A. S. G. "John Lydgate, Medieval Antifeminism, and Harley 2251." *Annuale Medievale* 13 (1972), 32–44.

———. "The McGill Fragment of Lydgate's *Fall of Princes*." *Scriptorium* 28 (1974), 75–77.

———. "Fifteenth-Century Middle English Verse Author Collections." In *The English Medieval Book: Studies in Memory of Jeremy Griffiths*. Ed. A. S. G. Edwards, Vincent Gillespie, and Ralph Hanna. London: British Library, 2000. Pp. 101–12.

———. "The *Speculum Guy de Warwick* and Lydgate's *Guy of Warwick*: The Non-Romance Middle English Tradition." In Wiggins and Field, *Guy of Warwick: Icon and Ancestor*. Pp. 81–93.

Edwards, A. S. G., Vincent Gillespie, and Ralph Hanna, eds. *The English Medieval Book: Studies in Memory of Jeremy Griffiths*. London: British Library, 2000.

Edwards, Edward, ed. *Liber Monasterii de Hyda*. Rerum Britannicarum medii aevi scriptores (Rolls Series) 45. London: Longman & Co., 1866.

Everett, Dorothy. "A Characterization of the English Medieval Romances." In *Essays on Middle English Literature*. Ed. Patricia Kean. Oxford: Oxford University Press, 1955. Pp. 1–23.

Farnham, Willard. *The Medieval Heritage of English Tragedy*. Oxford: Blackwell, 1963.

Farvolden, Pamela. "'Love Can No Frenship': Erotic Triangles in Chaucer's "Knight's Tale" and Lydgate's *Fabula duorum mercatorum*." In *Sovereign Lady: Essays on Women in Middle English Literature*. Ed. Muriel A. Whitaker. New York: Garland, 1995. Pp. 21–44.

Ferguson, George. *Signs and Symbols in Christian Art*. Oxford: Oxford University Press, 1954.
Fewster, Carol. *Traditionality and Genre in Middle English Romance*. Cambridge: D. S. Brewer, 1987.
Field, Rosalind. "Romance as History, History as Romance." In *Romance in Medieval England*. Ed. Maldwyn Mills, Jennifer Fellows, and Carol M. Meale. Cambridge: D. S. Brewer, 1991. Pp. 163–73.
Finlayson, John. "Definitions of the Middle English Romance." *Chaucer Review* 15.1 (1980), 44–62.
Foot, Sarah. "Æthelstan (893/4–939)." *Oxford Dictionary of National Biography*. Oxford University Press, 2004. Accessed 15 May 2014. Online at http://www.oxforddnb.com/view/article/833?doc Pos=2.
———. *Æthelstan: The First King of England*. New Haven, CT: Yale University Press, 2011.
Frakes, Jerold. *The Fate of Fortune in the Early Middle Ages: The Boethian Tradition*. Leiden: E. G. Brill, 1988.
Frankis, John. "Taste and Patronage in Late Medieval England as Reflected in Versions of *Guy of Warwick*." *Medium Aevum* 66 (1997), 80–93.
Galloway, Andrew. "Writing History in England." In Wallace, *Cambridge History*. Pp. 255–83.
Given-Wilson, Chris. *Chronicles: The Writing of History in Medieval England*. London: Hambledon and London, 2004.
Gower, John. *Mirour de l'Omme: The Mirror of Mankind*. Trans. William B. Wilson and revised by Nancy Wilson Van Baak. Medieval Texts and Studies 5. East Lansing, MI: Colleagues Press, 1992.
———. *Confessio Amantis*. Vol. 1. Second edition. Ed. Russell A. Peck. Kalamazoo, MI: Medieval Institute Publications, 2006.
Grabes, Herbert. *The Mutable Glass: Mirror-Imagery in Titles and Texts of the Middle Ages and the English Renaissance*. Cambridge: Cambridge University Press, 1982.
Gransden, Antonia. "Antiquarian Studies in Fifteenth-Century England." In *Legends, Traditions, and History in Medieval England*. Pp. 299–327. Originally published in *Antiquaries Journal* 60 (1980), 75–97.
———. *Historical Writing in England c. 1307 to the Early Sixteenth Century*. Vol. 2. London: Routledge & Kegan Paul, 1982.
———. "The Chronicles of Medieval England and Scotland." *Journal of Medieval History* 16 (1990), 127–50; 17 (1991), 217–43. Rpt. In *Legends, Tradition, and History in Medieval England*. Pp. 199–238.
———. *Legends, Traditions, and History in Medieval England*. London and Rio Grande, Ohio: Hambledon Press, 1992.
Gray, Douglas. "Hoccleve and Lydgate." In *Later Medieval English Literature*. Ed. Douglas Gray. Oxford: Oxford University Press, 2008. Pp. 307–25.
Green, Richard Firth. *Poets and Princepleasers: Literature and the English Court in the Late Middle Ages*. Toronto: University of Toronto Press, 1980.
Griffith, David. "The Visual History of Guy of Warwick." In Wiggins and Field, *Guy of Warwick: Icon and Ancestor*. Pp. 110–32.
Griffiths, Ralph A. *The Reign of King Henry VI: The Exercise of Royal Authority, 1422–1461*. Berkeley, CA: University of California Press, 1981.
Grossi, Joseph. "'Where Ioye is ay Lasting': John Lydgate's *Contemptus Mundi* in British Library MS Harley 2255." *Leeds Studies in English* 36 (2005), 303–34.
———. "Cloistered Lydgate, Commercial Scribe: British Library Harley 2255 Revisited." *Mediaeval Studies* 72 (2010), 313–61.
Guillaume de Lorris and Jean de Meun. *The Romance of the Rose*. See Dahlberg.
Hammond, Eleanor P. "On Two British Museum Manuscripts. (Harley 2251 and Adds. 34360): A Contribution to the Bibliography of John Lydgate." *Anglia* 28 (1905), 1–28.
———. *Chaucer: A Bibliographical Manual*. Clinton, MA: Macmillan Company, 1908.
———. "Boethius: Chaucer: Walton: Lydgate." *Modern Language Notes* 41 (1926), 534–35.
———. "A Scribe of Chaucer." *Modern Philology* 27 (1929), 27–33.
———. *English Verse between Chaucer and Surrey*. Durham, NC: Duke University Press, 1927. Rpt. New York: Octagon Books, 1969.

Hardman, Phillipa. "Lydgate's Uneasy Syntax." In Scanlon and Simpson, *John Lydgate*. Pp. 12–35.

Harriss, Gerald. *Shaping the Nation: England 1360–1461*. Oxford: Clarendon Press, 2005.

Havelock the Dane. In *Four Romances of England*. Ed. Ronald B. Herzman, Graham Drake, and Eve Salisbury. Kalamazoo, MI: Medieval Institute Publications, 1999. Pp. 85–159.

Hearne, Thomas. "Gerardi Cornubiensis Historia Guidonis de Warwyke. E Cod. MS. vet. In Bibl. Boll. Magd. Oxon. N. 147 fol. 227.a." In *Chronicon sive Annales Prioratus de Dunstaple*. Ed. Richard de Morins. Vol. 2. Oxford: Sheldonian Theatre, 1733. Pp. 825–30. Accessed 19 August 2012. Online at http://find.galegroup.com/ecco/.

Herrtage, Sidney, ed. *The Early English Versions of the Gesta Romanorum*. EETS o.s. 33. London: N. Trübner & Co., 1879.

Herzmann, Ronald B., Graham Drake, and Eve Salisbury, eds. *Four Romances of England*. Kalamazoo, MI: Medieval Institute Publications, 1999.

Hicks, Michael A. "The Beauchamp Trust, 1439–87." *Bulletin of the Institute of Historical Research* 54 (1981), 135–49.

———. *English Political Culture in the Fifteenth Century*. London: Routledge, 2002.

The History and Antiquities of Winchester. 2 vols. Winton: J. Wilkes, 1773.

Homer. *Iliad*. Trans. Richmond Lattimore. Chicago: University of Chicago Press, 1951.

Hopkins, Andrea. *The Sinful Knights: A Study of Middle English Penitential Romance*. Oxford and New York: Oxford University Press, Clarendon Press, 1990.

Horobin, Simon. "The Edmund-Fremund Scribe Copying Chaucer." *Journal of the Early Book Society* 12 (2009), 195–205.

Hyatte, Reginald. *The Arts of Friendship: The Idealization of Friendship in Medieval and Early Renaissance Literature*. Leiden: E. J. Brill, 1994.

Jackson, Peter. "*In translacione sancti Edwardi confessoris*: The Lost Sermon by Aelred of Rievaulx Found?" *Cistercian Studies Quarterly* 40.1 (2005), 45–83.

Jaeger, C. Stephen. *Ennobling Love: In Search of a Lost Sensibility*. Philadelphia, PA: University of Pennsylvania Press, 1999.

James, M. R. *On the Abbey of St. Edmund at Bury: I. The Library. II. The Church*. Cambridge: Cambridge Antiquarian Society, 1895.

Jenkins, Simon. *England's Thousand Best Churches*. London: Penguin Books, 1999.

Johnston, Michael. *Romance and the Gentry in Late Medieval England*. Oxford: Oxford University Press, 2014.

Jones, Joseph Ramon, and John Esten Keller. *The Scholar's Guide: A Translation of the Twelfth-Century Disciplina Clericalis of Pedro Alfonso*. Toronto: The Pontifical Institute for Mediaeval Studies, 1969.

Keen, Maurice. *Chivalry*. New Haven: Yale University Press, 1984.

———. *Origins of the English Gentleman: Heraldry, Chivalry, and Gentility in Medieval England c.1300–c.1500*. Stroud and Charleston: Tempus, 2002.

———. *England in the Later Middle Ages: A Political History*. Second edition. London: Routledge, 2003.

Ker, N. R. *Medieval Manuscripts in British Libraries*. Oxford: Clarendon Press, 1969.

King Horn. In *Four Romances of England*. Ed. Ronald B. Herzman, Graham Drake, and Eve Salisbury. Kalamazoo, MI: Medieval Institute Publications, 1999. Pp. 17–56.

Krueger, Roberta, ed. *The Cambridge Companion to Medieval Romance*. Cambridge and New York: Cambridge University Press, 2000.

Langer, Ullrich. *Perfect Friendship: Studies in Literature and Moral Philosophy from Boccaccio to Corneille*. Histoire des Idées et Critique Littéraire 331. Geneva: Libraire Droz, 1994.

Lawton, David. "Dullness in the Fifteenth Century." *English Literary History* 54 (Winter 1987), 761–99.

Leach, MacEdward, ed. *Amis and Amiloun*. EETS o.s. 203. 1937. Rpt. London: Oxford University Press, 1960.

Lee, A. C. *The Decameron: Its Sources and Analogues*. London: Nutt, 1909.

Legge, M. Dominica. *Anglo-Norman Literature and its Background*. Oxford: Clarendon Press, 1963.

Lenaghan, R. T., ed. *Caxton's Aesop*. Cambridge, MA: Harvard University Press, 1967.

Lerer, Seth. *Chaucer and His Readers. Imagining the Author in Late-Medieval England*. Princeton, NJ: Princeton University Press, 1993.

Lester, G. A. "The Books of a Fifteenth Century English Gentleman, Sir John Paston." *Neuphilologische Mitteilungen* 88 (1987), 200–17.

Literature Online, ProQuest. 1996–2015. Accessed 15 March 2015. Online at http://literature.proquest.com/.

Liu, Yin. "Richard Beauchamp and the Uses of Romance." *Medium Aevum* 74 (2005), 271–87.

———. "Middle English Romance as Prototype Genre." *Chaucer Review* 40.4 (2006), 335–53.

Lochman, Daniel T., Maritere Lopez, and Lorna Hutson, eds. *Discourses and Representations of Friendship in Early Modern Europe 1500–1700*. Burlington, VT: Ashgate Publishing Company, 2011.

Loomis, Laura Hibbard. *Mediæval Romance in England: A Study of the Sources and Analogues of the Non-Cyclic Metrical Romances*. New York: Bert Franklin, 1969.

Lowes, John Livingston. "The Loveres Maladye of Hereos." *Modern Philology* 11 (1914), 491–546.

Lydgate, John. *Lydgate's Temple of Glas*. See Schick, Josef.

———. *Fabula Duorum Mercatorum*. See Schleich and Zupitza.

———. *Lydgate's Fall of Princes*. Ed. Henry Bergen. EETS e.s. 121–24. Washington, DC: Carnegie Institute of Washington, 1924. Rpt. Oxford: Oxford University Press, 1927.

———. *Lydgate's Troy Book*. Ed. Henry Bergen. 4 vols. EETS e.s. 97, 103, 106, and 126. London: Kegan Paul, Trench, Trübner & Co., 1906, 1908 and Oxford University Press, 1935.

———. *Lydgate's Reson and Sensuallyte*. Ed. Ernst Sieper. 2 vols. EETS e.s. 84, 89. London: Oxford University Press, 1901, 1903. Rpt. 1965.

———. *The Siege of Thebes*. Ed. Robert R. Edwards. Kalamazoo, MI: Medieval Institute Publications, 2001.

———. *The Temple of Glas*. Ed. J. Allan Mitchell. Kalamazoo, MI: Medieval Institute Publications, 2007.

———. *Pageant of Knowledge*. In *Mummings and Entertainments*. Ed. Claire Sponsler. Kalamazoo, MI: Medieval Institute Publications, 2010.

Macaulay, G. C., ed. *Mirour de L'Omme*. In *The Complete Works of John Gower*. Vol. 1: *The French Works*. Oxford: Clarendon Press, 1899. Pp. 1–334.

MacCracken, Henry N., ed. *The Minor Poems of John Lydgate*. 2 vols. EETS o.s. 107, 192. Bungay: Richard Clay & Sons, 1911. Rpt. London: Oxford University Press, 1962. Vol. 2. London: Humphrey Milford for Oxford University Press, 1934.

Machan, Tim W. "Glosses in the Manuscripts of Chaucer's *Boece*." *The Medieval Boethius: Studies in the Vernacular Translations of* De Consolatione Philosophiae. Ed. A. J. Minnis. Cambridge: D. S. Brewer, 1987. Pp. 125–38.

Madan, Falconer. *Catalogue of Additions to the Manuscripts in the British Museum*. London: British Museum, 1894.

———. *A Summary Catalogue of Western Manuscripts in the Bodleian Library at Oxford*. Vol. 3. Oxford: Clarendon Press, 1895.

Mandeville, John. *Mandeville's Travels*. Ed. Paul Hamelius. EETS o.s. 153, 154. London: Kegan Paul, Trench, Trübner & Co., 1919, 1923.

Manly, John M., and Edith Rickert. *The Text of the Canterbury Tales: Studied on the Basis of All Known Manuscripts*. 8 vols. Chicago: University of Chicago Press, 1940.

Mann, Jill. *Geoffrey Chaucer*. Atlantic Highlands, NJ: Humanities Press International, 1991.

Mannyng of Brunne, Robert. *The Chronicle*. Ed. Idelle Sullens. Medieval and Renaissance Texts and Studies 153. Binghamton, NY: Binghamton University, 1996.

Mason, Emma. "Legends of the Beauchamps' Ancestors: The Use of Baronial Propaganda in Medieval England." *Journal of Medieval History* 10 (1984), 25–40.

———. "Mauduit, William, Eighth Earl of Warwick (1221x3–1268)." *Oxford Dictionary of National Biography*. Oxford University Press, 2004. Accessed 15 May 2014. Online at http://www.oxforddnb.com/ view/article/ 18361?docPos=4.

Mathew, Gervase. "Ideals of Friendship." In *Patterns of Love and Courtesy: Essays in Memory of C.S. Lewis*. Ed. John Lawlor. London: Edward Arnold, 1966. Pp. 45–53.

McDonald, Nicola, ed. *Pulp Fictions of Medieval England: Essays in Popular Romance*. Manchester: Manchester University Press, 2004.

McIntosh, Angus, M. L. Samuels, and Michael Benskin, et al. *A Linguistic Atlas of Late Mediaeval English*. 4 vols. Aberdeen: Aberdeen University Press, 1986.

Meale, Carol, ed. *Readings in Medieval English Romance*. Cambridge: D. S. Brewer, 1994.

Mehl, Dieter. *The Middle English Romances of the Thirteenth and Fourteenth Centuries*. London: Routledge & Kegan Paul, 1968.

Meyer-Lee, Robert J. *Poets and Power from Chaucer to Wyatt*. Cambridge: Cambridge University Press, 2007.

Mils, Maldwyn, Jennifer Fellows, and Carol Meale, eds. *Romance in Medieval England*. Cambridge: D. S. Brewer, 1991.

Mills, Lauren. *One Soul in Bodies Twain: Friendship in Tudor Literature and Stuart Drama*. Bloomington, IN: The Principia Press, Inc., 1937.

Minnis, Alistair J. "Aspects of the Medieval French and English Traditions of the *De Consolatione Philosophiae*." In *Boethius: His Life, Thought, and Influence*. Ed. Margaret Gibson. Oxford: Basil Blackwell, 1981. Pp. 312–61.

———, ed. *The Medieval Boethius: Studies in the Vernacular Translations of* De Consolatione Philosophiae. Cambridge: D. S. Brewer, 1987.

Minnis, Alistair J., and Tim W. Machan. "The *Boece* as Late-Medieval Translation." In *Chaucer's* Boece *and the Medieval Tradition of Boethius*. Cambridge: D. S. Brewer, 1993. Pp. 167–88.

Mitchell, J. Allan. "John Gower and John Lydgate: Forms and Norms of Rhetorical Culture." In *A Companion to Medieval English Literature and Culture c. 1350–c. 1500*. Ed. Peter Brown. Malden, MA: Blackwell, 2007. Pp. 569–84.

———. "Queen Katherine and the Secret of Lydgate's *Temple of Glas*." *Medium Aevum* 77 (2008), 54–76.

Mooney, Linne R."Lydgate's Kings of England and Another Verse Chronicle of the Kings." *Viator* 20 (1989), 255–89.

———. "More Manuscripts Written by a Chaucer Scribe." *Chaucer Review* 30 (1996), 401–07.

———. "A New Manuscript by the Hammond Scribe, Discovered by Jeremy Griffiths." In *The English Medieval Book: Studies in Memory of Jeremy Griffiths*. Ed. A. S. G. Edwards, Vincent Gillespie, and Ralph Hanna. London: British Library, 2000. Pp. 113–23.

———. "Professional Scribes? Identifying English Scribes Who Had a Hand in More than One Manuscript." In *New Directions in Later Medieval Manuscript Studies*. Ed. Derek Pearsall. York: York Medieval Press, 2000. Pp. 131–41.

———. "Scribes and Booklets of Trinity College, Cambridge, Manuscripts R.3.19 and R.3.21." In *Middle English Poetry: Texts and Traditions: Essays in Honour of Derek Pearsall*. Ed. A. J. Minnis. York: York Medieval Press, 2001. Pp. 241–66.

———. "John Shirley's Heirs." *Yearbook of English Studies* 33 (2003), 182–98.

Mooney, Linne, Simon Horobin, and Estelle Stubbs, eds. *Late Medieval English Scribes*. York: University of York, 2011. Accessed 10 February 2015. Online at http://www.medievalscribes.com.

Mortimer, Nigel. *John Lydgate's Fall of Princes: Narrative Tragedy in its Literary and Political Contexts*. Oxford: Clarendon Press, 2005.

Mosser, Daniel. "Dating the Manuscripts of the 'Hammond Scribe': What the Paper Evidence Tells Us." *Journal of the Early Book Society* 10 (2007), 31–70.

Nolan, Maura. *John Lydgate and the Making of Public Culture*. Cambridge: Cambridge University Press, 2005.

———. "Lydgate's Worst Poem." In Cooper and Denny-Brown, *Lydgate Matters*. Pp. 71–87.

Norton-Smith, John. "Lydgate's Metaphors." *English Studies* 42 (1961), 90–93.

———. *John Lydgate: Poems*. Oxford: Clarendon Press, 1966.

Olson, Paul A. "*The Parlement of Foules:* Aristotles's Politics and the Foundations of Human Society." *Studies in the Age of Chaucer* 2 (1980), 53–79.

Ormrod, Mark W. "John Mandeville, Edward II, and the King of Inde." *Chaucer Review* 46 (2012), 314–39.

Patch, H. R. *The Goddess Fortuna in Medieval Literature*. Cambridge, MA: Harvard University Press, 1927.

Patterson, Lee. "Making Identities in Fifteenth-Century England: Henry V and John Lydgate." *Acts of Recognition: Essays on Medieval Culture*. Notre Dame, IN: University of Notre Dame Press, 2010. Pp. 120–54.

Pearsall, Derek, ed. *The Floure and the Leafe and The Assembly of Ladies*. London: Thomas Nelson and Sons, 1962. Rpt. Manchester: Manchester University Press, 1980; Kalamazoo, MI: Medieval Institute Publications, 1990.

———. "The English Chaucerians." In *Chaucer and Chaucerians: Critical Studies in Middle English Literature*. Ed. D. S. Brewer. London: Thomas Nelson and Sons Ltd., 1966. Pp. 201–39.

———. *John Lydgate*. London: Routledge, 1970.

———. "The Development of Middle English Romance." In *Studies in Medieval English Romances: Some New Approaches*. Cambridge: D.S. Brewer, 1988. Pp. 11–36.

———. "Lydgate as Innovator." *Modern Language Quarterly* 53 (March 1992), 5–22.

———. *John Lydgate (1371–1449): A Bio-Bibliography*. English Literary Studies, Monograph Series No. 71. Victoria, BC: University of Victoria Press, 1997.

Peck, Russell. *Kingship and Common Profit in Gower's* Confessio Amantis. Carbondale, IL: Southern Illinois University Press, 1978.

Petrina, Alessandra. *Cultural Politics in Fifteenth-Century England: The Case of Humphrey, Duke of Gloucester*. Leiden: Brill, 2004.

Pollard, A. J. "Talbot, John, First Earl of Shrewsbury and First Earl of Waterford (*c*.1387–1453)." *Oxford Dictionary of National Biography*. Oxford: Oxford University Press, 2004. Accessed 15 May 2014. Online at http://www.oxforddnb.com/view/article/26932?docPos=2.

Purdie, Rhiannon, and M. Cichon. *Medieval Romance, Medieval Contexts*. Cambridge and Rochester: D. S. Brewer, 2011.

Purdy, R. R. "The Friendship Motif in Middle English Literature." In *Vanderbilt Studies in the Humanitites*. Vol. 1. Ed. Richmond C. Beatty, et al. Nashvillle, TN: Vanderbilt University Press, 1951. Pp. 113–41.

Radulescu, Raluca L., and C. Rushton. *A Companion to Medieval Popular Romance*. Woodbridge; Rochester: D. S. Brewer, 2009.

Ramsey, Lee. *Chivalric Romances: Popular Literature in Medieval England*. Bloomington, IN: Indiana University Press, 1983.

Rawcliffe, Carole. *Medicine and Society in Later Medieval England*. Stroud: Alan Sutton Publications, 1995.

Reimer, Stephen R., and Pamela Farvolden. "Of Arms and the Manuscript: The Date and Provenance of Harley 2255." *Journal of the Early Book Society* 8 (2005), 239–60.

Reinecke, George F., ed. *Saint Albon and Saint Amphibalus by John Lydgate*. New York: Garland, 1985.

Renoir, Alain, and C. David Benson. "John Lydgate." In *A Manual of the Writings in Middle English 1050–1500*. Vol. 6. Ed. J. Burke Severs, Albert E. Hartung, and Peter G. Beidler. New Haven, CT: Connecticut Academy of Arts and Sciences, 1980. Pp. 1809–1920; 2071–2175.

Richmond, Colin. *The Paston Family in the Fifteenth Century: The First Phase*. Cambridge, Cambridge University Press, 1990.

———. *The Paston Family in the Fifteenth Century: Fastolf's Will*. Cambridge: Cambridge University Press, 1996. Rpt 2002.

———. *The Paston Family in the Fifteenth Century: Endings*. Manchester: Manchester University Press, 2000.

Richmond, Velma Bourgeois. *The Popularity of Middle English Romance*. Bowling Green, OH: University Popular Press, 1975.

———. *The Legend of Guy of Warwick*. New York and London: Garland, 1996.

Robertson, D. W. *A Preface to Chaucer: Studies in Medieval Perspectives*. Princeton, NJ: Princeton University Press, 1962.

Robertson, Kellie. "Common Language and Common Profit." In *The Postcolonial Middle Ages*. Ed. Jeffrey Jerome Cohen. New York: St. Martin's Press, 2000.

Robinson, F. N. "On Two Manuscripts of Lydgate's Guy of Warwick." *Harvard Studies and Notes in Philology and Literature* 5 (1899), 177–220.

Rose, Valentinus, ed. *Egidii Corboliensis. Viaticus de Signis et Synmptomatibus Aegritudinum*. Lipsiae: B. G. Teubneri, 1907.

Rouse, Robert Allen. *The Idea of Anglo-Saxon England in Middle English Romance*. Cambridge: D. S. Brewer, 2005.

———. "An Exemplary Life: Guy of Warwick as Medieval Culture-Hero." In Wiggins and Field, *Guy of Warwick: Icon and Ancestor*. Pp. 94–109.

Rudborne, Thomas. *Historia Major Wintoniensis*. In *Anglia Sacra*. Vol. 1. Ed. Henry Wharton. London: Richard Chiswell, 1691. Pp. 179–286.

Rumble, Alexander R. "Gerard of Cornwall (supp. fl. c.1350)." *Oxford Dictionary of National Biography*. Oxford: Oxford University Press, 2004. Accessed 19 August 2012. Online at http://www.oxforddnb.com/view/ article/10770.

———. "Rudborne, Thomas (fl. 1447–1454)." *Oxford Dictionary of National Biography*. Oxford: Oxford University Press, 2004. Accessed 19 August 2012. Online at http://www.oxforddnb.com/ view/ article/24244?docPos=2.

Saunders, Corinne, ed. *A Companion to Romance: From Classical to Contemporary*. Malden, MA: Blackwell, 2004.

Scanlon, Larry. "Lydgate's Poetics: Laureation and Domesticity in the *Temple of Glass*." In Scanlon and Simpson, *John Lydgate*. Pp. 61–97.

Scanlon, Larry, and James Simpson, eds. *John Lydgate: Poetry, Culture, and Lancastrian England*. Notre Dame, IN: University of Notre Dame Press, 2006.

Schick, Josef, ed. *Lydgate's Temple of Glas*. EETS e.s. 60. London: Humphrey Milford, Oxford University Press, 1891. Rpt. 1924.

Schirmer, Walter. *John Lydgate: A Study in the Culture of the XVth Century*. Trans. Anne E. Keep. London: Methuen, 1961.

Schleich, Gustav, ed. "Lydgates Quelle zu seinem Guy of Warwick." *Archiv für Studium der neueren Sprachen und Literaruen* 146 (1923), 49–52.

Schleich, Gustav, and J. Zupitza, eds. *Fabula Duorum Mercatorum*. Vol. 83. Strassburg: Trübner, 1897.

Schwarzbaum, Haim. "International Folklore Motifs in Petrus Alphonsi's *Disciplina Clericalis*." *Sefarad* 21 (1961), 267–99.

Seaton, Ethel. *Sir Richard Roos: Lancastrian Poet*. London: Rupert Hart-Davis, 1961.

Seneca, Lucius. *L. Annaei Senecae. Dialogorum Libri Duodecim*. Ed. L. D. Reynolds. Oxford: Oxford University Press, 1977.

———. *Dialogues and Essays*. Ed. John Davie and Tobias Reinhardt. Oxford: Oxford University Press, 2007.

———. *Moral Epistles 1–65*. Trans. Richard Mott Gummere. Cambridge, MA: Harvard University Press, 1917.

Seymour, Maurice C. "Some Lydgate Manuscripts: Lives of SS Edmund and Fremund and Danse Macabre." *Edinburgh Bibliographical Society Transactions* 5.4 (1983–84, 1984–85), 10–24.

———. *A Catalogue of Chaucer Manuscripts*. 2 vols. Aldershot: Scolar Press, 1995–97.

Shakespeare, William. *Twelfth Night*. In *The Riverside Shakespeare*. Ed. G. Blakemore Evans. Second edition. Boston: Houghton Mifflin, 1997.

Sharpe, R. *A Handlist of Latin Writers of Great Britain and Ireland before 1540*. Brussels: Brepols, 1997.

Simpson, James. "The Energies of John Lydgate." In *Reform and Cultural Revolution*. Ed. James Simpson. Oxford: Oxford University Press, 2002. Pp. 34–67.

———. "John Lydgate." In *The Cambridge Companion to Medieval English Literature 1100–1500*. Ed. Larry Scanlon. Cambridge: Cambridge University Press, 2009. Pp. 205–16.

Siraisi, Nancy G. *Medieval and Early Renaissance Medicine: An Introduction to Knowledge and Practice*. Chicago, IL: University of Chicago Press, 1990.

Smith, D. Vance. "Lydgate's Refrain: The Open When." In Cooper and Denny-Brown, *Lydgate Matters*. Pp. 185–95.

Sponsler, Claire. "Lydgate and London's Public Culture." In Cooper and Brown, *Lydgate Matters*. Pp. 13–33.

———, ed. *John Lydgate: Mummings and Entertainments*. Kalamazoo, MI: Medieval Institute Publications, 2010.

Stenton, Frank. *Anglo-Saxon England*. Third edition. 1971. Rpt. Oxford: Clarendon Press, 2004.

Stevens, John. *Medieval Romance: Themes and Approaches*. London: Hutchinson University Library, 1973.

Stevens, Martin. "The Winds of Fortune in the Troilus." *Chaucer Review* 13 (1979), 285–307.

Straker, Scott-Morgan. "Propaganda, Intentionality, and the Lancastrian Lydgate." In Scanlon and Simpson, *John Lydgate*. Pp. 98–128.

Stretter, Robert. "Rewriting Perfect Friendship in Chaucer's *Knight's Tale* and Lydgate's *Fabula Duorum Mercatorum*." *Chaucer Review* 37 (2003), 234–52.

———. "Engendering Obligation: Sworn Brotherhood and Love Rivalry in Medieval English Romance." In *Friendship in the Middle Ages and the Early Modern Age: Explorations of a Fundamental Ethical Discourse*. Ed. Albrecht Classen and Marilyn Sandidge. Berlin: Walter De Gruyter, 2010. Pp. 501–24.

Strohm, Paul. "The Origin and Meaning of Middle English Romaunce." *Genre* 10 (1977), 1–28.

———. "Hoccleve, Lydgate and the Lancastrian Court." In Wallace, *Cambridge History*. Pp. 640–61.

Symons, Dana M., ed. *Chaucerian Dream Visions and Complaints*. Kalamazoo, MI: Medieval Institute Publications, 2004.

Thompson, Stith. *Motif-Index of Folk-Literature*. 6 vols. Bloomington, IN: Indiana University Press, 1955.

Thorndike, Lynn. *A History of Magic and Experimental Science*. 2 vols. New York: Macmillan, 1923.

Thrupp, Sylvia. *The Merchant Class of Medieval London, 1300–1500*. Chicago: University of Chicago Press, 1948. Rpt. Ann Arbor: University of Michigan Press, 1962.

Tolan, John V. *Petrus Alfonsi and His Medieval Readers*. Gainesville, FL: University Press of Florida, 1993.

Tolkien, J. R. R., and E. V. Gordon, eds. *Sir Gawain and the Green Knight*. Second edition. Oxford: Oxford University Press, 1967.

Trevisa, John. *On the Properties of Things: John Trevisa's* Translation of Bartholomaeus Anglicus De Proprietatibus Rerum, *A Critical Text*. Ed. Maurice C. Seymour. 3 vols. Oxford: Clarendon Press, 1988.

Van Dorsten, J. A. "The Leyden 'Lydgate Manuscript.'" *Scriptorium* 14 (1960), 315–25.

Vincent, Nicholas. "Plessis, John de, Seventh Earl of Warwick." *Oxford Dictionary of National Biography*. Oxford: Oxford University Press, 2004. Accessed 15 May 2014. Online at http://www.oxforddnb.com/view/article/ 22379.

Vinsauf, Geoffrey of. *Poetria Nova*. Trans. Margaret F. Nims. Toronto: Pontifical Institute of Mediaeval Studies, 1967.

Voigts, Linda Ehrsam. "A Handlist of Middle English in Harvard Manuscripts." *Harvard Library Bulletin* 33 (1985), 17–22. Accessed 19 August 2012. Online at http://pds.lib.harvard.edu/pds/view/2573358?n=15875 &s=4.

Wack, Mary. *Lovesickness in the Middle Ages: The* Viaticum *and Its Commentaries*. Philadelphia, PA: University of Pennsylvania Press, 1990.

Wallace, David, ed. *The Cambridge History of Medieval English Literature*. Cambridge: Cambridge University Press, 1999.

Wallis, Faith. "Giles de Corbeil." In *Medieval Science, Technology, and Medicine. An Encyclopedia*. Ed. Thomas Glick, Steven J. Livesey, and Faith Wallis. New York: Routledge, 2005. Pp. 198–99.

Ward, H. L. D. *Catalogue of Romances in the Department of Manuscripts in the British Museum*. Vol. 1. London: Longmans and Co., 1883. Rpt. London: Printed by Order of the Trustees, 1962.

Warner, Sir George F., and Julius P. Gilson. *Catalogue of Western Manuscripts in the Old Royal and King's Collections in the British Museum*. Vol. 1. Oxford: Oxford University Press, 1921.

Warren, Michelle R. "Lydgate, Lovelich, and London Letters." In Cooper and Denny-Brown, *Lydgate Matters*. Pp. 113–38.

Warton, Thomas. *History of English Poetry in Four Volumes*. Ed. René Wellek. New York and London: Johnson Reprint Corporation, 1968.

Weiss, Judith. "Guy of Warwick at Home and Abroad: A Hero for Europe." In Wiggins and Field, *Guy of Warwick: Icon and Ancestor*. Pp. 1–11.

Weiss, Judith, ed. and trans. *Boeve de Haumtone and Gui de Warewic: Two Anglo-Norman Romances*. Tempe, AZ: Arizona Center for Medieval and Renaissance Studies, 2008.

Wells, Marion A. *The Secret Wound: Love Melancholy and Early Modern Romance*. Stanford, CA: Stanford University Press, 2007.

Whiting, Bartlett Jere, and Helen Wescott Whiting. *Proverbs, Sentences, and Proverbial Phrases*. Cambridge, MA: Belknap Press of Harvard University Press, 1968.

Wiggins, Alison. "The Manuscripts and Texts of the Middle English *Guy of Warwick*." In Wiggins and Field, *Guy of Warwick: Icon and Ancestor*. Pp. 61–80.

Wiggins, Alison, ed. *Stanzaic Guy of Warwick*. Kalamazoo, MI: Medieval Institute Publications, 2004.

Wiggins, Alison, and Rosalind Field. "Editorial Introduction." In *Guy of Warwick: Icon and Ancestor*. Cambridge: D. S. Brewer, 2007. Pp. xv–xxi.

———. *Guy of Warwick: Icon and Ancestor*. Cambridge: D. S. Brewer, 2007.

Winny, James. "Chaucer's Science." In *An Introduction to Chaucer*. Ed. Maurice Hussey, A. C. Spearing, and James Winny. Cambridge: Cambridge University Press, 1968. Pp. 153–84.

Withrington, John. "The Arthurian Epitaph in Malory's *Morte Darthur*." In *Glastonbury Abbey and the Arthurian Tradition*. Ed. James P. Carley. Woodbridge: D. S. Brewer, 2001. Pp. 211–48.

Wogan-Browne, Jocelyn. "'Bet . . . to . . . rede on holy seyntes lyves . . .': Romance and Hagiography Again." In *Readings in Medieval English Romance*. Ed. Carol M. Meale. Cambridge: D. S. Brewer, 1994. Pp. 83–97.

Wolfgang, Lenora D. "'Out of the Frenssh': Lydgate's Source of *The Churl and the Bird*." *English Language Notes* 32 (1995), 10–22.

Woodcock, Matthew. "Crossovers and Afterlife." In *A Companion to Middle English Hagiography*. Ed. Sarah Salih. Cambridge: D. S. Brewer, 2006. Pp. 141–56.

Wright, H. G. *Boccaccio in England from Chaucer to Tennyson*. London: Athlone Press, 1957.

Zupitza, Julius, ed. "Lydgate's *Leben des Guy von Warwick*." *Zur Literaturgeschichte Des Guy Von Warwick*. Akademie der Wissenschaften LXXIV Bd. s. 623. Wien: Karl Gerold's Sohn, 1873. Pp. 23–46. Accessed 10 February 2015. Online at https://archive.org/stream/zurliteraturges00guy goog# page/n31/mode/2up.

———. *The Romance of Guy of Warwick: The Second or 15th-Century Version, Edited from the Paper MS. Ff.2.38 in the University Library, Cambridge*. EETS 25, 26. London: Trübner, 1875, 1876.

———. *The Romance of Guy of Warwick: Edited from the Auchinleck Ms. in the Advocates' Library, Edinburgh and from Ms. 107 in Caius College, Cambridge*. EETS e.s. 42, 49, 59. Bungay, Suffolk: R. Clay and Sons Ltd., 1883, 1887, 1891. Rpt. Oxford: Oxford University Press, 1966.

Glossary

abrood *spread all over*
afferd *afraid*
affray *fear, dismay*
aforn, afforn *before*
ageyn *again; against, in opposition to*
anoon *immediately, soon*
auctour *author, source*
avayll *assist, help*
ay *always*

ballaunce *balance, scale*; **hangyng in ~** *be in jeopardy or danger; feel uncertain*
ben *be*
benbassat, benbassatrie *by means of ambassadors, i.e. through negotiation*
bespreynt, spreynt *sprinkled with*
bond *binding agreement*
bonde (adj.) *bound, not free*
boone *prayer, petition, request*
brent, brennyng *burnt, burning*
byde (v.) *delay*

cheer *happiness; face, facial expression showing emotion*
coost *region*
chaunbre *(bed) chamber*
cure *attend, work, attention*; **bisy ~** *work diligently, do one's best*

dampned *declared guilty, condemned*
darreyne *to decide by combat*
degré, degree *rank, position in society; measurement of heat*; **by ~** *gradually*
do, do(o)n(e) *do, make*
dolour *intense sadness*
dool *grief; pain*
dreed(e) *dread, anxiety; warning, threat*
dressed *prepared*
dulle, dulled *numbed, bewildered*

echon, echoon *each one*
eek *also*
emprise, empryse *enterprise, undertaking*
equyté *fairness, justice*
erys *ears*
evir among *again and again; always*

feer(e), fyr *fire*
ferre *match, peer, companion, friend; company*; **in ~, ife(r)e** *together*
ferre *far*
firmament *the heavens*
flawme *flame*
fonde *try, attempt*
fro *from*
froward Of Fortune, *unfavourable, malicious*; of people, *hostile, warlike*
fyne (v. and n.) *end*

gaff *gave*
gan *did*
garnementis *garments, clothing*
gladly *usually; readily*

habiriownys *habergeons (coats of chain mail)*
han *have*
heer *here*
heere *hear; here*
hem *them, those*
her, here *their*

hir *her*
humblesse *humility*

icast *having been cast into; planned*

Kynde *Nature*
kynde *type, category*
kyndenesse *kindness, benevolence*

label *mark of cadency on coat of arms*
lat/let *allow, permit*; **~ be** *cease*; **~ me see** *tell me*
leche *doctor*; **lechys, lechis** *doctors*
list, lyst, lest *wish, desire*; **he ne ~** *he did not care*
louh *low*
lownesse *humility, meekness*

maner, maneer *manner, a way of being; type; in any such way*
mene *means, a way (to do something)*
mesoure, mesure *proportion, balance*
moorne, moornyng *mourn, mourning*
morowhil *just before or at dawn*
morwe *morrow, morning*
mot *must*
myscheef *misfortune, sorrow, hardship, disaster, wickedness*

necessité *need, hardship* (see Explanatory Note to *Fabula*, line 100, for philosophical sense)
nolde *would not*
nouht *not, nothing*
nyl, nylt *will not*

o, oo, oon *one, a man/person*
orysoun *prayer*
ouht *aught, anything*
outher. . . outher *either. . . or*

party *part, division, section; partly, part of; side, group, one side or the other*
peyne, peynes *pain, pains*; *penalty*
pleyn, pleynly *plain, plainly*
pleyne *complain*
pitous *benevolent*
pitously *piteously; humbly, devoutly*
plesaunce *pleasure, comfort*
pomp(e) *pride*
poraill, porayll *the poor, the wretched*
punssheth, punysshen, punsshyng *punish, punishing*

rage *anger, vexation, distress*
regitiff *governing, controlling*
rejoisshe *occupy, assume rule; glory in*
rewm *realm*

sepulture *burial*
sholde *should*
sike (adj.) *ill, sick*; (v.) *to sigh*; (subs. adj.) *sick man*
socour(e) *help*; **to do ~** *to render assistance*
sojourne *stay, sojourn*
sole, sool(e) *alone*
soleyn *alone*
spreynt see **bespreynt**
sterte *to leap or dart out suddenly*
sterte *a short time*
stre(e)mys *streams*
sue, sueth *to follow, pursue*; *oppress*
suych *such*

tencontre *to encounter, meet*
th'emprise see **emprise**
thenpreent *an imprint*
tho *those, then*
thu *thou, you*
tofore, toforn *before*
tother, tothir *other*
travayll *travel*, often in the sense of *being weary with travel; suffering, distress, torment, being troubled*
tretable *reasonable*
trowith *believe*
trowthe, trowly *truth, truly*

unkouth *unknown, unfamiliar*
unwarly *unexpectedly*

valyd *brought down, reduced*
viage, vyage *journey*

visage, vysage *face*
vygyl *the eve of; the night before*

weel (adv.) *well*
wele *prosperity*
wepnys *weapons*
wer *doubt, uncertainty*
wern *were*
whilom, whiloom *once, once long ago*
wi(g)ht *creature, person, being*
wol, wolde *will, would*
wood *crazed, angry; full of anger and rage*
wreke *take revenge*
wrouht *(has) done, brought about*

yif *if; in case of*

Middle English Texts Series

The Floure and the Leafe, The Assembly of Ladies, The Isle of Ladies, edited by Derek Pearsall (1990)
Three Middle English Charlemagne Romances, edited by Alan Lupack (1990)
Six Ecclesiastical Satires, edited by James M. Dean (1991)
Heroic Women from the Old Testament in Middle English Verse, edited by Russell A. Peck (1991)
The Canterbury Tales: Fifteenth-Century Continuations and Additions, edited by John M. Bowers (1992)
Gavin Douglas, *The Palis of Honoure*, edited by David Parkinson (1992)
Wynnere and Wastoure and The Parlement of the Thre Ages, edited by Warren Ginsberg (1992)
The Shewings of Julian of Norwich, edited by Georgia Ronan Crampton (1994)
King Arthur's Death: The Middle English Stanzaic Morte Arthur and Alliterative Morte Arthure, edited by Larry D. Benson, revised by Edward E. Foster (1994)
Lancelot of the Laik and Sir Tristrem, edited by Alan Lupack (1994)
Sir Gawain: Eleven Romances and Tales, edited by Thomas Hahn (1995)
The Middle English Breton Lays, edited by Anne Laskaya and Eve Salisbury (1995)
Sir Perceval of Galles and Ywain and Gawain, edited by Mary Flowers Braswell (1995)
Four Middle English Romances: Sir Isumbras, Octavian, Sir Eglamour of Artois, Sir Tryamour, edited by Harriet Hudson (1996; second edition 2006)
The Poems of Laurence Minot, 1333–1352, edited by Richard H. Osberg (1996)
Medieval English Political Writings, edited by James M. Dean (1996)
The Book of Margery Kempe, edited by Lynn Staley (1996)
Amis and Amiloun, Robert of Cisyle, and Sir Amadace, edited by Edward E. Foster (1997; second edition 2007)
The Cloud of Unknowing, edited by Patrick J. Gallacher (1997)
Robin Hood and Other Outlaw Tales, edited by Stephen Knight and Thomas Ohlgren (1997; second edition 2000)
The Poems of Robert Henryson, edited by Robert L. Kindrick with the assistance of Kristie A. Bixby (1997)
Moral Love Songs and Laments, edited by Susanna Greer Fein (1998)
John Lydgate, *Troy Book Selections*, edited by Robert R. Edwards (1998)
Thomas Usk, *The Testament of Love*, edited by R. Allen Shoaf (1998)
Prose Merlin, edited by John Conlee (1998)
Middle English Marian Lyrics, edited by Karen Saupe (1998)
John Metham, *Amoryus and Cleopes*, edited by Stephen F. Page (1999)
Four Romances of England: King Horn, Havelok the Dane, Bevis of Hampton, Athelston, edited by Ronald B. Herzman, Graham Drake, and Eve Salisbury (1999)
The Assembly of Gods: Le Assemble de Dyeus, or Banquet of Gods and Goddesses, with the Discourse of Reason and Sensuality, edited by Jane Chance (1999)
Thomas Hoccleve, *The Regiment of Princes*, edited by Charles R. Blyth (1999)
John Capgrave, *The Life of Saint Katherine*, edited by Karen A. Winstead (1999)
John Gower, *Confessio Amantis*, Vol. 1, edited by Russell A. Peck; with Latin translations by Andrew Galloway (2000; second edition 2006); Vol. 2 (2003; second edition 2013); Vol. 3 (2004)
Richard the Redeless and Mum and the Sothsegger, edited by James M. Dean (2000)
Ancrene Wisse, edited by Robert Hasenfratz (2000)
Walter Hilton, *The Scale of Perfection*, edited by Thomas H. Bestul (2000)
John Lydgate, *The Siege of Thebes*, edited by Robert R. Edwards (2001)
Pearl, edited by Sarah Stanbury (2001)
The Trials and Joys of Marriage, edited by Eve Salisbury (2002)
Middle English Legends of Women Saints, edited by Sherry L. Reames, with the assistance of Martha G. Blalock and Wendy R. Larson (2003)
The Wallace: Selections, edited by Anne McKim (2003)
Richard Maidstone, *Concordia (The Reconciliation of Richard II with London)*, edited by David R. Carlson, with a verse translation by A. G. Rigg (2003)
Three Purgatory Poems: The Gast of Gy, Sir Owain, The Vision of Tundale, edited by Edward E. Foster (2004)
William Dunbar, *The Complete Works*, edited by John Conlee (2004)
Chaucerian Dream Visions and Complaints, edited by Dana M. Symons (2004)
Stanzaic Guy of Warwick, edited by Alison Wiggins (2004)
Saints' Lives in Middle English Collections, edited by E. Gordon Whatley, with Anne B. Thompson and Robert K. Upchurch (2004)
Siege of Jerusalem, edited by Michael Livingston (2004)
The Kingis Quair and Other Prison Poems, edited by Linne R. Mooney and Mary-Jo Arn (2005)
The Chaucerian Apocrypha: A Selection, edited by Kathleen Forni (2005)
John Gower, *The Minor Latin Works*, edited and translated by R. F. Yeager, with *In Praise of Peace*, edited by Michael Livingston (2005)

Sentimental and Humorous Romances: Floris and Blancheflour, Sir Degrevant, The Squire of Low Degree, The Tournament of Tottenham, and The Feast of Tottenham, edited by Erik Kooper (2006)
The Dicts and Sayings of the Philosophers, edited by John William Sutton (2006)
Everyman and Its Dutch Original, Elckerlijc, edited by Clifford Davidson, Martin W. Walsh, and Ton J. Broos (2007)
The N-Town Plays, edited by Douglas Sugano, with assistance by Victor I. Scherb (2007)
The Book of John Mandeville, edited by Tamarah Kohanski and C. David Benson (2007)
John Lydgate, *The Temple of Glas*, edited by J. Allan Mitchell (2007)
The Northern Homily Cycle, edited by Anne B. Thompson (2008)
Codex Ashmole 61: A Compilation of Popular Middle English Verse, edited by George Shuffelton (2008)
Chaucer and the Poems of "Ch," edited by James I. Wimsatt (revised edition 2009)
William Caxton, *The Game and Playe of the Chesse*, edited by Jenny Adams (2009)
John the Blind Audelay, *Poems and Carols*, edited by Susanna Fein (2009)
Two Moral Interludes: The Pride of Life and Wisdom, edited by David Klausner (2009)
John Lydgate, *Mummings and Entertainments*, edited by Claire Sponsler (2010)
Mankind, edited by Kathleen M. Ashley and Gerard NeCastro (2010)
The Castle of Perseverance, edited by David N. Klausner (2010)
Robert Henryson, *The Complete Works*, edited by David J. Parkinson (2010)
John Gower, *The French Balades*, edited and translated by R. F. Yeager (2011)
The Middle English Metrical Paraphrase of the Old Testament, edited by Michael Livingston (2011)
The York Corpus Christi Plays, edited by Clifford Davidson (2011)
Prik of Conscience, edited by James H. Morey (2012)
The Dialogue of Solomon and Marcolf: A Dual-Language Edition from Latin and Middle English Printed Editions, edited by Nancy Mason Bradbury and Scott Bradbury (2012)
Croxton Play of the Sacrament, edited by John T. Sebastian (2012)
Ten Bourdes, edited by Melissa M. Furrow (2013)
Lybeaus Desconus, edited by Eve Salisbury and James Weldon (2013)
The Complete Harley 2253 Manuscript, Vol. 2, edited and translated by Susanna Fein with David Raybin and Jan Ziolkowski (2014); Vol. 3 (2015); Vol. 1 (2015)
Oton de Granson Poems, edited and translated by Peter Nicholson and Joan Grenier-Winther (2015)
The King of Tars, edited by John H. Chandler (2015)
John Hardyng Chronicle, edited by James Simpson and Sarah Peverley (2015)
Richard Coer de Lyon, edited by Peter Larkin (2015)
Guillaume de Machaut, The Complete Poetry and Music, Volume 1: The Debate Poems, edited and translated by R. Barton Palmer (2016)

Commentary Series

Haimo of Auxerre, *Commentary on the Book of Jonah*, translated with an introduction and notes by Deborah Everhart (1993)
Medieval Exegesis in Translation: Commentaries on the Book of Ruth, translated with an introduction and notes by Lesley Smith (1996)
Nicholas of Lyra's Apocalypse Commentary, translated with an introduction and notes by Philip D. W. Krey (1997)
Rabbi Ezra Ben Solomon of Gerona, *Commentary on the Song of Songs and Other Kabbalistic Commentaries*, selected, translated, and annotated by Seth Brody (1999)
John Wyclif, *On the Truth of Holy Scripture*, translated with an introduction and notes by Ian Christopher Levy (2001)
Second Thessalonians: Two Early Medieval Apocalyptic Commentaries, introduced and translated by Steven R. Cartwright and Kevin L. Hughes (2001)
The "Glossa Ordinaria" on the Song of Songs, translated with an introduction and notes by Mary Dove (2004)
The Seven Seals of the Apocalypse: Medieval Texts in Translation, translated with an introduction and notes by Francis X. Gumerlock (2009)
The "Glossa Ordinaria" on Romans, translated with an introduction and notes by Michael Scott Woodward (2011)
Nicholas of Lyra, Literal Commentary on Galatians, translated with an introduction and notes by Edward Arthur Naumann (2015)
Early Latin Commentaries on the Apocalypse, edited by Francis X. Gumerlock (2016)

SECULAR COMMENTARY SERIES

Accessus ad auctores: Medieval Introduction to the Authors, edited and translated by Stephen M. Wheeler (2015)
The Vulgate Commentary on Ovid's Metamorphoses, *Book 1*, edited and translated by Frank Coulson (2015)
Brunetto Latini, La rettorica, edited and translated by Stefania D'Agata D'Ottavi (2016)

DOCUMENTS OF PRACTICE SERIES

Love and Marriage in Late Medieval London, selected, translated, and introduced by Shannon McSheffrey (1995)
Sources for the History of Medicine in Late Medieval England, selected, introduced, and translated by Carole Rawcliffe (1995)
A Slice of Life: Selected Documents of Medieval English Peasant Experience, edited, translated, and with an introduction by Edwin Brezette DeWindt (1996)
Regular Life: Monastic, Canonical, and Mendicant "Rules," selected and introduced by Douglas J. McMillan and Kathryn Smith Fladenmuller (1997); second edition, selected and introduced by Daniel Marcel La Corte and Douglas J. McMillan (2004)
Women and Monasticism in Medieval Europe: Sisters and Patrons of the Cistercian Reform, selected, translated, and with an introduction by Constance H. Berman (2002)
Medieval Notaries and Their Acts: The 1327–1328 Register of Jean Holanie, introduced, edited, and translated by Kathryn L. Reyerson and Debra A. Salata (2004)
John Stone's Chronicle: Christ Church Priory, Canterbury, 1417–1472, selected, translated, and introduced by Meriel Connor (2010)

MEDIEVAL GERMAN TEXTS IN BILINGUAL EDITIONS SERIES

Sovereignty and Salvation in the Vernacular, 1050–1150, introduction, translations, and notes by James A. Schultz (2000)
Ava's New Testament Narratives: "When the Old Law Passed Away," introduction, translation, and notes by James A. Rushing, Jr. (2003)
History as Literature: German World Chronicles of the Thirteenth Century in Verse, introduction, translation, and notes by R. Graeme Dunphy (2003)
Thomasin von Zirclaria, *Der Welsche Gast (The Italian Guest)*, translated by Marion Gibbs and Winder McConnell (2009)
Ladies, Whores, and Holy Women: A Sourcebook in Courtly, Religious, and Urban Cultures of Late Medieval Germany, introductions, translations, and notes by Ann Marie Rasmussen and Sarah Westphal-Wihl (2010)

VARIA

The Study of Chivalry: Resources and Approaches, edited by Howell Chickering and Thomas H. Seiler (1988)
Studies in the Harley Manuscript: The Scribes, Contents, and Social Contexts of British Library MS Harley 2253, edited by Susanna Fein (2000)
The Liturgy of the Medieval Church, edited by Thomas J. Heffernan and E. Ann Matter (2001; second edition 2005)
Johannes de Grocheio, *Ars musice*, edited and translated by Constant J. Mews, John N. Crossley, Catherine Jeffreys, Leigh McKinnon, and Carol J. Williams (2011)
Aribo, De musica *and* Sententiae, edited and translated by T.J.H. McCarthy (2015)

Typeset in 10/13 New Baskerville
and Golden Cockerel Ornaments display

Medieval Institute Publications
College of Arts and Sciences
Western Michigan University
1903 W. Michigan Avenue
Kalamazoo, MI 49008-5432
http://www.wmich.edu/medievalpublications